FOR RENT BY OWNER

A GUIDE FOR RESIDENTIAL RENTAL PROPERTIES

By John Lack

FOR RENT BY OWNER: A GUIDE FOR RESIDENTIAL RENTAL PROPERTIES

Copyright © 2015 Atlantic Publishing Group, Inc.
1405 SW 6th Avenue • Ocala, Florida 34471 • Phone 800-814-1132 • Fax 352-622-1875
Web site: www.atlantic-pub.com • E-mail: sales@atlantic-pub.com
SAN Number: 268-1250

Library of Congress Cataloging-in-Publication Data

Lack, John
 For Rent by Owner: A Guide for Residential Rental Properties / by John Lack.
 p. cm.
 Includes bibliographical references and index.
 ISBN-13: 978-1-62023-100-5 (alk. paper)
 ISBN-10: 1-62023-100-X (alk. paper)
1. Real estate management. I. Title.
 HD1394.L335 2015
 333.5068--dc23
                          2015013355

Printed in the United States

Printed on Recycled Paper

Reduce. Reuse.
RECYCLE.

A decade ago, Atlantic Publishing signed the Green Press Initiative. These guidelines promote environmentally friendly practices, such as using recycled stock and vegetable-based inks, avoiding waste, choosing energy-efficient resources, and promoting a no-pulping policy. We now use 100-percent recycled stock on all our books. The results: in one year, switching to post-consumer recycled stock saved 24 mature trees, 5,000 gallons of water, the equivalent of the total energy used for one home in a year, and the equivalent of the greenhouse gases from one car driven for a year.

Over the years, we have adopted a number of dogs from rescues and shelters. First there was Bear and after he passed, Ginger and Scout. Now, we have Kira, another rescue. They have brought immense joy and love into not just into our lives, but into the lives of all who met them.

We want you to know a portion of the profits of this book will be donated in Bear, Ginger and Scout's memory to local animal shelters, parks, conservation organizations, and other individuals and nonprofit organizations in need of assistance.

*— **Douglas & Sherri Brown,***
President & Vice-President of Atlantic Publishing

Dedication

DEDICATED TO:

The near future:
David, Michael, Gregory and Jennifer

The further future:
Andrea, Amber, Jade, Shelby, Jessica, Spencer,
Rebecca, Madison, Clayton, Sarah, Deaton,
Olivia, Kyla, Ana, Azby, and Izzy

And the distant future:
Payton, Elira, and Zoey

Table of Contents

Introduction

was interested in building from a very young age. I can remember a building block set with small brick-like blocks that I would use to build houses, castles and buildings. My father added a room to our house when I was 8 years old, and then a second-floor bedroom when I was 11 or 12. In the latter room addition, he let me "help" him, giving me my first experience in construction. In junior high school, at about the age of 13, I was asked at a career-counseling day what I was interested in doing when I grew up. My answer was, "I want to be a guy that designs and builds houses."

At 17 years old I read a book entitled, "How I Turned $1000 into $1 Million in Real Estate." This was a perfect book for me because I had always wanted to be a millionaire; my mother reported that I told her such at an early age. The book was fascinating. I can remember most of it today, more than 50 years later. When the book was written, you could buy a small inexpensive rental for a thousand dollars down.

One of the key points of the book was how to pick a property that had the potential for increased value. It outlined improvements that were economical, and would make the property able to rent for more money each month. This increased income, coupled with the cosmetic improvements to the place, would increase the value of the property.

I read it more than once. However, for the next 25 years, I would build and have rentals, but never got on the track the book described. I had gotten into building duplexes and renting them, but even with my free labor, the cost was too high to keep the ball rolling. I had forgotten the basic point of the book: buying fair structures that could be improved upon, increasing their value and making a profit on the capital value going up, not just on the rents received. Fortunately, I had another chance to follow the book later in life. When that time came, I would not blow the chance a second time.

For years, our children have asked me to give them the information on rental properties that I had learned. We have chatted from time to time on the subject, but I finally sat down at the computer to get at least some basics down that were important to me. My writing production consisted of a few hours now and then – mostly while on vacation with nothing better to do than play on the computer. Over the next five years, I only got a basic outline done with a few notes of important points. I did write a little more on areas that were especially important to me, but the entire effort at that time would not have filled a long letter to a friend.

We met a developer friend on vacation that was writing a book and was fairly far along in his effort. This inspired me to get writing on a regular basis and get something done. With a little discipline, it is not that difficult; it is just a matter of getting in the habit of working on it. The progress inspires me to keep going. Picking a time to write is important. My best time is in the morning, preferably after a couple cups of caffeinated coffee. The words seem to flow easily.

Computers with spell check and grammar suggestions are wonderful, especially compared to writers like Longfellow or Poe, who wrote by quill and had none of our modern writing conveniences. My hat is off to all of them. Great credit goes to my wife, Anita, who proofread my work and provided many important corrections, as well as to our granddaughter, Jessica, who did the editing work to make the document fit acceptable literary standards.

We had always kept our kids tied to our company. The family partnership included them and all the grandchildren. Over the years, we expanded their roles in the company. Greg was still doing the maintenance manager function. His wife Stacy is our resident manager at one of the apartment complexes. Our daughter Jennifer would take over the middle management roll between the resident managers and us. Her husband, Doug is a general contractor and assists with projects. David worked on computer issues and acts as manager for our commercial properties on the south side of town. His wife Kara and his children (our grandchildren) do some of our accounting, bookkeeping and computer entry functions. Michael and his wife Stephanie are the computer experts, keeping up our websites and the PCs in all the offices. These kids are all wonderful people as well as a great asset to our company. We have also taken advantage of the skills of our other grandchildren, using them for painting and maintenance work.

We have been reasonably successful in buying and managing residential and commercial real estate. There are loads of people who have made a great deal more money than we have. Considering that we did not really get going at it until I was in my mid-forties, our progress has certainly been respectable.

The information contained here is from our personal experiences. We have looked for investments in many states and have owned property in California, Florida, Texas and the Cayman Islands. There will surely be differences from community to community on laws, regulations and traditions. What we show here is how we did it. We talk about our forms and procedures, but there are no doubt countless other ways to do the same thing. This is a documentation of a way to do it, not the way. I do feel very strongly on many points and I did not hesitate to make my opinions clear.

Some topics appear in several chapters by design. Information on these topics is divided up by chapter to give different levels of our organization the information they needed. For example, we do semi-annual inspections of our property. In the Administration chapter, I explain why we do these inspections. In the Resident Manager section, I give managers instructions on how to complete the inspection. There is also information in the Maintenance chapter on the maintenance workers part of the inspection. In the form section, you will find the form used and how to complete it. Some information is intentionally duplicated to keep it understandable in each section.

In the following chapters, you will find our rules and guidelines that have helped us become successful as landlords in the apartment and commercial real estate business. It contains information to assist in acquiring properties and making them more valuable. You can benefit from our triumphs and disasters and hopefully not make the same mistakes we did. Remember, it is always good to learn from the mistakes of others, as you cannot live long enough to make all the mistakes yourself.

I think our success was partly due to our continued effort to maintain our properties and make repairs in a timely manner. We had little or no deferred maintenance on our properties. Yes, we always had things on our list to do, but they were just jobs we had not gotten to yet. "Good enough for a rental" did not apply for us. We wanted our properties done right and we wanted the work to be completed in a professional manner.

We kept improving our properties. We always put profits back into the company, making our rentals better. We planted bushes and trees early because they need time to grow. We put in patios, concrete walks, and garbage can areas. Even when things are flat or headed south, they will come back; the improvements you make today will make the property much more valuable and easier to sell when times are good.

Take care of your properties; it is like money in the bank.

Chapter 1

BASICS TO LIVE BY

Character

Character is doing the right thing when no one else will know about it. It is a collection of traits that define your personal qualities. Helping a friend, giving directions to a stranger, loaning money when you might not get it back and many, many other actions can show you are a person who does the right thing. It is somewhat hard to define character but you sure know it when you see it.

The racer that helped another competing racer across the finish line in a marathon a short time back had character. The high school basketball coach that came off the sidelines, a year or so ago, to help a young girl who had forgotten the words to the "Star Spangled Banner" had character. Even if he could not sing well, he put his arm around the girl and helped her sing the best he could. It was classy.

Character is doing the right thing even though it is not necessarily good for you personally. Character is doing what is right when no one is watching, respecting opposing views and not putting down other people. Character is acknowledging the good done by others, even those you dislike. Many of the following good qualities in a person are also part of character. Honesty, respect, fairness, courage, and other qualities are all about Character. If a person does not have Character then they are in trouble because nothing else can substitute for it.

Never compromise your ideals to make money. A person with good character is going to live by his convictions and not turn his or her back on their ideals. Yes, making money is what being in business is all about, but making money is secondary to standing by the things that are important to you.

Keep your word

Keeping your word is about having character and honor. When people trust your word, they believe you and trust what you have told them. Keeping your word is a trait common to successful people. You build business relationships as you go along, and when people know you can be trusted to follow through on what you tell them, they are going to respect you and want to do business with you. Keep your word and banks and lenders will be beating down your door to lend you money.

Make your promises carefully. If things do not work out as you planned, you still need to follow through on what you have agreed to.

Say what you mean; mean what you say

This is one of those important traits that set you apart from the less trustworthy people. Whether promising to pay money, do work or be somewhere, it is in your best interest to follow through. Friends, family, and business associates are going to remember you as a person they can trust and rely on.

This is most important when you can get out of fulfilling your promises. Do not look for loopholes to get out of an obligation or for excuses not to follow through. It is easy to keep your word when all is going well, but your friends and associates will recognize your true character when you follow through even when everything is going to hell.

I am reminded of an apartment complex we bought. When escrow closed we went around to each tenant, introduced ourselves, and talked about the plans we had for the complex. We also assured them we had no plans to raise rents. Several months later, a tenant came up to me and shook my hand, telling me that we had done everything we said we would, and followed through on all our promises.

Saying what you mean spills over into raising children also. You need to set rules and consequences. Never promise or threaten anything you do not plan to follow through on. If they misbehave then you have an obligation to them and yourself to enforce the appropriate punishment. Likewise, when they do well you give them the reward you promised.

You need to say what you mean every time. It takes 100 percent for this to be successful and reneging only once can destroy your trustworthiness forever. When people know that you say what you mean they will trust and believe you in future dealings. (Don't you wish politicians read some of this stuff?)

Trust everyone but cut the cards

This saying is from an old Will Rogers, or W. C. Fields movie. This means that you give people a chance to prove their integrity, but you make sure they are not deceiving you. Of course you only trust them until they prove they are not worthy of your trust. A real estate agent that tells you a property is a good deal may be exaggerating the information to make a sale. Always check information yourself: if you get into a poor deal you only have yourself to blame. It is your job to verify everything.

We had an incident with a prospective tenant that came to be known as, "The preacher and the bill collector." We were renting one of our duplexes and the prospective renter arrived in a nice car. He was well dressed and he had his mother with him. He was in his late 30s or early 40s and appeared to be a perfect prospect to be a tenant. On top of the positive appearance, he said he was a preacher from the Midwest looking for a place before bringing his wife and family out west.

It would have been easy to rent to him, but we followed our rules of doing a credit check on all applicants. The credit check came back with red flags all over it. I doubt if he had ever paid a bill in his life. He was probably moving west because the bill collectors were fast on his heels. We did good checking him out. This falls into the category of trusting everyone but cutting the cards. Cutting the cards in this case meant doing the credit check, which saved us a headache down the road.

You also would like all real estate agents to feel comfortable talking with you, and you want them to know they cannot lead you astray. You want them to know you are going to cut the cards and there is no way they can deal from the bottom of the deck.

A handshake is the same as a 50 page legal document

This does not mean that you do not want legal documents, purchase agreements and contracts. They are all part of buying property. It means that, as far as you are concerned, if you shake someone's hand on something it is binding to you. Even when it all goes to hell after, you stick by what you have agreed to. This fits right in with character, keeping your word and saying what you mean. You want everyone to know you are the type person that will follow through and that your word or handshake is like gold: you can take it to the bank.

It is not really even just a handshake; your word fits into this category also. If you agree to it verbally then it is in ink for you. People who work for you, subcontractors, and suppliers will hold you in the highest regard if you honor your commitments. Be honest, tell it like it is, shake their hand, and it is a done deal.

Smile a lot and be courteous, say hello

This sounds like a no-brainer, but it is very easy to become a little stiff in the rental business. A smile goes a long way towards keeping relationships on a positive level. I always say hello to tenants when I am on a property. A short chat with tenants about nothing important puts you in a completely different place than landlords or management companies that put themselves above their tenants. This goes for all parts of your life. Courtesy and a smile will make you a joy to be around and make relationships with everyone else easier. Remember to smile, your friends will love it and your enemies will wonder what the hell you are up to.

Be on time personally or with documents

When a person is on time it shows respect of other peoples' time. Always allow enough time to get where you are going plus a little extra time for a problem. If you are where you are supposed to be on time, others will soon learn that they need to be on time too. This is a major personality trait of those who are efficient and cognizant of their responsibilities. A responsible person will call if they are held up or late. Be on time, call or join the ranks of the irresponsible nitwits.

Being on time with documents is also a trait of a responsible landlord. Paychecks, bills, notices and other documents need to be done on time. You want everyone to know that you are going to have the correct paper work done at the proper time.

Actually, you should figure that there are only two categories of being on time; you are either early or you are late. Just being 'on time' is so close to late that there is not that much difference. Then there is my wife, who, when getting a unit ready to rent, has only one category: getting it done as early as possible.

Pay bills on time or early

Paying bills on time is just like being physically on time. A responsible business owner pays bills early and never pays them late. You want to be paid on time by your tenants and those who owe you money. You want to have a reputation as a "good pay." Workers and subcontractors will appreciate being paid on time. They also have payrolls and expenses, and knowing that they can depend on you will make their lives easier. You want subcontractors to want to work for you. If they know you are fair and pay your bills on time, they are going to go out of their way to do a good job for you. They do not want to lose your business.

A subcontractor who is treated fairly and paid on time is going to be there for you when there is a problem and you need help. When the air conditioner goes out on a summer holiday weekend or a toilet quits on Thanksgiving, the subcontractor that has been taken care of will be there for you.

There are two kinds of people in this world; those who paid their bills on time and those who wished they had.

Financial Responsibility and Credit Rating

Financial responsibility generally comes from spending less than you make. In this world of easy credit, it is very easy to get into a debt hole you may not be able to dig out of. My wife always saved 10 percent of her income. Even as a little girl with a 25-cent allowance, when she asked her mom for more in a week and was asked what happened to her quarter, she would respond, "I saved it." Saving money is its own reward. If people got as much enjoyment from saving as they do from spending, they would be much better off financially.

Have a budget and stick to it. Live within your means. Pay cash for as much as possible; when you use a credit card, pay it off each month. You should have enough money in liquid savings to cover six to eight months of expenses. This is your safeguard for a loss of a job, injury or other disruption in your income. Do not get tied into a long-term car loan just because it does not seem like that much money each month. Buy a car you can afford and sleep better at night knowing you have not over extended yourself. Make purchases based on need and not on want. If you need it, buy it; if it is only a want then you had better be sure you have the money to pay for it.

You should not be organizing your finances by increasing your income to cover your expenses. It should be the other way around; your expenses should be less than your income. You do not deserve anything; you earn everything. Some people really have no idea about their money and where it goes. Have a budget and the good sense to stick with it. Save money for rainy days and future investments. Be the master of your finances, not the servant to your creditors.

Maintaining a high credit rating is extremely important in becoming successful in real estate. Buying real estate is going to take loans, and banks like to loan to people who are going to pay them back. If your record shows that you always pay your bills when due and repay loans on time, banks are going to jump through hoops to get your business. This means paying all bills all the time. It is very difficult to come back from a poor credit rating.

Be very careful with credit cards. It is easy to depend on them and very easy to be buried in credit card debt. If you do not have enough money this month to live on and use a credit card, how are you going to pay all the bills next month plus the credit card bill? It is not easy, but everyone needs to live within their means and not depend on credit cards to survive.

Live below your means and within your needs. Save money and borrow responsibly. Your credit rating will follow you for the rest of your life. Use it to your advantage by paying bills on time and loans on time or early. Guard your credit rating like your future depends on it, because it does.

Track Record

This is one of the most overlooked but very important traits of a successful business owner or landlord. You build a record of being responsible and trustworthy over the years, which will pay dividends the rest of your business career. When people know you are going to do what you say and have a proven record of following through on your commitments, they are going to trust you.

Your track record needs to be perfect. You cannot be responsible 90 percent of the time and be a flake the other 10 percent. It might as well be 90 percent flake, because that is all that is going to be remembered. You need to be perfect to have a good track record. You need to have no screw ups. Even if all goes bad and it does not turn out as planned, you put on your big boy pants, take the blame, and do everything you can to make it right. Making things right might include a monetary loss to yourself to safeguard the money entrusted in you.

You want everyone to know that a loan to you or any other trust in you is rock solid; that no matter what, you have the capabilities and the desire to do what is right. Track record is a key part of our success in real estate. It never occurred to us not to pay back a loan on time or fail to do something we had promised. Following through on commitments will set you above and apart from many people that just do not get the importance of doing what they have agreed to and doing what is right.

An example of our good track record and the trust in us by lenders occurred one day when we got a call from the loan officer at our bank. He told us he had a couple wanting to buy a house that did not have the money to make it happen. However, they did have a duplex in a nice area of town that he was willing to part with to be able to buy this new home. The bank officer told us it was probably worth $145,000 and we could get it for $125,000. It is hard to turn down a bank loan officer telling you he has a great deal for you and a loan to go along with it. We looked at it, and even though it was not in the neighborhood with our other duplexes, it was a nice property in a good part of town. We bought it and still own it today.

We maintained rock solid credit and always followed through with what we told our loan officers. It has paid off many times by getting good loans and quick loans when we needed them. In this case, it was money in our pockets.

Treat tenants like real people

Always remember that this is just a business, it is not personal. Yes, tenants will do all the wrong things – fail to pay, damage our property etc., etc. – but that is just part of this business. Treat tenants fairly, make them play by the rules and do not be surprised when they screw up. It is all part of being a landlord.

Expect poor behavior and attitude from a tenant, and you will not be surprised often. They can be inconsiderate, but we are not. We smile and explain, but do not take it personally. It is just normal day-to-day tenant relations. If you stay above anger, name calling, and raised voices and just try to be a pleasant manager, the tenant will know that you are just doing your job. You may not win them all over, but being consistently pleasant and businesslike will put you in control.

Real people work; you do a tenant a favor by requiring them to work. We have always required a good work history for consideration to rent from us. There are some people, we accept, that simply cannot work due to physical or mental abilities. However, those that can work but do not will have to rent from someone else. It is more than the ability to earn money; it is the basic responsibility of being a contributing member of a society. We feel that those who have the self-worth to earn a living will have the personal qualities to pay their rent and take care of our property.

When dealing with tenants or others, always give the benefit of the doubt when you are not sure. Yes, you will be wrong often, but that is better than wrongly jumping to conclusions. If you are not sure about what a tenant is telling you, get facts. A tenant will appreciate and respect you for getting the correct information. They may not agree with it or like it, but they will know they are being treated fairly. If after getting the correct information you agree with them, they will be delighted.

As a general rule, give tenants more than they expect or paid for. This does not sound like a good business principle on the surface. A common attribute of all successful businesses is customer loyalty and satisfaction. People do not patronize places when they are not satisfied. Consider an auto repair shop that does work on your car, when you pick it up you notice that they have washed it for no charge. Not a big deal or a big expense for the shop, but special for the customer. In the real estate rental business, we have opportunities to give tenants a little extra now and then as well. Maybe this means supplying a fresh roll of toilet paper or paper towels when they move in, or leaving a few bottles of water in the fridge. We have waived late fees occasionally for a good tenant. We want to keep the good tenants happy without costing us much money.

My wife is a tough, no nonsense female. In her 20s, at 5 foot 4 inches and 125 pounds, she passed the entrance examination to become a firefighter, no easy task. She was hired as one of the first female firefighters in her department, as well as one of the first in the United States. She passed all the training and became a full-fledged firefighter, and subsequently was promoted to Apparatus Operator driving fire engines or hook and ladder trucks. She was on the smaller size, but pity the poor male firefighter that might state she was too small to rescue someone. She would grab him by the collar and drag him out of the room, preferably down some stairs. I put this information about her here to set the background of the following tenant story.

We had living in one of our duplex units a single female who had two small children. Her husband had left a few month prior and her car was stolen earlier that month. Times were bad for her and she was forced to take a bus across town to work. It was early December and we had heard from our manager that she had paid her rent on time for the month, but had told her children that there was not going to be a Christmas this year for them. It was sad, but when you are in the business of renting property on the lower end of the scale sad stories are common. This one was different because she was such a nice tenant and she had paid us before spending money on Christmas for her kids.

In the week before Christmas, my wife fixed up a small tree we had with lights and decorations. She also went to Toys"R"Us and purchased a couple toys each for the tenant's children, wrapped them and delivered it all personally to them. She did this all on her own and I did not even know about it until our manager in the neighborhood told me. It was just a simple, inexpensive and very nice way to treat a tenant.

Carolyn, another tenant in one of our apartments, was a wonderful, older lady. We had her as a tenant for the ten years we owned the complex and she had lived there before that. She kept her apartment spotless and was the perfect tenant. She left us to move to an assisted living facility. She was more than a tenant, she was a friend and we miss her.

Disagree without being disagreeable

People disagree all the time. It is the nature of human beings. We are all wired differently and we all think differently. Always hear the other person out and give your arguments calmly and clearly. If you and another person cannot agree, part as friends that see things differently. It is not personal, but just a difference of opinions. Respect people, and when your opinions do not mesh with another person's, disagree without being disagreeable. Maintain your cool and treat the other person with respect even if you think their position or idea is wacko.

Attention to Detail

I believe attention to detail is a good trait which I have had for all of my adult life. I like things done right and I am never comfortable with, "Good enough." Unfortunately, this trait can be called 'nitpicky' or 'anal.' There are people you want in your life that are anal. You certainly want your doctor and airline pilot to be very anal, as well as a police officer or firefighter who comes to help you. Even your attorney should pay good attention to details.

My years in the fire department added to my desire that everything be done correctly. As an officer with the responsibility of saving life and property, I figured there was no place for 'just getting by.' Even at 15 years old cutting lawns, I wanted them to be perfect, all trimmed and not a leaf out of place. I still want all the canned goods and spices on the shelf lined up with labels to the front and all my tools in the garage in a specific place.

This attention to detail served us well in the rental business. I always wanted our property to be in good condition and to show well. If we had the option to spend the money and do it right or to rent the place the way it was, we always chose to do it right unless time or money prevented it. Many times, taking the time and money to do it right meant we actually saved money by renting a place more quickly or preventing a more costly repair down the road. Attention to detail in accounting and paperwork is important for the health of your business and will be noticed by banks, improving your track record.

I still keep list of parts and paint colors for our apartments, pick lint off the floor, and keep my gas tank above quarter full. If you read books about Ray Kroc from McDonalds or Steve Jobs of Apple, you will find that they were ultimate nitpickers. They wanted perfection all the time. Many successful business people share this trait. The old proverb, "If it is worth doing it is worth doing right," is as true today as it was a hundred years ago. Those who do not worry about doing it right and are only interested in just getting by will always just get by.

Chapter 2

TERMS, DEFINITIONS AND FORMULAS

Listed here are common terms and definitions found in real estate in general and this work in particular. We provide formulas for many of the calculations as well as examples with actual numbers to show the relationships.

Amortization

Amortization is a big word for the period of time in which you pay off a loan. Thirty year amortization means you pay for 30 years. Most apartment and commercial loans are written for five to 10 years, and then they need to be rewritten for the next period. However, the payment is set on a 25 or 30 year amortization. Your payments for the loan are just as if you had a loan for the 25 or 30 year period.

After the initial five, seven or 10 year period of the loan, it rolls over to an adjustable loan with interest based on market rates. You usually get a better deal refinancing with a new loan for the shorter periods and starting the amortized payment (on the 25 or 30 year repayment schedule) all over again.

Amortization is also a term used on your tax return to deduct certain costs associated with rental properties, which cannot be claimed in the year paid. Escrow fees, loan fees, and loan points must be "amortized" over the life of the loan, similar to depreciation. Escrow and loan fees are considered part of the cost of the building, and cannot be taken as an expense in the year paid. They must be spread over the life of the loan. Points are considered pre-paid interest and are also amortized. In commercial properties, lease commissions to a real estate agent and the cost of tenant improvements to the property usually need to be amortized.

Aggressively Priced

This is another great term used by real estate "professionals." It just means that the asking price is more than the place is worth. This is a selling technique used when the market is going up and sellers have the advantage; there are more buyers than sellers and the chances of selling for a higher price are increased.

In a seller's market and even sometimes in a buyer's market, buyers are faced with a 1031 exchange situation, wherein they are subject to a large capital gains tax if they cannot find a suitable exchange property to purchase. The seller is clearly in the driver's seat, as they do not have to sell anything but the buyer has to buy something.

When we were looking for our first apartment complex we found one we liked and we had the selling agent over to discuss it. The property was listed at $2,800,000 but the Net Operating Income only justified a price of $2,600,000. I told the selling agent this and he said the property was "aggressively priced." New to this term, I asked him what aggressively priced meant. He stalled and beat around the bush, and finally said it was priced on the high end to catch someone in a 1031 exchange situation that was going to have to buy something and was willing to over pay for it.

Basis Points

"Basis points" is a term you see often in real estate monthly, quarterly and annual reports. It is a term used by "real estate professionals." "Basis points" is a hundredth of a percent. If vacancies go up from 5.00 percent to 5.01 percent, they have raised one basis point. It is probably easier to describe than, "Vacancies went up 1/100 of a percent."

For example, if cap rates went from 6.5 percent to 7 percent it could be said that they went up half a percent, that they went up .5 percent, or, if using "Basic Points," that they went up 50 basis points.

The term makes a little more sense when the increase is a decimal. If a cap rate goes from 6.00 percent to 6.74 percent, it went up 74 basis points, 74 one-hundredths of a percent, or .74 percent.

Do not confuse this with Points paid when getting a loan, or the Basis used in computing capital gains taxes.

CAM, Common Area Maintenance

In commercial real estate, tenants are often charged for expenses to cover common area maintenance. Common area expenses usually deal with a multi-tenant commercial property where maintenance charges are pro-rated by the percentage of the floor area a tenant occupies. Items included in CAM charges can vary depending on the terms of the lease and the agreement between the tenant and the landlord.

Cap Rate, Capitalization Rate

Capitalization Rate is a percentage that represents the return on a property based on the income produced (NOI), compared to the price of the property.

To calculate the NOI, the income used is actual income of net rent income plus other income. (This is the amount taken to the bank.) This income is reduced by actual expenses including an allowance for reserves. In this calculation, interest expense for the mortgage is not included, as mortgage payments come out of the Net Operating Income.

The Cap Rate percentage is found by dividing the annual Net Operating Income on the property by the cost of the property. It is only as accurate as the accuracy of the net income minus all expenses, including an allowance for reserves.

> FORMULA:
> (NOI) divided by (Cost of Property) = Cap Rate as a percent

> This formula can be figured backwards as well. If you know the income, expenses, and a known or desired Cap Rate, you can figure what the property is worth.

> (Cost or Value of Property) = (NOI) divided by (Cap Rate)

This Cap Rate percentage varies depending on supply and demand of properties, quality of property for sale, and market interest rates. When demand for property is high, the Cap Rate goes down. When the interest rate is low, the Cap Rate also goes down. Properties that are more desirable will command a lower Cap Rate.

Cap Rates have been going up and down for the last decade. In 2003, Cap Rates were around 7.5 percent. By 2006, at the height of demand, the Cap Rate was as low as 4.5 percent for Class A properties. By the end of 2008, it was back to about 6.5 percent or higher. In late 2009 to 2012, the cap rate was at 7 percent or higher. Then in 2013, as the economy brightened and apartments increased in value, Cap Rates began to drop again, hitting about 6 percent in mid 2013.

A small difference in Cap Rate will result in a large difference in price. Therefore, it is very important to have accurate rent and expense figures to work with. Using a real estate broker's figures will always result in a higher Cap Rate than the property warrants, because income will be inflated and expenses deflated, resulting in a NOI above what it should be.

As a general rule, you should not buy a property with a Cap Rate that is lower than the interest rate on the loan.

Cash on Cash

Cash on Cash is a percent figure that real estate agents use to show the potential profit from a property. It is a percentage of return based on the out of pocket down payment compared to the profit after all expenses and debt service interest have been paid. The principal part of the mortgage is part of the profit and is included as profit in the "Cash on Cash" figure.

Cash on Cash is not a good figure to base judgment of a property upon, as it depends on the size of the down payment and terms of the loan.

FORMULA:
Annual Profit equals... (Income) − (Expenses)
Divided by.................. (Total out of pocket cost)
Equals.....................Cash on Cash as an annual percentage

EXAMPLE 1: A property cost $100,000 that produces $10,000 profit after all expenses. If purchased for cash, you have $100,000 out of pocket cost.

Annual Profit equals.... $10,000
Divided by .... $100,000 (Your out of pocket cost)
Equals.................... 10 percent cash on cash for the year

EXAMPLE 2: Same property, except you put $20,000 down and obtain a loan for $80,000 at 6 percent interest for 30 years. The $10,000 profit is reduced by the amount of interest expense paid on the loan. In the first year there will be about $4,500 in interest paid, reducing profit to $5,500 for the year.

Annual Profit equals.... $5,500
Divided by............... $20,000 (Your out of pocket cost)
Equals...................   27.5 percent cash on cash for the year

This is why I do not place much importance on cash on cash figures in sales brochures. In Example 2 above, the cash profit is less but the cash on cash percent is much larger than in the first example. Better to look at the basics of income and expenses to determine the value of a property. This does make a good argument for financing properties. By leveraging, you can significantly increase your return on your out of pocket investment.

Credit Score

A credit score is a number representing the creditworthiness of a person. This number is used by creditors and banks to judge the likelihood that a person will pay a loan back. It provides a snapshot of risk that banks and other institutions use to help make lending decisions.

FICO is the leading provider of credit score information. This is a private company that compiles credit scores on people and sells this information to lenders. FICO is the most known company providing this service, but there are others. FICO scores range between 300 and 850 and are based on a number of factors from your credit history.

We always do a credit check on a prospective tenant. This is not a cut and dried deal. As many factors affect their credit rating, we look for how long ago problems occurred and what they did about them. Since 2007, half the country has a poor credit rating. A good apartment owner will use the credit score and rating as a tool along with other factors, like job history, to make a determination if a prospective tenant is a good risk.

CDR, Credit to Debt Ratio

Credit to debt ratio, sometimes called CDR, or just DR, is a ratio of the NOI of a property to the debt service payment. (Debt service payment includes principal and interest.)

This is a figure banks use to determine how large a loan the income of the property can support. It is found by dividing the NOI by the annual mortgage payment for the interest rate and term desired. The banks want the property owners to be able to pay their mortgage payment and have money left over each month. CDR can be expressed as a percentage but is usually shown as a decimal.

Depending on the quality of the property and the financial times, the desired CDR can range from 1.15 for a top property in good times, to 1.35 for lesser properties in poor times. Commercial properties are usually figured at the higher CDR numbers. Generally, a CDR of 1.2 to 1.25 should work for most banks. The borrower's financial strength might sway the banks a little.

> As CDR is based on a total mortgage payment, it changes as interest rates change or the amortization term changes.
>
> FORMULA:
> (Annual Net Operating Income)
> Divided by (Annual Mortgage Payment)
> _____
>
>   = (CDR)
>
> Or figuring from a known CDR

(Annual Net Operating Income)

Divided by (CDR)

= (total annual mortgage payment with principal & interest)

EXAMPLE: A property has a NOI of $135,000 per year. The annual mortgage payment including principal and interest after a proposed down payment is $115,000 per year.

($135,000 NOI)   divided by ($115,000 Payment) = 1.17 CDR

If the bank wants the loan to be at or above a CDR of 1.25, it will be necessary to increase the down payment so that the annual mortgage and interest payment will not exceed $108,000.

($135,000 NOI) divided by (1.25 CDR) = $108,000 Payment

Classes of Properties

Apartment properties are loosely classified in groups as to the quality, amenities and desirability.

CLASS A

Class A properties are generally newer, in nice parts of town, rent for more and have all the top features. In a class A property, you would expect fitness centers, community rooms, nice pools, spas, maybe tennis courts, upgraded appliances, ceramic floor tile and granite counter tops. Fireplaces and washer/dryers are common in class A properties. Oftentimes these are very large complexes getting top rents.

CLASS B

Class B properties are nice, but lack many of the upscale features of a class A property. Class B apartments can be in most any neighborhood in town. They are clean, well maintained, and provide a basic apartment at a competitive rent. All of the properties owned by our company are class B properties.

We have always felt that class B apartments are the most stable investment as they are reasonably priced, offer clean basic housing, and are in demand by tenants who usually pay their bills. The best combination is a class B property in a class A area, especially if the class B property has a few class A features, but can still rent economically.

CLASS C

Class C properties are less desirable. They have little or no landscaping, are poorly maintained, and are generally older buildings in poorer areas of town. Many times class C properties will have wall heaters and/or wall air conditioner units. All the duplexes we owned were class C properties when we bought them, but we got them up to a B- at least. Their advantage to investors is that C properties cost half as much as an A property, but can generate 70 percent of the rents.

Class C is the lowest official class, but there are plenty of properties out there that we would call class F. There are plenty of lower class apartments around making money if the landlord has the tolerance for dealing with the cliental.

Concessions

Concessions are discounts on rent or free rent, usually given as an incentive to lease or rent a property. Most times if the complex uses leases, an amount of free rent is given, such as two weeks or a month free with the signing of the lease.

Occasionally, at the beginning of a rental term rents might start a week or two after moving in. This is usually due to splitting the cost with a tenant that is giving notice somewhere else and has another rent obligation.

This lost rent is not usually considered a concession but rather part of the vacancy percentage.

During the downturn in the real estate market of 2008 to 2011, we found ourselves giving more concessions to stay competitive and fill vacancies.

When buying a property it is important to delete all concessions from scheduled rents to arrive at a true net rent income amount.

Dating and Anticipation

These are terms used in business but not much in real estate. Dating is when a business purchases items and gets the merchandise, but does not have to pay for it until a specific date in the future. This is common in seasonal businesses where the store owner wants to get his store full of merchandise and be ready when the season gets in full swing. It is just a type of credit offered to sell a product.

Anticipation is kind of the opposite of Dating. If a business pays their bill early, not waiting for the full dating period to pass, they will be given a discount. This discount is known as anticipation and is usually shown as a percent discount per month for the amount owed.

Debt Service

Debt service is the term used for the amount of the mortgage payment, including principal and interest. It is usually shown as an annual payment, but can be shown monthly.

Deferred Maintenance

When repairs are not done and are put off, it is called "deferred maintenance." These repairs can cost a considerable amount of money and must be taken into account when calculating the value of a property.

Some reserves type repairs, like roof replacement, are done infrequently. Estimate the life of the roof, figure how much should have been set aside each year, and include it in the deferred maintenance figure. Use the same type of calculations for exterior painting, parking lot resurfacing and stripping, and pool plastering and pool equipment replacement. The value of a property should be reduced by an amount equal to the reserve funds that should have been set aside for these expenditures.

Deferred maintenance can also involve individual rental units, gutters, office, landscape or other parts of the complex where routine day-to-day maintenance has been neglected or patched instead of fixed.

Due Diligence

Sellers provide information on the property to the buyer. The buyer provides, in the Purchase Agreement, a list of documents they wish to review, and the seller must provide these documents in the time frame stated in the Purchase Agreement.

The Purchase Agreement will have a "Due Diligence" time period. This is a time period for the buyer to read, check and approve all of the disclosure information and documents provided by the seller (or documents the buyer obtains elsewhere.) The buyer may make independent inspections, review, and check anything they wish to during this period.

During the Due Diligence period, the buyer may cancel the purchase for any reason. This time period can be whatever the buyer and seller agree to in the Purchase Agreement, but is usually 30 days or less. Once the Due Diligence period ends, the buyer sends a letter to the seller accepting all of the information and documents. The contract becomes more binding at that time and deposit monies are usually increased and/or become non-refundable. There may still be a loan contingency to be satisfied later.

The buyer, in their Due Diligence acceptance letter, can list "exceptions" which must be satisfied for the purchase to progress. At this time, the seller can cancel the purchase if they are unable or unwilling to correct exceptions.

The Due Diligence period is an important part of the purchase, as it allows the Purchase Agreement to be signed without having to spend a lot of time on inspection and research before moving forward. It allows interested parties to make a deal based on reasonable expectations of the property and to have time to verify the information. It provides the buyer with an escape clause in case the property turns out to be less than expected.

Estoppel Certificate

An estoppel certificate is used in commercial leases so a tenant can confirm details of their tenancy to a third party. This is usually done when the property is being sold or when the landlord is applying for a loan. The certificate is typically prepared by the owner/landlord with the facts needed and only requires a signature from the tenant. The tenant, of course, must make sure all the information on the certificate is correct.

The certificate can contain any information about the property, which the tenant can confirm. This information will include rents, rent increases, and any other terms of the lease that might be important to the third party. This certificate enables a buyer or a loan officer to verify information supplied by an owner or real estate agent. This is a simple and common procedure and a tenant only needs to verify the information.

The bottom line on estoppels is simple. The third party wants to have correct information on the property verified by the tenant.

Execute

When an agreement or document is signed by all parties involved. A purchase agreement becomes a fully executed purchase agreement when both the buyer and the seller have signed the document.

Expenses

Many expenses for an apartment complex are nearly the same from complex to complex. However, a few exceptions are noted here. Look for big differences from county to county for utility costs (water, sewer and waste removal.)

Electricity and natural gas are somewhat constant in an area. There can be major electrical and natural gas differences if the buildings have central hot water paid by the landlord, or a heated pool or spa. Tenants usually pay their own electricity, natural gas, telephone, TV and internet.

Some complexes require much more advertising than others due to a hidden location or competition in the area. Check the seller's income and expense records to see how much is spent on advertising. If advertising and attorney fees are both high, it is an indication of tenant problems, evictions and vacancies.

Insurance and property taxes are a function of value and sales price. They can increase substantially at a change of ownership. Property taxes especially can increase significantly if the property has been held for some time by the seller and taxes are currently low on the property. Be sure to calculate your new total expenses using the new property tax amount.

Insurance costs can increase at a change of ownership due to the property being revalued at a greater amount and having the current insurance coverage based on the previous value. Check with your insurance agent for a new quote to be sure.

Expenses, Capital

Capital expenses are over and above normal day-to-day expenses and expenses paid from Reserves. Capital expenses are upgrades that improve the property, and should usually result in higher rents or fewer vacancies. Fewer vacancies can be the result of the complex being more rentable or nicer. Examples of capital expenses are ceramic tile floors, microwaves, washer/dryers, patio covers, carports, pool bathrooms, or fitness centers.

Some capital expenditures are done for management purposes and do not effect rents (a new work shed or manager's office improvements, for example.)

Capital expenses are not included on the income and expense report and are not part of the Net Operating Income because they are optional.

FSBO, For Sale by Owner

FSBO stands for: *For Sale by Owner*. You might find this in a newspaper advertisement or sales brochure or on a for sale sign. This just means that there is no real estate broker involved in the sale.

GRM, Gross Rent Multiplier

Gross Rent Multiplier is an easy way to compare properties or calculate values. It is sometimes called GIM (Gross Income Multiplier.) The GRM should only consider rent income. Some real estate brokers like to confuse buyers with the "GIM" using all income and making the property appear to be a little more valuable. Non-rent income would be income from the laundry room, late fees etc. Stick with a GRM using only rent income to provide a better comparison value.

GRM is a ratio of annual rent income to value. It does not consider vacancies or expenses. This is not as detailed a figure as a value based on cap rates, vacancies and expenses, etc., but it is easy and quick and a good indication of the approximate value of a property.

The GRM ratio is shown as a decimal and calculated by dividing the cost of the property by its annual rent income.

> FORMULA:
> (Cost of Property) divided by (Annual Total Rent) = (GRM)
>
> EXAMPLE: A property costing $1,000,000, with a total annual rent of $100,000 would have a GRM of 10.0.
>
> ($1,000,000) divided by ($100,000) = 10.0 GRM

A low GRM is better for the buyers, because it means that they are getting more income from the property. A small difference in GRM will result in a sizable difference in income. Like cap rates, making sure these figures are accurate is very important in determining the value of a property.

Cap rates and GRM amounts vary in relationship to the economy. In a buyer's market when the supply of properties for sale exceeds demand, prices drop and GRM gets smaller. (Cap rates increase in a buyer's market.) When the real estate market shifts to a seller's market, the cap rates drop and the GRM gets larger. There is no right or wrong amounts for cap rates and GRM. They vary in relationship to market conditions. In the early 1950s, the standard GRM was around 10.0.

Over the years, GRM slowly dropped and leveled off at about 8.5 for much of the late 1900s, with some ups and downs. This continued until about 2003, when GRM started climbing with the real estate boom of 2004 to 2006. Asking prices during this time had GRM of over 12.0 many times.

By 2008, real estate values were in free fall and the GRMs dropped. Asking prices were slow to reflect actual values and GRM took a while to adjust.

By 2010, realistically priced properties had GRMs of around 8.0, with many distressed properties selling at GRMs even lower.

Wise real estate investors keep familiar with what properties are listed and sold for to keep themselves up to date on both current cap rates and GRMs. This will enable a potential buyer to recognize a good deal on a possible investment when it comes along.

Hard Money

Hard money is money that is being held somewhere and is non-refundable. For example, this might be in escrow as a deposit on a purchase; if you fail to complete the purchase under the terms of the agreement, the deposit is forfeited to the seller.

Hard money is also money you pay the bank to lock interest at a certain level in anticipation that interest rates are going to go up. If you complete the loan as agreed to, the "hard money" goes to pay loan fees. However, if you fail to complete the loan, the hard money will be forfeited to the bank and gone forever.

We had a situation once refinancing two apartment complexes where interest rates were headed down; when they got to record lows, we paid $40,000 in "hard money" to lock in the low interest rate. Unfortunately, the rates kept falling and by the time the property was ready to close it was in our advantage to lock in the new lower interest rate and forfeit our $40,000 to the bank. It pained us to lose our hard money, but the difference in interest rates was worth more than the $40,000 in reduced payments over the five-year life of the loan.

Income

The terms "rents" and "income" are often used interchangeably. (See below under "Rent" for all the different ways rental income can be stated.) Rental income is by far the largest portion of income received. For commercial properties, you probably receive what is called "Additional Rent" or some similar term, which is a monthly charge to the tenant for their share of common area expenses.

Laundry rooms generate a modest income, followed by late fees, credit checks, etc. These are usually all lumped together under "Other Income" on an income and expense statement for a property.

Often "Other Income" is not used when figuring Net Operating Income because it is such a small percent of the entire income total. When this shows up on a broker's calculations for a property, it is probably because the broker is struggling to justify the asking price of a property and wants to make the property look like a better deal than it really is. Other incomes run about 5 percent of the total income and therefore will have a modest effect on NOI.

Issue

An issue in real estate is a problem. If there is an issue then something is wrong. We looked at a commercial property in Texas once and we were told, "There was an issue with the roof." I did not know what the agent was talking about and questioned him about what was wrong with the roof. Finally, he admitted that when it rained water came in. "Oh," I told him, "that is what a roof issue is. Back home we would call that a leak." This is not a common term here and agents usually explain what the problem is or just ignore it all together. We have disclosure laws, and a seller is required to disclose any "issues" with the building. In some other states, disclosure laws may not be as stringent, and it is very important for the buyer to beware.

Leases

Leases for commercial property will include how taxes, insurance and maintenance expenses are going to be handled. There are a number of different systems in use depending on the state or tradition for the area. As a general rule, the more desirable the property, the more expenses are passed to the tenant. Rents will be based on how much of the expenses the landlord is required to pay.

Full Service Lease

As the name implies, this type of lease covers pretty much everything. The landlord will be paying the property taxes, insurance, utilities and common area maintenance, as in the Gross Lease below. However, in a full service lease, most other expenses for the business are included in the tenants' rent, such as janitorial service and even changing light bulbs. These leases can vary somewhat, but generally provide a tenant with everything included in their monthly rent payment.

Gross Lease

A gross lease is similar to the full service lease, except tenants pay their own janitorial service and other minor maintenance expenses in their unit. The landlord pays all the property taxes, insurance and common area maintenance expenses. Utilities, most times, will be paid by the property owner. Utilities are definitely the landlord's expense if utility services overlap suites in a multi-tenant property.

Modified Gross Lease

In a modified gross lease, some of the expenses are passed to the tenant or are paid directly by the tenant. This generally includes utilities or maybe insurance, but can be whatever the landlord and tenant agree to. We prefer that tenants pay for utilities. This gives them an incentive to conserve.

Triple Net Lease, (Nnn)

This is the standard lease used for the best properties and top tenants. In this lease, the tenant pays for everything. Property taxes, insurance, utilities and all common area maintenance expenses are pro-rated back to the tenants. There are usually a few expenses reserved just for the landlord that will be specified in the lease. These expenses typically include the roof and the main structure of the building. For the most part the tenant pays their rent and all other expenses.

Single Net Lease And Double Net Lease

These are hardly ever used. These can fall into the modified gross lease category. In a single net lease, the tenant pays the real estate taxes. In a double net lease, they also pay the insurance. It is just easier to write a modified gross lease and indicate who pays what.

Letter of Commitment (Commitment Letter)

The bank will send this letter on a commitment to loan money. Sometimes they have an escape clause in the letter, but generally when you get this Commitment Letter the loan is pretty much approved. The letter can have contingencies in it such as a minimum appraisal amount, reserve cash in bank, etc. You must satisfy these contingencies to get the loan.

Leveraging

Leveraging a property is when you put a small percentage down and get a large loan. This amounts to using borrowed funds for a significant amount of the investment and expecting the profits made to be greater than the interest payable. In our duplex days, we liked to leverage properties as much as possible with the smallest down payment, lowest interest rate and longest term. Leveraging allows you to buy more or larger properties with the least amount of your own funds involved.

It can be dangerous when the real estate market is depressed and values are dropping. For commercial properties or apartments, banks are not going to let investors leverage as much as they might for a smaller property. Loan to value amounts required by the bank will make an investor put down a sizable down payment and reduce leveraging.

LOI, Letter of Interest, Letter of Intent, Expression of Interest

This is a non-binding letter from a possible buyer to a seller or property owner, showing that you would like to buy their property. Very basic terms are listed, including price, proposed loan details and any special terms. This is just a letter, and most times it is a single page or two. It is signed by the buyer and, if accepted, by the seller. It is totally non-binding and either party can walk away for any reason. Only the Purchase Agreement legally binds the buyer and seller. The LOI is a good faith offer to buy a property.

A letter of interest is a good way to start, as it does not require a multi-page, attorney language document. If the letter is accepted, the buyer prepares a Purchase Agreement with detailed terms of the purchase, including options, contingencies, etc. All terms of the Purchase Agreement are negotiable and only become a contract when both parties sign.

A similar letter of interest is received from a bank concerning a loan. The bank sends such a letter when it feels that the basics of the purchase are sound. It will outline the loan amount and terms, and, like above it is also non-binding. The interest letter from the bank will contain such things as application fee, documents required, and anything else the bank feels is important. This is different from a Commitment Letter from the bank, which is more binding and will contain specific conditions required before a loan will be approved.

LTV, Loan to Value

Loan to Value, or LTV, is a term used by banks. It is the amount of loan the lender will give on a property. It is shown as a percent of the value of the property. In good economic times a loan to value of 80 percent was common, but when values got too far ahead of rent income, the LTV got smaller. Properties purchased during the peak of the real estate boom in 2005 or 2006 generally ran around a 65 percent LTV. By 2009, even though values were down, banks were so shell-shocked from all the bad loans that LTVs were many times 60 percent, disregarding a high CDR.

> FORMULA:
> (Loan Amount) divided by (Value of Property) = (LTV percent)
>
> (100 percent) minus (LTV percent) = (Down Payment percent)
>
> Loan amount is a function of Income and Expenses (NOI), using the CDR (Credit to Debt Ratio) desired by the bank.

Managers

Resident Manager

In our community, a landlord is required to have a management person living in one of the apartments if the complex has 16 units or more. Besides being the law, it is good business to have someone there to handle the day-to-day management duties, and to be available for problems after hours. Many smaller complexes only need a part-time manager. When the manager lives on site, it is easy to handle the daily activities without having to sit in the office. You are still within the law if you have a maintenance person living on premise instead of the resident manager, but you are far better off having a manager there.

Property Manager

The term property manager is often times used for the management level above the resident manager. The property manager supervises several apartment complexes. "Property manager" can also mean the professional property management company itself.

Margin

Margin is a percentage increase over a known amount. For example, in retail sales, if a merchant buys an item for $100 and marks it up 25 percent, they will sell the item for $125. The extra $25 is their profit margin.

Banks do similar "marking up", in the case of an adjustable rate mortgage, by using a known index rate and increasing this amount by the agreed upon margin to set the interest rate. The margin is a fixed percentage rate, while the index rate varies according to market conditions. The interest rate for the loan can change annually over the life of the loan.

Most apartment loans will provide an option to rollover to an adjustable rate mortgage after the initial fixed rate period. When applying for an adjustable rate loan, you want the lowest margin possible. This is somewhat negotiable based on your credit rating, down payment amount, points paid and initial interest rate.

Negative Cash Flow

Cash flow is the income less expenses and mortgage payments. When vacancies or expenses increase to the point where there is not enough income to pay all the bills, you enter into a negative cash flow situation where it is necessary to use other funds. This usually happens more with smaller properties when the bank does not require loans to qualify based on a pre-set CDR.

NOI, Net Operating Income

NOI is the amount of income the property will produce before mortgage payment (Debt Service.)

When estimating income on a property for sale, we use market rents as if all units were rented for the amount currently obtained for a new tenant renting a vacant unit. The manager's apartment is included in market rents just as if it was rented. The expenses will reflect management costs, which will include the value of the manager's apartment.

This gross market rent amount is reduced by a vacancy percent, usually figured at 5 percent. After the annual market rents have been reduced by a vacancy factor, the result is known as Net Rental Income. Add any other income to arrive at Net Annual Income.

Next, subtract estimated expenses from the Net Annual Income. Take into consideration expenses over normal amounts for new taxes, insurance, utilities, heating spas or providing hot water to tenants. This expense estimate should also include an amount for reserves, based upon the exterior siding type, roof type, size of parking lot, and pool and spa reserves needed.

The result of Net Annual Income less expenses and reserves is Net Operating Income (NOI.)

FORMULA:

	Annual Market Rent
Less	Vacancy percent
	Net Rental Income
Plus	Other Income
	Net Annual Income

Less	Estimated Expenses
	(without Interest Expenses)

Less	Reserves
	Net Operating Income

AS PART OF AN ANNUAL OPERATING STATEMENT

Net Operating Income is also calculated as part of the annual Operating Statement for a property. We want to know the incomes, normal routine expenses and the NOI to compare them to prior years or other properties. In our annual statement, we do not include any capital improvements or discretionary spending. We are looking for the basic income and expenses of the property and the NOI it is producing. The annual report also uses actual income as opposed to market rents, and therefore there no need for a vacancy allowance. Because this statement is for comparison purposes, we do not include any expenses known as reserves. The reason for this is that reserve expenses vary widely from year to year and their inclusion would make comparisons difficult. Below are the actual figures for one of our apartment complexes in 2011.

FOR EXAMPLE:

	$551,336	Actual Rent Income
Plus	$31,057	Other Income
Equals	$582,393	**Net Annual Income**
Less	$235,472	Actual Expenses (without Interest Expense)
Equals	$346,921	**Net Operating Income**

Points

Points are a fee paid to the bank when getting a loan. Points are considered pre-paid interest by the IRS. Each point is one percent. For example, if you were borrowing $1,000 and had to pay two points to get the loan, you would have to pay the bank the fee of $20. Not a great deal on a small loan, but on a million dollar loan the same two points would cost you $20,000. When banks lower the interest rate, they raise the points to be paid. Both are fluctuating amounts. Sometimes you have the choice of paying more in points up front and getting a lower interest rate on the loan. This is known as *Buying Down.*

We always figure the bank is not going to be setting itself up to make less money one way or the other, so it does not make a lot of difference which way you choose to go. If you were low on down payment funds then the low point's higher interest rate would be more appealing. Like most dealings with the bank, they set the rules and terms and we accept them or not.

Points paid on a loan cannot be taken as an expense on your taxes in the year paid. The IRS requires them to be amortized over the life of the loan. If the property is sold or refinanced you can take any remainder of points from previous loans as an expense in the year the property is sold or refinanced.

REIT, Real Estate Investment Trust

This is a security that sells like a stock. It can be privately run or a public company similar to mutual funds. This type company invests in real estate either by the purchase of properties, making mortgages, buying of existing mortgages or some combination of these. We have not invested in any of these.

Rents

Rents can be expressed in many ways. The number most important is the amount on the deposit slip: the amount we will deposit in the bank. Some of the other rent and rent income terms are listed below:

Gross Scheduled Rent, (Scheduled Rent)

This is the current rent for the apartment type. If the complex has ten apartments renting for $700 per month each, the Gross Scheduled rent for the complex is $7,000 per month. This is the rent each unit is NOW scheduled to pay. Even the vacant units are counted in this number. This total is kind of a mix, with occupied units shown at their current rents and vacant units shown at market rent.

Market Rents

Market rents are the price you would rent an apartment at if it came vacant today. This would include a reduction for any concessions normally offered to a new tenant. This price should be compatible with similar units in the area.

When calculating the value of an apartment complex, use Market rents. This should be the best rent return on units, while keeping vacancies low. This means that if rents are raised above this point, vacancies will increase and the net result will be less profit. After a complex is purchased, rents can be raised in stages until they are all at Market rent. As long as raised rents do not exceed the competition, few tenants will move.

Even though some apartments in the complex may be renting for more or less than this amount, if you multiply the number of apartments in the complex (including the manager's apartment) by the Market rent, it will give the best income information when calculating values.

The value of the manager's apartment will show up under management expenses when calculating net operating income (NOI.)

Effective Rents

What tenant pays after concessions are deducted. This term is used by some real estate brokers but not very often. It is really the same as Market Rents less concessions. Concessions are a discount for signing a lease, or some free rent up front. Effective rents are pretty much what you are really getting for the unit. (Most brokers would still consider this Market Rent.) It does not deal with vacancies (see Net rents.)

Pro-Forma Rent

Pro-forma is French for baloney. Pro-forma rent is a number picked out of the air by real estate brokers to indicate some future rent income possibilities. As this number is totally made up, do not ever use it. It is just a way to justify an overpriced property. Use Market rents to figure values.

It is certainly possible that current rent income for a property is too low, but using Market rents will result in a fair value for the property. As a general rule, if a list of figures begins with "Pro-forma," you can pull it out and toss it in the garbage.

Actual Rent

Actual rent is the amount on the deposit slip that went to the bank. Actual rents charged can be anything. Many times, landlords fail to increase rents over the years and they end up with some tenants paying the going market rate while other are still paying whatever they paid when they moved in. Owners and managers are often reluctant to raise rents and long term tenants end up paying less than the going rate.

The actual rent for a property is all the rents added together collectively. Actual rents will almost always be lower than market rents and much lower than Pro-forma rents. It is good business for a landlord to keep his rents close to market rent values. This will keep profit and property values up because both are a function of rents. Keep the value of the property where it should be by keeping rents current.

If actual rents get too far behind market rents it can be very difficult for landlords to raise them to the proper level. By the time the landlord adjusts rents the market rent has gone up again. It is not a good practice to raise rents often to try to catch up, as you will alienate your tenants. By having rents too low in an increasing market you probably will not catch up until things level off unless you impose a large rent increase. Some cities have laws that prevent rent increases larger or more often than you might need to catch up. If rents are kept close to market then keeping abreast of rent values in a changing market is far easier.

Net Rent, (Net Current Rents, Net Market Rents)

Net rent is the amount left after concessions and vacancies. The formula for figuring net rents of an apartment complex is:

(Market Rent) – (Concessions) – (Vacancies) = Net Rent

The industry generally uses a 5 percent vacancy factor. This does vary by area, with some places a little less and some places higher. Five percent is usually a little lower than reality but a good figure for comparing properties. It is not easy to maintain only a five percent vacancy. A complex that can maintain only a 5 percent vacancy rate is doing very well. Determining net rents are one of the steps in calculating net operating income (NOI.)

Reserves

Reserves are money set aside annually for major repairs that occur on a non-annual basis. You do not necessarily have an account somewhere for this, but it is included in the cash reserves for the company.

Reserves include a new roof or major roof repair; exterior painting or major exterior siding repair; replacing large sections of fencing; resurfacing the parking lot; and plastering the pool or replacing equipment for the pool. These repairs occur from every five years to every 20 years or more.

The amount set aside for reserves, for the complex, comes from past history or is estimated, taking into consideration roof and siding types. Flat roofs need to be resurfaced more often than pitched roofs, but they are less expensive. Flat roofs need to be redone about every 10 to 15 years, while a pitched roof should last 20 to 25 years. Exterior siding needs more repairs than stucco and it must be painted about every five years.

A pool plaster needs to be refinished about every 15 years and the pool equipment will probably need to be replaced about every five years. If the complex has a spa, then there will be twice the amount of pumps and filters, and a heater that will need periodic replacement.

It is very important when figuring the value of a property to include an annual amount for these reserve expenses. In 2009, for example I would figure $250 per year per apartment, if the apartment complex had T-111 wood siding. Apartment complexes with a stucco exterior would be figured at $200 per year per apartment. Most complexes have a swimming pool, but if they did not have one, I would reduce the reserve amount by $50 per year per apartment.

The amount allowed for reserves is important in the calculation of value. For example, in the case of one 44 unit apartment complex we were looking at, figuring the normal expenses came to just over $4.000 per unit in 2009. Allowing the $200 for reserves was just about 5 percent more (an important amount to add.) Keeping in mind that $200 times 44 apartments is $8,800 per year, which reduced the NOI by $8,800. At a 7 percent cap rate, this reduced the value of the complex by **$125,000**.

Reserves are a general amount of money figured per unit annually. In 2009 the amount ran between $200 and $250 depending on features of the complex. When figuring the value of an apartment complex, the reserve allowance is added to expenses, usually as a separate line when figuring the net operation income of a property.

Reserve funds can be put into a separate bank account, but are usually just left with other operating funds. A wise investor makes sure reserve funds are always available for these periodic expenses as well as for some unexpected large repair.

Condominium projects also use Reserve in a similar manner. It is necessary to include many more items in the reserve fund because, unlike apartments, there is no income to pay for these repairs. Therefore, the condo owners must pay each month into a fund designated to pay for all common area repairs. For example, normal repairs paid from income in an apartment complex, like painting curbs now and then must be allowed for and funds set aside for, in a condominium homeowner association.

Stabilization (Stabilized Income, Stabilized Rent)

Stabilization is a term seen in sales brochures that means the property is rented for less than Market rent, has too many vacancies, has deferred maintenance, or has some other problem causing income to be low.

This means that if you fill the vacancies and make all the repairs, get the rents up to market, etc., then the "Stabilized" income can be realized. Never mind that the selling party has not been able to accomplish these tasks and get rents up to market levels.

Stabilization is not as bad as the term "Pro-forma" because it is based on somewhat controllable variables. But keep in mind if it was easy to stabilize a property, then the seller would have do so before putting it up for sale.

1031

1031 is a section number of the IRS tax code. This deals with the rules for a tax deferred exchange of properties. It is important when selling a property that has been held for a number of years, or one that has experienced a large increase in value. A 1031 exchange allows you to move your basis from the old property to the new one without incurring any capital gains tax liability at the time of the sale.

TIC, Tenant in Common

This is an investment where a management company gets a group of investors to pool their money to purchase a large commercial property. The property can be apartments, offices, retail shopping centers or just about anything else that can be imagined. It is different from a partnership in that the investors have few rights and no say in the operation of the investment. This investment offers a good rate of return and is permissible as a 1031 deferred tax purchase. These features make it appealing to many investors who have money to invest and are looking for a good rate of return.

These investments were popular when values were escalating and it was easy to show a profit. However, when values decreased in the real estate melt down, this type of investments tanked; they were generally overpriced, had large loans, and in some cases were run by shady management. Some, like apartments, have weathered the downturn, but office-type investments were soon underwater from reduced rental rates and huge vacancies.

This investment is very dangerous and for those with too much money, needing to get rid of some. On the surface they appear like a reasonable investment, but they are not. In 2006 in needing to re-invest 10-31 funds, we bought a couple of these TIC investments and fortunately only put in a modest amount of funds. We know others who lost a substantial part of their retirement funds from TIC investments. Our experience is that these investments are set up to be too easy for unscrupulous manages to run into the ground with no way for the actual investors to do anything about it. Run; do not just walk away, from anyone trying to sell you a TIC investment.

Turnover

A turnover occurs when one tenant leaves and it is necessary to get the rental unit ready to rent to the next. This would include any repairs, changes or cleaning necessary to bring the unit back up to our standard quality.

Vacancy Factor (Vacancy Rate, Vacancy percent)

Vacancy factor is a percentage subtracted from Market Rents and used when calculating the value of a property. Vacancies vary from property to property and an estimate of the vacancy percentage is used based on current conditions. Many times a vacancy rate of 5 percent is used. This percentage is not all that accurate, but is usable when comparing similar properties in generally the same area. You will want to be more accurate with the vacancy percentage when calculating Net Operating Income, because this affects the value of the property.

In 2008 to 2010 vacancy rates were as high as 10 percent. They have slowly dropped in the last few years and are around 5 percent, even a little under in some locations at this time.

In reality, a 5 percent vacancy percentage is very good and many properties will not be able to maintain such a low rate. Even if a property is usually full with a waitlist, it might have some unpaid rents, a little vacancy time between tenants, and time for renovations; it will end up with close to 5 percent vacant. I like to consider the "economical vacancy," the actual money put in the bank compared to the scheduled rents. A 5 percent or 6 percent economical vacancy is very, very good.

Chapter 3

ADMINISTRATIVE STUFF TO KNOW

Information Used at Main Offices

Real Estate Agents You Can Trust and Why

You trust people in real estate because they exhibit good traits. They are trustworthy, they tell the truth, and your dealings with them have shown they can be relied upon. As you have dealings in real estate, you build relationships and friendships. You will like some agents and will be unsure about others. The traits we have discussed will put some agents in a more respected position.

Because of their track record and reasonable advice, you may regard them as friends as well as business associates. Just remember that they only make money when they sell something. While the best agents will not lead you into a bad deal just to make a sale, many agents cannot be trusted to give good advice, and are only interested in the sale. I see many, many properties that I know are not good deals being closed in a sale to someone. I suspect an inexperienced buyer has been convinced that they are getting a good deal by an unscrupulous agent or broker. You only need to read sales brochures for a property to see exaggerations designed to make a property look like a better buy than it really is. The rule is always 'buyers beware.'

However, it is also true that the seller needs to be careful. We have seen real estate brokers attempt to get us to list a property with them at a higher-than-normal commission rate and terms designed to benefit the broker, not us.

The more you know about rental properties, the better you can evaluate a property's value. I have always stayed on top of what is for sale in our area and often look at properties just to learn more. Most times, I know more about them than the agent trying to sell them. If an agent gives me bad information, I am likely to know better. You may be able to rely on the advice of trusted agents, but you need to personally make sure a property is right for you. There are agents in the business that will make it easier for you to make the right decisions.

RANDY

We met Randy as the selling agent on the first apartment complex we purchased. It was a 38-unit, 20-year-old complex in a fair part of town. I liked it because it showed well. It had the open look I like with mature trees and plenty of parking. Randy was a big guy who looked like he would be more comfortable in Levi's than the suit he wore. I called him while I was on the property for the first time, and he said they had a possible offer and that he could come over to our home with details on the property.

He showed us the income and expense reports for the previous year and a rent roll. The information he presented did not justify the asking price for the property: my calculations showed the property to be worth about $200,000 less than the asking price. He told us that the property was priced to appeal to a buyer in a 1031 exchange situation who had to buy something. They had just such a buyer interested in the property. If that fell through, he would let me know and we could go from there. I told him that we did not have any exchange issues and that if he called me back I would not exceed the lower price.

Randy was pleasant and honest. He had told me what was going on without making a big deal out of it. I liked him from the start, partly because I am more comfortable in Levi's than a suit too. About a month later, I got a call from Randy because the buyer had told them to stuff it and walked. He said the property was available and I reaffirmed the price we were willing to pay for it.

Randy's stock really skyrocketed in 2005, when I met him by accident pushing a cart at the local grocery store. He told me that duplexes were selling for record amounts and that if we were smart, we would sell our duplexes and buy apartment complexes. He knew we owned 30 duplexes at this time and it was a big deal. His logic was that duplexes are worth about $200,000 per unit and apartments would cost less than $100,000 per unit; with apartments renting for about 75 percent to 80 percent of what duplexes were getting, it made sense. Randy had opened our eyes to the possibility of selling our duplexes. We had never thought about selling them before, but after looking at the numbers, it was a total no-brainer. Randy was right, duplexes were selling for somewhere between "wow," and "I do not believe it." Duplexes were valued in the stratosphere somewhere and people were buying them as fast as they came on the market. Because of Randy's advice, our financial position more than doubled in one swift maneuver.

I have talked a few times about us lucking out sometimes. This was one of those incredible times, when the chance meeting pushing grocery carts resulted in a major shift in our focus. No other real estate agent called me or emailed me to give me a heads up that we were sitting on a valuable bunch of duplexes that could be sold, or that the proceeds could be used to buy much betters properties. The timing was perfect. We sold the duplexes within in less than two months, at the height of the duplex market and were safely into apartment complexes by the time duplex values crashed and burned.

We kept in contact with Randy and looked at properties now and then that he was trying to sell. We did not buy anything else from Randy until about four years later, when he told us about a commercial property that he knew we had liked a couple years before. It had been in escrow to sell but had fallen out, and the current price was worth an attempt to purchase. This was in the middle of the real estate meltdown, and the 13-suite commercial shopping center had five vacancies. It was priced about 25 percent less than it had been only two years before when we had made an unaccepted offer. Not buying this property two years before was one of the more lucrative non-investments we never made.

Randy made it happen. He was on top of the negotiations and kept the ball rolling until it closed, giving us our first multi-unit commercial property. Randy had also worked many years as a loan officer, as well as a real estate agent, and had a down-to-earth approach. There was nothing stilted about him, just good information that was easy to understand. A year later, Randy guided us through the purchase of a 48-unit, broken condominium project that had been taken back by the bank and finally the FDIC. It took a couple years to put this together, but with Randy's help, we pulled it off and added at very nice property to our portfolio.

This is the kind of agent you want on your side. He tells it like it is with no embellishments to make a sale. He is a friend as well as our agent.

Rick

Rick is one of the agents I met when we were looking to purchase property years ago. He worked for a large national Commercial Real Estate company. He had shown us a few properties over the years, but we had not bought anything from him. In all the dealings I had with him, he never exaggerated the quality of a property. His advice on properties always matched information I already knew to be true. Rick never even came close to deception.

When Randy gave us the information and advised us to sell our duplexes and buy apartments, we thought about it for a while and decided that he was right. We did not want to simply list 30 duplexes, so I called around to all the real estate agents I knew and told them we were thinking of selling all or part of our duplexes.

When I explained this to Rick, he said that he had just been talking to a large company that was looking for several duplexes all in one area. We had 28 duplexes in a three-block community of 32 duplexes. Rick said he would see if there was any interest from the potential buyer. Rick made no mention of commissions or listings, just offered to check it out. We sat down with Rick to talk about our duplexes, and told him all that was good and bad about them. It was mostly good because we had put all of the profits we had received from them back into improving them.

Rick set up a tour of the property with the owner of the company interested in our duplexes. We showed representative units, and I was open and honest about what I knew needed fixing and all the upgrades we had done. This was one of only a couple times we showed the property before receiving an offer. Rick's potential buyer liked the property. There was still no mention of commission or listing. I trusted Rick and he apparently trusted us. We always offered more information on our properties than they asked for; we like plenty of documents when we buy a property, and figured they would appreciate it also.

Only a short time passed before we received a verbal offer that was dirt simple; they would buy all 28 duplexes "as is" for a price that was 10 percent below whatever the comps turned out to be. This meant we could just walk away from them with no pest reports, no repairs, or anything other than us picking up a check and heading to the closest bank. We loved it.

Rick brought the official offer to our house with the papers necessary to move forward. Finally, he had a purchase agreement that included a modest 2 percent commission. Rick had trusted us throughout this period and his company had charged us a minimum amount for their services. We sold our 28 duplexes in a transaction that was essentially agreed to with a handshake.

After the sale of our duplexes, I worked closely with Rick looking for replacement properties. I talked to Rick every day on the phone about possibilities. He understood how "aggressively priced" properties had become. He and I always agreed on values and other issues with the potential properties.

I am sorry to say I lost contact with Rick over the years. The big company he worked for was bought out by another and he was off to new adventures.

Merry

We met Merry early in our duplex buying days in 1984. She was the listing agent on a duplex we wanted to buy. She was honest, easy going and knowledgeable. We liked her and developed a friendship from then on. She was our agent on many purchases and a couple of sales. She provided forms and kept us out of trouble. Even when we got big enough not to need an agent most of the time, she offered advice and guidance.

It is great if you can find agents like Merry, Rick and Randy. It is a pleasure to work with nice, genuine people. My definition of genuine is that there is no phony front to them. They tell it straight and what you see is what is there. There is no hidden agenda, it is just, "Here are the facts and let's move forward."

Administrative Guidelines

Administration is the upper management of the company. Here is where policies and rules for the company are formed. Bill paying and money matters along with most purchases are an upper management responsibility. Acquisitions of property are an administrative function.

When we began we did everything, including dealing with tenants and making repairs ourselves. As your company gets larger duties can be spread around better with a resident manager and repair people. The administrative duties, however, remain with the property owner who makes the big decisions on the direction of the company. There are a number of good management principles and guides, which will make running the company easier.

Company Manual of Operations

For our real estate company, we have organized our rules, guidelines and specifications into a Manual of Operations. This was similar to the way we worked in the fire department. We always wanted to standardize procedures and guidelines so that all personnel would operate the same and crews would be interchangeable. In the residential real estate business, I wanted to have a document that workers could refer to on how we do things. We also keep track of specifications and paint colors in each complex. As with any guidelines, it is important to review them frequently and make necessary updates to keep them accurate and up to date.

Our Manuel of Operations is divided into five sections. The first contains administrative directions, vendor lists, guidelines on specific procedures and general office procedures for managers. We also keep internet passwords, email addresses and personal contact information.

Part two of the manual is devoted to specifications. This section includes the paint colors, window blind sizes and information specific to each apartment complex. The specific information has model numbers of appliances and other equipment in a unit. Any small bit of information that might make it easier to repair an apartment should be included. When we buy a complex, we spend several hours making a list of every part in the units that might need to be replaced at some time in the future. All this information is kept in our specification section of our manual.

The third section deals with specific maintenance issues. Our turnover, or make ready procedure, is outlined here, as well as instructions for trouble-shooting the air conditioning system. There are individual topics on several day-to-day maintenance problems faced by our repair personnel.

The fourth section list forms we use and how to complete them. The fifth and final section is for office use only and contains the procedures for handling accounting issues with our computer system.

Each company needs to have established policies on day-to-day procedures to keep maintenance personnel on track. With standardized procedures, it is much easier for a maintenance worker to travel to another complex to do repairs and find the same system of parts inventory and procedures as was used at our other properties. Written procedures keep your company organized. Workers want guidelines; make it easy for them and provide a document with the information they need and the way you want jobs done.

Organizational Chart

An organizational chart is a document that shows the people in an organization arranged by level of authority. This means that the big boss is at the top; under this person is the next level of supervision, and on down the line to the lowest level. It shows each person's immediate supervisor. The span of control and the unity of command are readily apparent. The organizational chart is very important to large organizations, but not usually needed for small to medium real estate companies.

When a real estate company gets large enough that there is some confusion at times about who answers to whom, then it is time for an organizational chart. It is pretty easy to know who is at the top of the chart and who is at the bottom. Filling in the in-between personnel in is a bit more of a challenge. Most organizations end up with several people in the middle management positions with overlapping responsibilities supervising the same people.

Each employee needs to have only one boss. There can be several people they work for from time to time, but they need to have a single supervisor that they report to and go to if there is some conflict in instructions. For example, a repairperson is subordinate to a maintenance manager. But, they will work at several different apartment complexes getting instructions and directions from several resident managers. The repairperson's boss is still the maintenance manager even though they are working for someone else at the time. If there is any conflict in duties then the repairperson checks with his immediate supervisor, the maintenance manager, for clarification. The key is communication between workers, managers and supervisors. When everyone knows what is going on things always work better.

If your company starts having problems as to who is the boss over whom, then it is time to make an organizational chart. If it is not readily apparent how the chart should be laid out then that alone is enough to prove you need one. Everyone should know who their boss is and who their subordinates are. The best way to determine if you need an organization chart is to take a pencil and paper and lay one out. If you can organize all the people in your company easily then you probably do not need an organizational chart. You only need one when it is not easy to make one.

Accounting

Fiscal Year

Businesses can set up their accounting in a fiscal year of their choice. A fiscal year is any 12 month period ending on the same day each year. Many companies use the calendar year as their fiscal year beginning on January 1st each year and ending on December 31st. We use a calendar year basis, as do most rental real estate companies.

Businesses of a seasonal nature many times will end their year during the slowest part of their business year. The IRS only requires you to establish a fiscal year you are going to use when you start your company and that you close your business year (fiscal year) on the same date each year.

Accounting Basis, (Cost Basis Vs. Accrual Basis)

In cost basis accounting, income and expenses are recorded at the time money changes hands. For example, if someone pays you rent for December on December 20th, the income would be in that year. However, if payment were received on January 2nd, the income would be for the following year, even though it was rent for December of the prior year. When you get the money determines in what month, quarter or year it is included.

Likewise, if you pay a bill near the end of one year, it is part of that year, even if the bill is not due until the next year. A bill paid in January for a December purchase will be an expense in the coming year.

Businesses that use cost basis accounting can manipulate their tax liability by paying bills before the end of the year, and deferring income until the following year. Or possibly the reverse, if there is some tax law taking effect on January first of the following year and there is an advantage to get as much income as possible in a particular year.

Buying merchandise on accounts allows you to receive the merchandise in one year and pay for it in the next.

Cash accounting is easier than accrual accounting. Your checkbook could work as your tax records. Income is deposited on a certain date and expenses are paid. On December 31st, (or the end of your fiscal year) you close out the year. You can simply subtract your opening balance at the beginning of the year from your ending balance, giving you the profit for the year (or loss if your ending balance is smaller.)

In accrual basis accounting, income and expenses are recorded when they occur, regardless of whether money has changed hands or not. For example, if you run a business selling merchandise and billing customers for their purchases, you sell an item and you consider it as income. The money owed you for the item is shown as "account receivable." Likewise, if you buy something on account and will have to pay for it in the future, it is shown as an expense now with the amount owed carried as "account payable."

The accrual basis system is much more complicated than cost basis accounting, but is more accurate in reflecting the monetary health of the business. All major companies and any businesses that deal with large inventories of merchandise for sale use the accrual basis of accounting.

Companies in the business of providing rental property can use either system of accounting. Generally, cost basis accounting is preferred because it is simpler. We use cost basis for our income and expenses for tax return purposes, but use a modified accrual method for our business records, shown later in this Accounting section. Purchases and expenses paid with credit cards are included in the year purchased even though they are not paid until the following year, when the bill comes due.

Co-Mingling Of Funds

Co-mingling of funds is when money from more than one person is kept in the same bank account. Incomes are deposited in the account and expenses are paid from it. This practice is illegal when handling other people's money and is not permitted. It would seem you could keep track of the ins and outs, but in reality it is too easy to pay bills from other peoples' money. This used to be common practice by property management companies dealing with many owners. If someone was short, it was just covered by the joint funds. It was only a matter of time before things got screwed up.

Though not against the law, it is best not to co-mingle personal money and business money. It is not uncommon for small sole-proprietor businesses to keep funds in a single account and keep track of business expenses separately. Keeping business funds in their own bank account will make it much easier to keep track of income, expenses and balances of funds available. It is totally permissible to transfer funds from personal to business or business to personal as needed. Such transfers will be shown in each bank statement.

Financial Statements

Income And Expense Statements, (Profit And Loss)

All businesses use an "Income and Expense" report to record the cash flow of the company. This can also be called a "Profit and Loss" statement, or P & L report. All these are the same, with all the incomes of the company listed first, and followed by all the expenses the company has incurred in the same time. The difference is either a profit or loss for the reporting period.

The reporting period can be any period convenient to the business. There can be monthly reports, but usually they are found in quarterly reports and fiscal year reports. Reports do not need to be for any special time period and can be parts of months or any other period the company likes. Often banks will require a profit and loss report for a loan or refinance.

Apartments use the Income and Expense report also, usually calculated annually on a calendar basis. A calendar year will contain expenses like taxes and insurance that is not paid monthly. It is important for an owner of rental properties to keep good track of profits and losses for making decisions involving money and budgeting. This report will give owners information on routine expenses as well as provide guidelines for future upgrades and capital improvements.

Real Estate Schedule

A real estate schedule is a spreadsheet showing all the real estate owned by a company or individual. The schedule includes the address or description of the property, date of purchase, cost, current value and equity. The schedule may also contain the loan company and loan number. Additional information is sometimes also included, such as income and expenses for the property, and perhaps mortgage principal paid in the previous year.

Annual Operating Statement

What we call our Operating Statements can be called different names by different organizations. It is completed at the end of a fiscal year, but can also be done quarterly or any other time frame that would be beneficial to the company. We use an Excel spreadsheet showing the properties owned by the company in a side-by-side comparison, showing incomes and expenses. If a company is small enough, all of the properties can be listed on one or two sheets. As portfolios grow, it becomes necessary to group properties to keep the amount of data from becoming overwhelming.

The groups can be by property type. You can group residential properties on one sheet and commercial properties on another. They can also be grouped by size, or one can group smaller properties together in one column and larger properties in their own column. A larger company might group properties by city, state or even country. Properties need to be grouped so that the spreadsheet is easy to understand. Even if properties are grouped for the overall company operating statement, the group should be expanded on its own sub statement showing the comparison of the properties in the sub group.

The Annual Operating Statement for our company contains two sections. One section contains all properties and investments for the company called, "Operating Summary by Complex." The second is an analysis of only our apartment complexes called, "Apartment Analysis."

Operating Summary by Complex   2013

	Oak Tree	Lynnwood	Rocky Mountain	The Plaza	Button Commercial	Victorian	Courtyard Center	General Admin	Total
INCOME									
Rent Income	294,383	295,821	559,113	452,467	106,315	31,055	172,322		1,911,475
Other income	14,108	11,185	27,496	15,935	46,231	250	1,632	433	117,269
TOTAL INCOME	308,490	307,005	586,608	468,402	152,546	31,305	173,954	433	2,028,744
EXPENSES									
Advertising	419	608	1,107	527		114	160		2,936
Auto Travel	85	394	681	54	218		54	4,800	6,285
Clean Maint	19,368	19,901	16,265	20,400	3,225	3,292	8,084	797	91,331
Insurance	5,392	6,400	9,708	4,769	1,893	876	3,027	13,166	45,230
Legal Professional	2,274	6,572	1,825	4,558		37	104	20,272	35,642
Interest	104,228	103,021	173,295	117,488	50,618		84,679		633,329
Repairs Routine	30,042	24,949	26,986	40,473	1,287	1,049	2,077	20,300	147,163
Repairs Replace	17,580	18,918	15,904	10,887		733	421		64,443
Taxes	27,645	26,653	52,374	36,919	20,407	3,529	16,470		183,998
Utilities	34,608	41,988	59,532	73,994	14,601	7,423	33,555	4,768	270,469
Wages	4,628	17,055	19,260	1,445		45	158	42,281	84,871
Other	1,038	1,290	620	1,328	19	30	1	3,716	8,042
TOTAL EXPENSES	247,307	267,748	377,557	312,842	92,269	17,128	148,789	110,100	1,573,740
GROSS PROFIT	61,183	39,258	209,051	155,560	60,277	14,177	25,165	-109,666	$455,004
Reserves	12,008	8,551	27,969	11,950	2,700		60		63,238
Capital & Upgrade	9,188	15,400	36,636	9,465		67	472	1,717	72,945
Tools	275	266	282	118			72	2,884	3,897
NET PROFIT	39,711	15,041	144,164	134,027	57,577	14,110	24,561	-114,267	314,923
Principal Paid	33,836	33,500	56,919	39,109	15,248		26,491		205,103
Cash after debt service	5,875	-18,459	87,245	94,918	42,329	14,110	-1,930	-114,267	109,820
NOI	165,412	142,279	382,347	273,048	110,895	14,177	109,843	-109,666	1,088,333
CDR	1.198	1.042	1.661	1.744	1.684		0.988		1.298

OPERATING SUMMARY BY COMPLEX SHEET

The first section is our Operating Summary by Complex sheet listing all properties, including investments. All incomes and expenses are shown, as well as any capital expenses, money spent from reserves, and any other onetime expense or income for that particular period of time. This page we call our "Operating Summary by Complex." It contains all money that has been received or spent and is the same as the total figures from our accounting system and what we send to our CPA for our annual tax returns.

The spreadsheet lists properties or groups of properties across the top and income, expenses and other information vertically. This sheet contains principal paid for the year, net operating income, and credit to debt ratios for each property. The far right column is a total for our entire portfolio for the time period reported. Income and expense amounts are taken from our accounting system totals. Yearend mortgage information comes from lenders' end of year statements, or our real estate schedule. The totals column on the right shows the company totals for profit, net operating income, and our overall credit to debt ratio for our entire portfolio.

Apartment Analysis Sheet

The second section is called "Apartment Analysis Sheet." This sheet adapts entries to better reflect actual expenses for each apartment complex and puts them in a format that can be compared to industry standards or other properties for sale. Only apartment complexes are on this spreadsheet. Most of the numbers are calculated automatically. The only entry required to be inputted into the sheet is the average rent per unit for each type of apartment in each apartment complex. All other cells are calculated automatically.

Review the rent reports for each complex for the year. Calculate an estimated average scheduled rent for each unit type (one bedroom, two bedrooms etc.) Scheduled rent is the normal rent for a unit. It does not use any concessions, discounts, or specials. Vacant units and non-payment of rent are not considered. This is the only entry needed on our report. The program calculates annual and scheduled total rents for each complex. This calculation will deduct the manager's apartment from the total. Only rent income is used for this analysis.

Expense totals for each complex are automatically adjusted from end of year figures by adding part of the general expenses of the company into each apartment complexes expenses. This amount is a proration based on a comparison of total income percentages of each complex.

Some category lines use a percent of all properties while others use a percent of only apartments. The percentages are calculated from the Operating Summery sheet and are carried forward to the Apartment Analysis Sheet by the program. The calculations on this sheet are designed to be comparable to apartment properties that are for sale. This gives us a good reference for normal expenses when evaluating a possible property acquisition in the future.

The Apartment Analysis Sheet does not include taxes, reserves, upgrades, or tools. Repairs include normal repairs and carpet, appliance, etc. replacement costs, but do not include any capital expenses. Money spent from reserves is also not included in these calculations because money for reserves is set aside separately when calculating the value of a property. Interest or debt service is not used in this analysis.

Only regular expenses are used because they are the only expenses used in calculating Net Operating Income (NOI). Mortgage principal and interest are paid out of NOI and are not included in this analysis. Wage categories are increased automatically by the cost of the manager's apartment. Any medical or vehicle costs are also included in the wages shown on the Operating Summary sheet and carried forward to the Apartment Analysis Sheet.

Apartment Analysis Sheet 2013

	Oak Tree Apts			Lynwood Apts			Rocky Mountain Apts			The Plaza Apts			Totals		
	Totals	Per Unit	Percent of income	Totals	Per Unit	Percent of income	Totals	Per Unit	Percent of income	Totals	Per Unit	Percent of income	Totals	Per Units	Percent of income
Number of units	38			38			59			48			183		
Monthly 1 Br rent	660			675			780			830					
Monthly 2 Br rent	850			775			865			950					
Monthly 3 Br rent	n/a			n/a			1,200			n/a					
Total Annual Scheduled Rent w/o Manager apt	313,560			320,100			583,620			501,240			1,718,520		
Manager apartment	10,200			9,300			10,380			11,400			41280		
% of all income	15.21%			15.13%			28.91%			23.09%					
% of income, apts & Courtyard	16.73%			16.64%			31.80%			25.40%					
Actual Income															
Rent Income	294,383	7,747		295,821	7,785		559,113	9,476		452,467	9,426		1,601,783	8,753	
Lossed Income	19,177		6.12%	24,279		7.59%	24,507		4.20%	46,773		9.73%	116,737		6.79%
EXPENSES															
Advertising	419	11	0.13%	608	16	0.19%	1,107	19	0.15%	527	11	0.11%	2,662	15	0.15%
Auto Travel	815	21	0.26%	1,120	29	0.35%	2,069	35	0.36%	1,162	24	0.23%	5,166	28	0.30%
Clean Maint	19,501	513	6.22%	20,034	527	6.26%	16,518	280	2.83%	20,602	429	4.11%	76,655	419	4.46%
Insurance	7,394	195	2.36%	8,393	221	2.62%	13,515	229	2.32%	7,809	163	1.56%	37,110	203	2.16%
Legal Prof	5,357	141	1.71%	9,639	254	3.01%	7,687	130	1.32%	9,238	192	1.84%	31,921	174	1.86%
Repairs/Replace	51,017	1,343	16.27%	47,245	1,243	14.76%	49,346	836	8.46%	58,516	1,177	11.28%	204,124	1,115	11.88%
Utilities	35,333	930	11.27%	42,709	1,124	13.34%	60,911	1,032	10.44%	75,095	1,564	14.98%	214,048	1,170	12.46%
Wages	21,899	576	6.98%	33,393	879	10.43%	43,087	730	7.36%	23,582	491	4.70%	121,961	666	7.10%
Other	1,603	42	0.51%	1,852	49	0.59%	1,694	29	0.25%	2,186	46	0.44%	7,336	40	0.43%
TOTAL EXPENSE	143,339	3,772	45.71%	164,993	4,342	51.54%	195,934	3,321	33.57%	196,717	4,098	39.25%	700,983	3,831	40.79%
GROSS PROFIT	151,044	3,976		130,828	3,443		363,178	6,156		255,750	5,328		900,800	4,922	
Reserves	12,008	316	3.83%	8,551	225	2.67%	27,969	474	4.79%	11,950	249	2.38%	60,478	330	3.52%
Capital & Upgrades	9,476	249	3.02%	15,685	413	4.90%	37,182	630	6.37%	9,901	206	1.98%	72,244	395	4.20%
Tools	758	20	0.24%	746	20	0.23%	1,199	20	0.21%	850	18	0.17%	3,553	19	0.21%
NET PROFIT	128,803	3,390		105,845	2,785		296,828	5,031		233,049	4,855		764,525		

These kinds of reports, like any reports, are only as accurate as the accuracy of the data entered. Therefore, we emphasize the importance of coding expense in the correct category and assigning it to the correct complex. We do not want any personal items mixed up in the company expenses and are careful to keep business expenses and personal expenses totally separate.

Many administrative costs are paid from our general fund and coded as such in our accounting program. For this analysis sheet we pro-rate many of these expenses by complexes based on size of complex and amount of gross income. We want these common expenses included in each complex's annual figure to have an accurate total of costs. Likewise, we pro-rate the cost of such items as our umbrella insurance policy or workers' comp insurance to each complex based on value, gross income and wages.

BALANCE SHEETS

Balance sheets are common financial statement documents that show the assets and liabilities of a company at a particular point in time. They are always used at the end of your fiscal year, but can really be done any time they are needed, such as to include in a quarterly report or when applying for a loan or refinance.

The sheet is divided into assets at the top and liabilities at the bottom. Assets are what the company has and liabilities are what the company owes. Assets will include cash, real property, personal property, tools and any accounts receivable owed to you.

Liabilities are loans the company has, unpaid bills and owner's personal equity. Owner's equity may not seem like a liability, but it is a part of the balance between assets and liabilities. Basically, assets less liabilities equal owner's equity or net worth.

Annual Lender Reports

Banks that hold the loans on apartments or commercial property usually require an annual report as part of the loan requirements. Generally, they want a rent roll by apartment with amount of rents, and an income and expense report for the property. Depending on the loan requirements, you might also have to provide income tax returns or just about anything else they thought was necessary at the time of the loan approval.

Worker Compensation Insurance Policy Report

The insurance carrier that is providing worker compensation insurance will want an annual report showing information that will assist them in setting your workers' comp insurance rate for the following year. This report generally contains the gross rental income of the company, normal workers by name, a lodging schedule for resident managers and the amount paid for workers during the year.

IRS

Depreciation

Depreciation is a paper loss permitted on your IRS tax return on property used as a rental. This deduction was instituted to encourage the construction of residential housing. This deduction allows a landlord to take a depreciation expense each year, thereby increasing his profit or minimizing losses for the year and making his investment in rental property a better deal.

Generally, rental property is depreciated over a period of 30 years. This permits the landlord to take 1/30 of the cost of the building each year as a deduction. Only the building is allowed to be depreciated and land costs are not included.

When the property is sold, however, the depreciation must be recaptured as part of your capital gains taxes on the property. "Recaptured," means that the depreciation you claimed over the years must now be included in your taxes as income. This "recapture" amount is usually taxed at a lower rate than regular capital gains tax or standard income tax rates. (See Capital Gains following.)

Like most tax laws, there is a loophole to carry forward the depreciation from a sold property to a new property. (See 1031 Tax Deferred Exchange below.)

There are other expenses, like a new roof, that must also be depreciated over a number of preset years. Even though you pay this cost out of pocket you are not allowed to deduct the entire amount in the year paid and must be depreciated over the estimated life of the roof.

Capital Gains

When personal property and real property are sold for more than your cost, there is a "Capital Gains Tax" due on the transaction. Capital gains profits are shown on your income tax return for the fiscal year that includes the sale. Any improvements to the property or costs that have not been taken as an expense in a prior year are deducted from the sale price and not subject to the tax. There is no allowance for inflation, but the tax rate for capital gains is lower than the tax rate for ordinary income if the property has been held longer than one year. Capital gains tax on property held less than a year is calculated as ordinary income.

Deferring capital gains taxes as long as possible is a major objective in building a real estate portfolio. Borrowing against a property instead of selling does not trigger a capital gains obligation. A tax-deferred exchange is a tax code provision that allows a rental property owner to sell his property and move the profit into the down payment for another similar property without incurring any capital gains tax burden at the time of the exchange.

1031 Tax Deferred Exchange

1031 is a section number from the tax code. There are strict rules regarding the amounts of money used for the down payment and the obligations for the new loan. When it comes time to sell a property and buy a new one under this provision, get information and rules from a qualified tax advisor. It is not all that complicated, but as with most IRS rules, you want to make sure all your "T"s are crossed and your "I"s dotted.

The rules do not let you actually touch any of the money from the sale of your property. There are 1031 holding companies that do this for you. They are also known as "Qualified Intermediaries" or "Exchange Accommodators." After your sold property closes escrow, all of the proceeds will go directly to the holding company. They hold your money and disperse it at your direction as deposits, down payments or fees for the new property being purchased as a replacement. You will receive the going rate interest on the money held in the meantime. These 1031 holding companies are experts on the rules and regulations regarding these tax deferred transactions.

1031 rules require you to identify replacement properties within 45 days of the close of escrow on the sold properties. You are allowed to identify more properties than you are going to buy; however, the property you eventually purchase must be on the 45 day identification list. You must also close on a replacement property within 180 days of the close of escrow of your sold properties. These rules also require the debt on the replacement property to be equal to or exceed the debt you carried on the sold property.

This was important to us when we sold our duplexes because we had had some for as long as 20 years and had taken a depreciation loss on them. Two of the duplexes had been fully depreciated and we had a very large capital gains liability if we did not defer the proceeds from this sale.

Identifying and entering into contract on new properties was a bit of a daunting task as there were plenty of vultures out there waiting to find someone running out of time on their identification period and try to sell them an overpriced property.

The problem is that the properties you identify are not locked up in a purchase agreement, which means that you could easily get in the position that you could not actually purchase the identified property. You are permitted to identify some extras, but it is a roll of the dice if you are going to pull it off without being forced to overpay for a property just to satisfy the rules.

My thoughts on this were to identify properties and get into a purchase agreement as soon as possible. We began looking seriously for replacement properties as soon as we were in contract to sell the duplexes. That gave us a couple months before the close of escrow and forty-five days after to get them all locked up. When we found a property that we liked and got through the Letter of Interest, we would enter into a purchase agreement with one of the contingencies being that the transaction was part of a 1031 exchange. In this manner, we were able to find, identify and purchase our replacement properties at an acceptable purchase price.

Amortization Of Some Closing Costs

Generally, expenses incurred in a tax year can be taken against the profits for that year. In the case of some purchase and loan expenses, the IRS requires that they be taken over a longer period of years. As far as the IRS is concerned, these expenses, even though the money was paid "up front" at the time of the sale or the loan, are considered either pre-paid interest or part of the cost of the property; therefore, it must be spread over the term of the loan or life of the property. These costs will include title and escrow fees, as well as points or other fees charged by the bank for the loan.

For a new purchase, the escrow and title fees are considered part of the purchase price and are depreciated along with the building. If the property is refinanced and it incurs additional escrow and title fees, these fees must be amortized. Points and fees charged by the bank are considered pre-paid interest and must be amortized over the life of the loan. If the property is refinanced or sold, any remaining amount that has not been taken as amortization expense may be taken in its entirety in the year of the new loan or sale.

Amortization is similar to depreciation. The amount is divided over a set number of years and an amortization expense is taken each year. In the case of a refinanced loan, you will be able to expense any amounts that have not been amortized from the old loan. However, there will be a new amortized amount beginning with the new loan.

In commercial properties, the expenses for tenant improvements and real estate commissions on a lease are also subject to amortization over the life of the lease.

Buying Properties

Buying properties is the fundamental function of administration. You are going to be on the lookout for good rental property most of the time. When starting you will be looking for a home or duplex, but as your company grows you will move into larger properties. Finding properties or just happening to come across some does happen from time to time.

Four Duplexes From An Owner In Foreclosure

One example of finding a property occurred when we heard that two duplexes on our block were heading to foreclosure. The properties were owned by a company that was experienced in real estate, but for some reason had become over extended. The two duplexes were in reasonably good shape and had rent-paying tenants in them. They had not been put on the market yet. We contacted the owner and offered to buy them. He told us he was interested and that if he did not sell them they would be taken back by the bank. It turned out that his loans were held by the same bank we normally did our real estate loans.

We contacted the bank and we were told that they held the note on the two duplexes and the owners were behind in payments, but they had not started foreclosures on them. The bank also informed us that the same owner had two other duplexes across the street that had already been foreclosed on and were in the control of the bank.

Contacting the seller, he informed us that once foreclosure proceedings started he did not think he had any control over the two duplexes across the street.

We began negotiations with the seller and the bank offering to take all four duplexes by paying all the back payments due with penalties and assuming the current balance on the loans. This was a good deal for everyone. The bank got rid of four problem properties. The seller got out of foreclosures, saving his credit rating, and we got four duplexes for below their value with a smaller than normal down payment.

Once Bought 3 Duplexes In 12 Days From Chinese-Speaking Sellers

One day our son called and said there were a couple of "For Sale" signs on duplexes in our neighborhood. We checked it out and found that there were three duplexes for sale. We called the real estate agent on the for sale sign. We were told they were all three owned by a couple in San Francisco who wanted to get rid of them. The price was close to fair, but we were heading out for a six week dive trip to Mexico in two weeks. To complicate matters, not only did the sellers live out of town, but also they only spoke Chinese.

That same day we made our offer for all three duplexes on the condition it had to close in two weeks. We knew a loan was possible in that time, as we had just purchased one other duplex a short time before and the bank had all our information. Our real estate friend, Merry, our bank loan officer, and our title company officer said it could happen that fast. We forwarded as much information as possible even before our offer was accepted. The sellers had a relative who could translate for them.

Within a day the offer was accepted, repairs were agreed upon and we were off and running. We helped the seller with repairs that were their responsibility. The real estate agent for the seller was amazed that we could get so much done so fast.

The transaction was completed without a hitch and we signed papers 12 days after the offer had been accepted. The purchase closed on time and we took off in our motor home to Baja Mexico with our real estate portfolio increased by three.

Enough For A Truck

Our real estate broker, Merry, came over to write up an offer for a duplex that had come up for sale. This was in our neighborhood and was a very nice property. The older owner had taken very good care of it and it did not have any maintenance issues. They were asking $118,000, which was about $15,000 more than the going rate in the area. We wanted it. My wife and Merry chatted about what to offer and decided to offer $115,000, which it surely was worth.

I was in the kitchen listening to them and suggested we offer $112,000 instead, which we could justify by the recent comps; if he took it I could buy a truck with the $3,000 we would save. They laughed, but did write the offer up for the lesser amount. A few days later, the seller agreed with our value logic and took the $112,000. A stroke of the pen on a letter of interest and I had a truck. Not a new truck but a free used truck. I could not have been happier if it had been a Rolls Royce with a chauffeur.

Owner Ashamed To Show Vacant Duplex

In our duplex days when we were in the buying mode, we kept track of all the properties in our neighborhood and who owned them. We figured we would have a better chance of buying a property if we knew who owned it and how long they had it. We had made an offer on a three-bedroom duplex that was vacant and in fair condition. Our offer was accepted and we were in the middle of the escrow process. I knew the same owner had another duplex on the next block that had been vacant for months and was in horrid condition. I asked the seller if they had any other properties they might want to sell. They were embarrassed to tell us they owned the duplex on the next street. We pushed them a bit and they admitted it was theirs. You know you are in a good negotiating position when the seller is ashamed to tell you they own a trashed property.

We convinced them to show it to us and we made an offer for what it was worth. They accepted our offer and we added another fixer-upper to the portfolio. These kinds of duplexes that look horrid when you get them are really just a normal nasty turnover. We move in, haul out the junk, replace bad stuff and spruce up the entire place. We can usually turn over a property like this in a couple weeks with a new tenant in place shortly thereafter.

Dealing with Tenants

Rent Rolls

Rent rolls are maintained at the apartment complex level. This is a duty of the resident manager, but supervisory personnel need to make sure this is done. These records will have all pertinent information about a tenant, their current rent, how much security deposit they have paid, and any scheduled rent increases pending. It is easy to fall behind on this information and hard to catch up. Supervisors should check the tenant records of the resident managers from time to time, as well as the individual files for apartments. This is done when a new tenant moves in or a tenant is moving out. We want our information on funds owed to us or security deposits held by us to be correct.

Over the course of our time in this business, we have, on more than one occasion, failed to raise rents as provided for in the rental agreement and given a tenant too large of a security deposit refund. If managers kept good records, these money-losing mistakes would have a much less chance of occurring.

Keep Rents Current

You want your rental to be making as much money as possible, so you need to keep your rents up to market levels. You do not want to be the most expensive apartment in the area, but you sure do not want to be at the bottom either. It is necessary to keep abreast of going market rents. Checking the apartment rental guides in grocery stores or newspaper ads can give you an idea of what similar units are renting for. Sometimes managers can exchange information with the managers of other complexes to find out what they are charging.

Keeping rents current will not only keep profits up, but will keep you from having to make large rent increases to catch up. It is not easy to catch up on rents if you fall too far behind. We experienced this in the late 1990s and early 2000s. Once behind, you either have to give tenants one large increase or several smaller increases close together. Neither of these will make your tenants happy. Some communities have limits on how much of a rent increase a property owner is permitted. Try to keep close to the going rate, and be ready to show angry tenants copies of what others are charging and how you determined the going rate from comparisons in the area. In the late 1990s when we were trying to play "catch up," we sent rent increase notices with a cover letter giving details of rent prices, specifications, and utility cost increases to show renters we were not just arbitrarily raising rents.

The value of your property is a direct function of the income received. When rents go up 5 percent then your building value goes up 5 percent. This is a big deal and important when it comes time to sell the property or refinance.

Evictions

When a tenant is just not going to pay their rent, or they have not left after being served with a notice to move, the next course of action is an official eviction. We follow the steps outlined by our eviction attorney.

Once we have gone through the eviction process and the forms are at the eviction attorney, it is a good idea to stay on top of the process. Check with the attorney often to be sure that all timetables are being observed and that things are moving forward as quickly as possible. The cost of an attorney is a small part of the total cost of getting rid of a non-paying or bad tenant. An eviction specialist attorney will know the system, judges, and court procedures. They will be in a better position to get the eviction done without a problem.

The eviction process takes four to eight weeks. It begins with forwarding the rental agreement and the notices you gave the tenant to the attorney. The attorney will file an eviction lawsuit in the court and serve a notice to the tenant. The tenant has five to 15 days to respond (depending on how they were served.) If there is no reply from the tenant, the case moves directly to the sheriff's department for a lockout. It will take a week to 10 days for the sheriff to post the apartment and do the lockout.

If the tenant replies to the notice, a court date is set, which takes 14 to 28 days. If the case is successful in court, it then goes to the sheriff for posting and lockout, which takes up to 10 days.

Money Judgments

In the eviction process, we always seek a monetary judgment against the tenant for back rent and damages. A court judgment allows for the attachment of wages, checking accounts or other assets. We always turn these judgments over to a collection agency. It is well worth the cost of the collection agency, as this is a time-consuming process and an agency has more avenues in place for collection.

If we do not get a court judgment, the collection agency must file in superior court. This is time-consuming and costly. A landlord can file in small claims court for amounts from $20 to $7,500.

We like having a monetary judgment against the tenant. These court judgments last for 10 years and will be hanging over their heads; the judgment will show up if they apply for credit, a loan or rent another property. During this time, many tenants will want to buy a home or need a clean credit report for some reason, and we can still collect from them years later. In one case, we got a call from an old tenant eight years after their eviction and court-ordered judgment for $1,200. They wanted us to sign off on it for a couple hundred dollars. No deal; it was our money and we had been waiting for it. If they wanted the judgment removed then they had to pay the full amount.

Workers As Tenants

We have regular workers that are tenants and put all or a part of their pay towards their rent. We use a "worker holding fund" program to keep track of this worked income and any cash advances given to a worker, or any other funds that will impact their paycheck. Managers and workers have also used this worker holding fund as a savings account; a pre-designated amount is withheld from their paycheck and held in the worker holding account until it is withdrawn. This is a convenient benefit for the workers, does not cost us anything, and helps to assure us that the rent is paid on time.

We use this worker holding category in our accounting system. It is used as an area for credits and debits of the worker. The ins and outs into this category should eventually balance each other out to zero. Any balance in this fund other than the saving part is waiting for the next paycheck or rent due. We require workers to do the work before they get the rent credit. On payday, a regular amount is put into the holding fund for each worker in the program. When the next rent is due, the manager at the complex credits the worker's rent due on their monthly Rent Deposit Report. In this way, the work from one month goes to pay the rent in the next month.

Leases versus Month-to-Month

Most apartments are rented with a lease. Landlords like to get the tenants locked in for as long a time as possible. Tenants like the protection of not having rents raised. It looks like a win-win situation on the surface. Our problem with leases is that they make getting rid of a problem tenant much more difficult. If a resident manager is having problems with a tenant, it becomes necessary to document such problems and build a case to break the lease.

We prefer month-to-month rentals so that we can just give a problem tenant a 30 or 60-day notice to leave. On a month-to-month rental agreement, it is not necessary or required to give a reason for ending the tenancy. We just give them the notice and only tell a tenant that, "It is not working for us." We never give a reason. We do not want to get into an argument with a problem tenant; we just want them out.

A good example of the value of being able to just give a 30 day notice occurred with a tenant in a duplex we had just purchased. The duplex had been in foreclosure with a very dysfunctional family renting one side of it.

They had a pit bull chained to a car's bumper in the driveway, the son was a bum and a crook, and the parents did not work. As soon as we bought it, we gave notice to get rid of the dog, which angered the son. At the time, we did not realize that the dog was the only normal one at the property.

We lucked out a few days later when several police units showed up with a helicopter to arrest the son. The father protested and they arrested him too, followed by the arrest of the interfering mother. They all went off to the slammer. The next day my wife served them, in jail, a 30-day notice to leave. Within a month, they were all gone, the place was cleaned up and we were ready for a normal tenant.

We are in the business of renting apartments and we like to keep them full. We do not get rid of good renters, only problem ones. These are people that are bothering other tenants, making too much noise, or not taking care of our property. The rule is that if you do not get rid of bad tenants then you will only have bad tenants. Good people will move out or will not rent from you at all. The month-to-month rental agreement makes it much easier to get the bad ones packing. The lease does not really protect the landlord much. If a tenant wants to move or their economic condition changes, they are going to leave. Court judgments against a tenant are just as easy to obtain on a month-to-month rental agreement as on a lease.

To relieve the fear a new tenant might have, we give them a letter assuring them we will not raise their rents for a specified period of time. This gives them the protection they like without locking us into a lease

Advertising and Promotion

Print Advertising

Advertising is expensive, and reaching the right cross section of possible future tenants is very difficult. Several of the complexes we bought were using the apartment rental guides found in grocery stores. This is a great publication, but the cost was more than a small apartment complex could afford. A half-page monthly ad cost almost as much as the rent for a one-bedroom apartment for a month. If the complex was large enough it could work, but in a 38 unit complex there was not enough income to afford this type of advertising. Large citywide newspaper advertising has also gotten prohibitively expensive. That, coupled with the decline of newspaper readership, makes it a poor place to put your advertising dollar.

There are a few places to promote your property that will not break the bank. If you are in a suburb or smaller community, there may be a smaller regional newspaper or weekly paper that runs ads for a modest cost. These smaller inexpensive newspapers are definitely nice for advertising your property. There are also tabloid-type publications in most major cities that sell inexpensive ads. Always look around when you are in restaurants or stores to see if there are any free publications offered. They will not be the only type of advertising you will need, but they are a start. The lack of one of these inexpensive methods of advertising is not a deal killer when considering a new property.

Online Advertising

We use Craigslist all the time. It is free, which makes it desirable. It is also well known and read by many people. The list rotates, with the latest ads at the top, so it is necessary to update your ad frequently. Check your ads on Craigslist weekly, as the ads are deleted after seven days. Open an account where you can store your prior ads and use them again when they fit the current vacancy. Craigslist also allows pictures in the ad, so make a file of nice pictures that show off your complex. Always put a picture in the ad. Remember, it is all free; you have nothing to lose. Craigslist does have limitations on the number of ads permitted from an email address. Placing ads from the email of each complex will allow you to maximize the use of Craigslist while working within their limitations.

In addition to Craigslist, there are many other websites advertising available apartments. Many times these online ad services are less expensive than other print versions and more effective. We have used several of them.

When we got into the apartment business, we started our website to promote the properties and give information to people looking for an apartment. Our son in the computer business put it together for us. There are many companies that can help with creating a website inexpensively. We have links to all of our complexes, contact information, map links, and pictures of each complex. On the main sign out front of each apartment complex, we have our website name prominently displayed in type large enough to be seen from the street. We figure that if we can get them to the website then they are more likely to come to the complex, where we will have a chance to show them how nice our properties are in person. Websites need to be checked from time to time to ensure that the contents trigger a high inclusion on the leading search engines. You will need a computer guy to do this, or to pay for the service from a company.

Facebook and other social media sites are important because they appeal to younger people. You should keep in mind that younger people make up a large percentage of renters. You need a Facebook page for each apartment complex. Watch out for negative reviews from bad or evicted tenants that post their comments to discredit your property.

Banners And Signs Out Front

Banners and signs out front large enough to catch the eye of a passing motorist are a way of getting our message out. Many local sign shops can make any size banner you might want. Online companies can make very professional banners and/or signs at reasonable prices. They have pre-made signs, or you can add custom features such as your phone number or a special message.

We have banners out front of all our complexes. They are usually about three feet tall and 10 to 12 feet wide. Some just have the phone number of the complex in very big print. Others have a standard message, such as, "Renting Now," "Move in Specials," etc. If you own several complexes, you can have different banners at each and rotate them around between properties. The rotating of banners gives your complexes a fresh look and a better chance of being seen.

Besides banners, we use smaller signs and bullet-type attention getters. These are available from online sources and companies specializing in supplying printed items for multifamily rental companies. The signs are about the size of a small "For Sale" sign and are available in dozens, if not hundreds of catchy phrases.

I do not like the front of our properties cluttered with a mishmash of signs. Keep it simple and tasteful. Get the message across without being tacky. There just needs to be enough color and signage to get the passerby's attention.

Tenant Referrals

We offer our existing tenants a cash reward for referring someone that rents an apartment. The cash amount usually works out to about 15 percent of a month's rent. The existing tenant gets the discount off their following months' rent. We carry the reward as an advertising cost in our accounting system.

We get a few tenants from each of these methods. Taking advantage of all the low cost ways to promote your property will help to keep advertising budgets modest.

Property Taxes

Property taxes vary by state and county. Within a state, property taxes will be somewhat similar, depending on local assessments and special taxes. Between states, however, rules can vary widely. States can have any possible system you can think of. When looking for property in one state, we learned that the assessor would assign a value and tax that was obviously too high. Everyone hired attorneys to fight it. The attorney always got the amount reduced, leaving the property owner with a lower tax bill, but legal fees to pay.

The moral is to make sure you know what the property taxes and any other taxes or fees are going to be when figuring the expenses and value of a property. You do not want any costly mistakes to bite you on your fanny after the close of escrow on the property.

Property taxes will be reassessed on the transfer or sale of the complex. This is a standard procedure that can result in a large tax increase if the property has been held for several years. It is important to calculate the new tax on the purchase price instead of using real estate property taxes from past expense records.

Certain transfers within family members are excluded from the general rule that a change in ownership will trigger a reassessment of values for property taxes. However, each tax jurisdiction can have its own rules on how this must be done. We gifted part-ownership of our duplexes as part of our estate planning to our children. We failed to follow the rules exactly and triggered the local property tax assessor to quickly jump into action, reassessing our properties and sending us a hefty increase in property taxes. We fought it, and after three years and thousands of dollars in attorney fees, we did prevail. We ended up a little poorer and a lot smarter.

To get property taxes reduced due to a decrease in values or other circumstances will require a battle with your city or county assessor's office. The old proverb, "You cannot fight City Hall," is not totally accurate; you can fight them and get a tax assessment reduction, but you would probably rather have a tooth pulled without Novocain. When real estate values are going up it only takes the assessor five minutes to reassess a property to increase taxes. When values are declining it requires copious amounts of paperwork and the time to attend hearings and jump through the hoops that are required to get them reduced. This is not a job for the weak of spirit and is one of the reasons they do not allow landlords to carry guns. In the major property devaluation since 2008, we have been successful in obtaining assessment value reductions and tax refunds for all our properties. There are companies that will perform this service for a percentage fee. Though costly, this is a good course of action for those who not up to fighting with local government.

Utilities

Utilities have become a major expense for a landlord. The cost of energy, water and sewer service has far exceeded increases in other expenses. These expenses can vary widely between local jurisdictions that are relatively close together. When calculating expenses for a prospective property, make sure you have good information on actual utility costs. We have been surprised on more than one occasion with utility bills greater than expected; even though we thought we had done our homework, we failed to verify costs, as we were unaware of the size of the difference from one community to another.

These wide differences can occur from city to city or county to county. Take trash removal, for instance. We had been in the apartment business for a few years and thought we knew what it cost for a dumpster of garbage. However, we found that the city in which we had just purchased an apartment complex required us to use a specific waste removal company, which charged 50 percent more than the company we used just down the street in a different county. We were not sure of the politics in this, but we were sure about our profit being reduced.

At this same complex we got a similar surprise when looking at expenses for water. Water costs for the complex were twice what we were used to paying with our other properties. Water and sewage treatment costs can be very high in some areas. When evaluating a possible property to purchase, verify all utility costs. That way, even though you may not like them, you will not be surprised.

Larger apartments will have a swimming pool, but many do not have a spa. Not only will a spa increase needed reserves for the pumps and heater, but it will use up a great deal of electricity and gas. Most spas are kept hot 24 hours a day, year round. Tenants are not good about keeping a thermal cover on. This results in considerably higher utility costs if a property has a spa. A spa is still a good feature for a property; you just have to be sure to allow for the cost in your expense figures.

It is always nice to pass utility costs to the tenants. Renters expect to pay their own electricity and gas bills. Most complexes built in the last 25 years or so will have individual electricity and gas meters for each apartment. These apartments will usually have individual hot water heaters. Before energy became an issue, many times, apartments would have a large water heater serving several apartments, with natural gas bills being paid by the landlord. A landlord is far better off with tenants paying for their own hot water. Rents should be a little higher when the landlord is stuck with the bill for hot water. In reality, you generally cannot get the higher rents. It is a nice sales feature, however, when showing an apartment to make the point about the tenant not having to pay this utility expense.

Generally, water and sewer bills are paid by the property owner, as these utilities are not usually individually metered. In complexes with very high water bills it is possible to pro-rate the water monthly charges and re-bill to the tenants. There are companies that perform this service for a fee. The water bill is paid by the landlord and then sent to the utility billing service. The company pro-rates the bill to each apartment based on the number of bedrooms and occupants. They send bills to each apartment and pay the landlords monthly from proceeds collected less their fee. This is a bit of a hassle, but far better than paying the bill yourself.

With all of the above variables, it should be obvious that a property under consideration for purchase must be evaluated for the utility costs it is going to incur. If you allow for the proper utility expenses, your offer to purchase will be correct and your profit on the property will be as expected.

Semi-Annual Inspection

Our semi-annual inspections come up in several of these chapters. We include it in the resident manager's duties, as well as the section for the maintenance person that is part of the inspection. The Forms chapter provides information on filling out the Semi-annual Inspection Log. We include this section here to give a background on how we came about doing the inspection. Prior to these inspections, we occasionally got a rude awakening when a tenant moved out and left the property in a horrid condition.

We began making thorough inspections twice a year when we heard horror stories about mildew and mold. In 2003, we purchased a complex that had gone through a "mold" issue; they had had to move everyone out and totally clean and replace many walls and floors to satisfy the local health and environmental departments. This had cost the owner almost half a million dollars and the loss of several months' rent. We took this property over and made a plan to try to keep us out of the same disaster.

At that time we instituted our twice-a-year inspection in which we inspect every unit we own. We look for any mildew and any water leaks. These are the main problems surrounding mold development. We also check for any repairs needed in the unit. We check the smoke detector, change the furnace filter and check the tenants' housekeeping. A tenant who is not taking care of our property or has a unit full of trash will be asked to clean up their act; if they fail to do so in a reasonable amount of time, they will be given a notice to move.

Some jurisdictions require inspections annually. For apartment complexes in these locals, we incorporate the required inspection with our own semi-annual inspection.

Mold and Mildew

Mold and mildew have been around forever. They grow and flourish in moist warm areas. Poor ventilation and poor housekeeping enhance the conditions that allow mold and mildew to grow. Construction in past years was not airtight and permitted some accidental ventilation. Walls might not have been filled with insulation, and doors and windows allowed a small amount of air to leak into the structure. During this time, bathrooms usually had a window allowing some fresh air.

When energy issues became a high priority, building codes were changed to make the structures as air tight as possible. Along with these code changes, builders and developers left off the windows in bathrooms as a cost-saving measure. They did provide an exhaust fan in bathrooms, but occupants, not liking the noise, did not turn them on when showering. Another bad building code change for developers was to leave off the duct pipe on range hoods and just let the hood blow back into the room. These code changes have all contributed to reducing ventilation and increasing moisture in buildings. Someone boiling noodles on the stove will be putting all the steam produced into the air of the building, as will the person taking a long hot shower.

Building construction changes set the stage for the mold and mildew problem, but lawsuit attorneys turned it into a major issue for property owners. All that was needed was a tenant who got the flu and ran to an attorney claiming mold poisoning. The attorneys loved it.

There are several things you can do to protect yourself. The first is to put the burden of notifying you of any mildew issues on the tenant. Apartment associations provide legally approved forms that inform renters of their responsibilities concerning mildew and mold. Include this form on the tenant's responsibilities regarding mold and mildew as part of your rental agreement. If mildew is found, the tenant is the first line of defense in cleaning the area. We have obtained mildew and mold eradication certificates for several of our key personnel. This certificate allows these people to clean and remove mold or mildew from up to 100 square feet of contaminated area.

To prevent mildew from getting a head start on our properties, we inspect every unit twice a year for any evidence of mold, mildew or water leaks. We have rewired bathroom switches to a single switch so that the light and fan come on together. Unfortunately, there is no easy fix for ductless range hoods.

HOA, Home Owners Association

An HOA or Home Owners Association is the governing body for a group of homeowners, usually owners of condominiums. An HOA is formed to deal with the day-to-day management of a condominium project. The homeowners association handles all common area maintenance, repair work and cleaning. Typically, the homeowners will elect several owners to serve on a committee to make sure the by-laws or condominium rules and regulations are followed for the benefit of all owners.

This committee can also be called the Board of Directors or Executive Committee. They will enter into a contract with a company that specializes in the management of HOAs. Most states have complicated rules for HOAs to follow to protect the owners. Even though the association is responsible for all activities, in reality the management company runs it all.

The problem we have seen after being in two of these HOAs is that most of the owners are first-time buyers or people that do not have a clue as to the management and day-to-day activities required in a condo association. The management company took on the full responsibility of running the complex and ran it as if they were the owners. It is easy for a management company to exceed their authority and make recommendations that are not needed adding an unnecessary expense for the HOA. In some cases they forget that they work at the direction of, and are subordinate to, the owners.

If you get involved in one of these associations, my advice is to do what I did: get yourself elected to the association committee or board. Once on the board you have the chance to keep the management company working with you for the betterment of the organization.

Money Issues

Leverage

Leverage is a financing term used to denote the ratio or percentage of loan to the value of the property. A property that is leveraged or heavily leveraged is one with a large loan and a minimum down payment. It is called leveraging because, with the smaller down payment, an investor can buy more properties and increase their potential for profit from increased values. Loan to value (LTV) is a percentage ratio of the loan. As an example, if you had a property that was valued at $1,000,000 and had a $600,000 loan, it would have a LTV of 60 percent. It is a simple percent problem of dividing the loan amount by the value.

In our early, younger days when loan amounts were modest on duplexes, we wanted the property to be leveraged to the greatest amount possible. We liked the lowest down payment, smallest monthly payments and longest term for repayment. This allowed us to purchase a duplex without tying up too much of our cash, and left us in a position to move forward if another property came up for sale. In our duplex-purchasing days this plan worked well because banks only wanted 20 percent down, and many times we could get a seller to carry part of that for a few years. We did have other full time jobs at the time and did not need income from these duplexes to live on. This allowed us to leverage our loans to the maximum. The danger of overly leveraged properties was mitigated by having our loans spread over several duplexes. One or two might get in trouble, but the others would keep our portfolio afloat.

Duplex loans were all 30 year pay back periods (amortization period.) This provided a lot of security, because we did not have to deal with another loan unless we wanted to refinance. Leverage became more of an issue for us when we got into apartment ownership. The numbers got bigger. With duplexes, the loans were in the tens of thousands of dollars; now all of a sudden the loans were in the millions. We could always handle the smaller duplex loan payments out of our other income in an emergency, but there was no chance we could make a payment that way on a multi-million dollar loan. To make matters worse, with apartments, the loans were all for a shorter period of time with a mandatory refinance after a few years, or a change to an adjustable rate loan that could result in loan payments increasing substantially. We would run the risk of interest rates increasing at the time of a required refinance.

Without large cash reserves in case of a financial emergency, borrowing against a large property with a high loan to value percentage was downright dangerous. In the mid-2000s before the real estate crash, most banks only required 20 percent to 25 percent down to obtain a loan. To make matters worse, property values tended to be inflated, making the actual loan to value number larger. When property values dropped, vacancies increased, and rent income slowed, pressure was put on high leveraged loans with high payments. This was a time of financial problems for owners holding overly leveraged loans.

The bigger danger in high LTV loans is in a time when interest rates are on the increase. The original loan might have been set for five or 10 years with a locked-in interest rate. At the end of this period the loan must be refinanced or it will move to an adjustable rate loan at market rates. If you refinance, the bank is going to want the loan to value number to be close to the going rate, which, after the disasters of the last decade, is now in the 30 to 35 percent down area. Rents may not have kept pace with the increase in mortgage payments from the adjustable option. It may be necessary to come up with more cash to refinance at a new LTV required by the bank. Either option will drain money from your bottom line.

In our duplex days we liked a LTV of 80 percent or higher if we could get it. When we moved to apartments, we backed off to 70 percent to 75 percent. Now in our older, conservative, cautious borrowing period of our life we always plan a LTV in the 60 percent to 70 percent range. These smaller loans diminish the rate by which you can increase your portfolio, but also diminish the chances a borrower will lose their property to foreclosure. The financial landscape is littered with the remains of borrowers that got in over their heads by getting loans that did not make sense for the property. We own a property today that we bought for 50 cents on the dollar from a bank that had taken the property back from an owner who got caught up in the financial frenzy of the boom.

Maintain Cash Reserves

Saving and cash reserves as a business priority has always been wise. Those who save are able to withstand the bad times and can bridge slow times until things get better. Savings are important in the early days to accumulate the funds required to put a down payment on a rental property. Later, savings are needed in case emergency repairs are required. A company that maintains cash reserves is going to be able to survive over a company that does not. The amount of cash reserves required will depend on several factors including other income you might have or funds you are able to draw from.

We always wanted relatively large cash reserves. My wife and I feel comfortable and sleep better if we know we have enough money in the bank to cover the unknown. How much cash is enough in your emergency fund? Personal financial planners recommend a six to eight month emergency fund in case of unemployment or other unknown disasters. When we began and had two duplexes, we maintained about that amount in reserves, meaning we kept an amount equal to about six months of the rental income in our cash reserve fund. This was a lot of money but it brought us the security we both demanded.

When we owned more duplexes, the amount per duplex diminished. Our logic was that it was unlikely that a disaster would happen to all of them and we only needed enough funds for the worst-case scenario. When we owned around 10 duplexes, we would maintain about 50 percent of the value of one in our reserve fund. This was probably more than we really needed, but in our security, conscious brains it made sense. When we got into apartment complexes and the loans and payments were significant, we increased the reserve cash fund to about the cost of one and a half units. This ratio of cash-to-unit value continued until the mid-2000s when borrowers and banks were failing. We doubled our cash reserves at this time and decreased our loan to value percentage. With real estate values only beginning to return to a respectable level and the economy still less than stellar, we are maintaining very large reserves in the anticipation that interest rates might begin to climb from their current record lows and put pressure on our bottom line. We are currently maintaining cash reserves around the value of eight individual apartments or about 4 percent to 5 percent of our net assets. When disaster hits there is great comfort when you can throw cash at it.

Saving Money

There are a number of smaller saving possibilities that grouped together can increase the profit of your company. The use of computer phones in each complex will reduce phone cost considerably. When buying a property, be sure to check any service contracts you are going to inherit. Many times these can be renegotiated to improve the terms to save money. The worst of these are the contracts for laundry service. These contracts usually pay the original owner an upfront fee and lock them into a long contract. Then if the property is sold, the original fee is gone with the seller and the buyer is stuck with the long contract.

When buying a property, always get a pest report. Generally, the buyer pays for the pest report, but if there is any work, many times it is the seller's responsibility or at least it is a negotiable point. It is better to get this information at the time of purchase instead of down the road when you are going to have to pay for the repair all by yourself.

You should also periodically check prices on existing services like yard care, pool service and garbage pickup. If these people know you check prices now and then, they are not likely to overcharge for their services. Most big retailers and home improvement stores have customer loyalty programs that offer discounts to larger customers. Take advantage of savings wherever you can and remember Ben Franklin's saying, "Take care of the pennies and the dollars will take of themselves."

Principles of Management

Praise In Public, Reprimand In Private

This is a key principle in keeping employees from feeling degraded. Most of us are receptive to suggestions from our bosses that are done in a constructive and friendly manner with no one else around. No one likes to be put down when friends, co-workers or other people are nearby. On the other hand, when an employee is being praised, they want the whole world to know about it. This is standard human nature. When you have to correct someone or actually have to discipline them, then do it in private with just you and them. Always be positive and point out the right way to do whatever it is that is a problem.

It is easy to make a mistake here and put someone down while making a joke, but if you do it in front of others, the person will not be happy about it. Always take them aside and council them like a friend.

Unity Of Command

Unity of command is a management term that means that each employee has only one boss. In any organization it is easy to fall into a system where all the "higher ups" tell the lower level employees what to do. Getting information and direction from multiple bosses always leads to problems. The famous old quote, "a man cannot serve two masters," is just as valid today as it was a thousand years ago.

Write your "chain of command" on a piece of paper. Who answers to whom? There will be people in your organization that are support people, who are not actually in charge of employees, such as a maintenance managers and part-time handy men. These people can give advice to complex managers, but the manager still only answers to their immediate supervisor.

In this kind of organization the responsibility moves up the chain. If the head, top of the heap, grand master, big boss questions a problem, they need only ask the person right below them to take care of it.

Responsibility moves up the chain and authority moves down the chain. You can delegate authority, but you cannot delegate responsibility. If your subordinate does not do his job then you are ultimately responsible. Give your subordinate enough authority to do the job; they are responsible to you, but you cannot get away from ultimate responsibility.

Span Of Control

Span of control is a management term referring to how many people one supervisor can control. This can vary some on the structure of the organization, but generally is not a very big number.

In the fire department as a Battalion Chief, I was in charge of seven fire stations housing 10 companies and 10 captains. The captain in each company only had three fire fighters under him or her.

It is generally accepted that a single supervisor can handle six to eight subordinates, depending on what work is being done. In supervising apartment resident managers, the mid-level supervisor should be limited to four to six managers. The geographical space between complexes increases the limitation as to the number in an effective span of control.

If it were an office situation, a single supervisor could handle dozens of subordinates. In residential rentals where the resident managers are on their own much of the day and the distance between complexes is great, the job of the mid-level supervisor is more difficult. To compensate for the geographical distance problem the mid-level supervisor needs to be available by phone or email to assist resident managers when needed.

Micro Managing

Micromanagement is a style of management whereby an upper level manager or boss uses excessive supervision to control subordinates or pays too much attention to minor details. Generally, this term has a negative connotation.

If your company follows a good chain of command and organizational chart then subordinates will be controlled by their direct supervisors. If an owner sees something wrong, it is not micromanaging to observe the problem and inform the next level down. I was chatting once with a high-level middle-management person in another company who told me of a problem she had observed by an entry-level employee in her company. I asked what she had done about it and I was told that she did nothing, because she did not want to be "micromanaging." It is not micromanaging to report the problem to the proper supervisor and let the chain of command do its job.

This does not mean a high-level person in the company cannot talk to lower level employees about a problem. For example, if the president of a manufacturing company, while walking through the warehouse, observes an oil spill on the floor that is slipping hazard; it would be fine to catch a nearby worker and make him aware of the problem. Micromanaging would be to give that same worker the assignment to check the floors each day for slipping hazards. This work might need to be done, but it needs to come down through the chain of command.

Chapter 4

FINDING THE RIGHT PROPERTY

Initial Consideration: Is It Right for Us?

We receive many sales brochures for apartment complexes that are for sale. Even when we are not in the position to purchase a property, I spend a great deal of time looking at brochures to keep abreast of what has been for sale, prices and cap rates. I even print some to keep on file for reference. If we are actively looking for a property then my job is more difficult and involves deciding if the property is going to be one that is right for us.

Size And Location

To get past the first reading of the brochure, a property has to have some minimum qualities required by me. It must be in a decent part of town. It does not have to be in the best part of town, but it cannot be in the worst or a bad part of town. The size has to be within our budget.

The cost is not a deciding factor at this time. I do not use the selling price as a deal killer, because I figure I am just going to offer what it is worth if we try to purchase it. However, I do a rough cost-per-unit based on market rents. This rough figure of value is just so I will have an idea of how far apart my calculations are from the seller's asking price. I base my rough value figures on the formula that the monthly rent is one percent of the value of the complex. For example: if the complex of 24 units has 12 one bedroom units renting for $900 per month and 12 two bedroom units renting for $1,100 per month then the average rent is $1,000 per month. If you consider that this $1,000 is one percent of the value of the unit, then the average value will be $100,000 per unit, and the entire complex of 24 units will have a value of 2.4 million dollars. This rough figuring will work out to about a 7.5 percent cap rate. There is no consideration for actual cap rates, expenses, vacancies, etc. This just gets you into the ballpark of the possible value.

Age

We will not currently consider a property built prior to 1979. Lead paint was outlawed in 1978 for use in residential buildings. Buildings built prior to 1979 are subject to extensive regulations concerning removing, sanding or in any way disturbing the paint. This can even include painting over the existing paint. These kinds of regulations make maintenance on the property more of a pain than it is worth. Older properties present more challenges for owners and the paint issue just makes it a deal killer. It is possible to test the paint for lead and perhaps get around the issue if the property has many other terrific qualities. In our younger days, before the more stringent regulations regarding lead paint, we had no concerns about purchasing properties of this vintage.

Parking

I am a big believer in adequate parking. I do not want to get a call in the middle of the night that someone is in the wrong parking place. One of my minimum parking requirements is one covered parking place for each apartment. I also want at least one parking place for each bedroom. For example, a 24 unit apartment complex with half one bedroom and half two bedroom units would need a minimum of 36 total parking places, of which a least 24 were covered. This is a bare minimum; it is much better to have too much parking than not enough. Older apartments often relied on street parking. Street parking is a plus but it should not be considered in the minimum parking requirement.

If a complex for sale does not have this ratio of parking then it is a no-go unless there is enough land to add parking, which is usually not possible. Carports can be added to a property, but this must be allowed for in the purchase price.

Density Or Units Per Acre

I like a property with open spaces around the units and room for nice landscaping. Most apartment complexes are two stories. If the property for sale is two stories then I would like a maximum of 20 units per acre. I would consider 25 units per acre if it has many other things going for it, but that is the absolute maximum. Better yet would be 15 units to the acre. If the complex is only one story, or includes both one story and two story portions, then the units-per-acre would have to be reduced to maintain the openness desired.

Landscaping

We expect apartment properties to have nice landscaping, including mature trees. I will consider the complex if there are possibilities to improve the landscaping and trees that will mature in a reasonable amount of time. The older I get, the less time I have for trees to grow. It is often difficult to determine the quality of the landscaping from the brochure, so this needs to be looked at on the first drive by of the property.

If any of the above attributes are missing from the property or do not fit our minimums or maximums, the property will be shelved for reference only and will not be considered for purchase. If the property gets by this first screening then it is off for a drive by to check it out further.

Drive By to Check Property and Area

The first drive by is to get a feel of the property and to see if it looks nice enough for us to get more detailed information on it. We want to like the property on this first look. It does not have to be love at first sight but it needs to be a minimum of pleasant attraction. You will want to check the immediate neighborhood around the property as well as the local businesses near the property and on the major streets in the vicinity. When I get to the property the first thing I look at is how it would look to a prospective tenant. Does it have curb appeal? This is extremely important; you want people driving up to your complex to have a good first impression. If it does not have an attractive street appearance then the property is probably not going to make it farther in the consideration process.

Street Location

It is good if the property sits on a busy street. Drive by traffic is free advertising. The more people who see the promotional signs on the property, the more potential renters you are going to attract. Being on a very busy boulevard can also be a negative because of noise. Many streets that are busy during the daytime when your signs can be seen may have reduced traffic in the evenings. Do not buy a property alongside a freeway, no matter how great everything else is. The noise from a freeway is horrid and it goes on 24 hours a day. In our duplex days we owned several that backed up to a freeway. They were inexpensive and were a good investment at the time, but I would not do it again. Sound walls do help some, but not enough to make it reasonable. You want someone else to own freeway property, so their tenants will want to move because of the noise – maybe to your more peaceful property.

It is bad to own a complex that is hidden or land locked, back in a neighborhood with other apartment complexes between your property and the flow of traffic. You do not want prospective tenants driving by your competition looking for your place. If the other owner's places look inviting, it will peel off possible renters. It is far better to be the first apartment complex seen when the customer turns into the area. We purchased a complex once in a nicer area that was just off the main street. It could be seen from the main street and was the first apartments you came to after turning. There happened to be several very nice apartments further down this side street from ours, many of which were newer than and at least as nice as ours. We had not thought about it at the time of purchase, but everyone heading to the other complexes had to pass by ours. We just needed to look nice and have a few for rent signs up and possible renters would stop by. We benefited from the advertising the other apartments had to do to get people back to where they were located.

Other apartments in the area are not bad. It produces more prospects for renters. You want to make sure your building stands out from the competition. We looked at a smaller, very nice complex once that was at the end of a dead end cul-de-sac with a nice, very large complex between it and the main street. It would be very hard to compete with the big, nice, and closer-to-traffic apartments that renters would have to drive by to get to yours.

General Looks From The Street

Verify information that might have been in the sales brochure. Does the landscaping meet your standards? Does the density give a feeling of open spaces? Are there any deal killers that you are not expecting that are visible from the street, such as flat roofs or major T-111 siding issues? Some of these should have been in the sales brochure, but it is always good to check them on site.

Immediate Neighborhood

Drive the immediate neighborhood looking at the homes and business within a block or so of the property. We want the homes nearby to look nice, with trees and bushes cared for, and lawns mowed. Do the homes have security doors on their front doors? This is not necessarily a deal killer because many people feel more comfortable with metal security doors. However, if most of the homes have these doors then it may be an indication of a crime problem.

Another clue to problems is the presence of metal chain link fences. These fences are sometimes called cyclone fences. They are usually about three feet tall and people put them around their front yards to keep people out or dogs in. Either way it is a good indication that the neighborhood is not desirable. Chain link fences are expensive and no one spends that kind of money unless they feel they need the protection. In the case of a dog in the yard, homes in a nice neighborhood never have dog runs in their front yards. The presence of chain link fences and security doors is reason enough to stop considering the property for purchase.

Look at the quality of vehicles close to the property. If the neighborhood is full of broken down older cars and trucks, it is a sign of people who either do not have much money, are not working, or just do not care enough to take care of their property. Worse yet is the presence of cars up in the front yard, or in some stage of being overhauled. In better neighborhoods, people keep their cars and trucks reasonably clean and in working order. The vehicle issue is not a deal killer in itself, but it is one of the indicators the buyer should be considering. Any one of these neighborhood problems may not in itself be all that bad, but coupled together; they give a good indication of the surrounding area. Security doors here and there, a few broken down vehicles and an occasional chain link fence add up to a negative impression of the neighborhood and put the property for sale out of consideration.

General Area And Businesses

If the property gets by the immediate area drive by, then we expand our tour to include nearby businesses and the closest main commercial street.

Again, we are trying to determine the character of the area and the problems that might be encountered owning an apartment complex there. We want good tenants who pay their rent, take care of the property, and get along with the other renters. The basic rule is that if there are bad people in the area, good people are not going to rent there. If they do rent then the bad tenants will drive them out and you will be left with only bad tenants. Our inspections of the area are to determine if it is an area that is receptive to responsible tenants.

The first thing I look for in the business area is security bars on windows and doors. In areas of high crime, businesses protect their buildings with heavy steel doors and window coverings. These types of security protection are ugly and expensive. A business will only spend money for these if there is a real danger of being the victim of a break in. If the closest businesses to the property being evaluated have bars on the doors and windows then the property will not be considered farther. You do not want to own an apartment complex in an area of high crime.

In the business area, are people just hanging around? Respectable people come and go to businesses. In bad parts of town people hang around in the middle of the day, drinking, selling drugs, or just visiting with others who also are not working.

We want the business areas to be well kept up, like the homes. They should be clean, nicely landscaped and in good repair. A business owner in a reputable part of town knows he must maintain his shop to attract customers. There should be no graffiti in the area. Good business owners will clean up or paint over graffiti as soon as possible. They do not want customers seeing anything negative about their business.

What kinds of businesses are in the area? If there is check cashing, payday advance stores, cigarette shops, tattoo parlors, liquor stores, bars, or adult video shops, it should alert you to possible problems. These can very well be located in nicer parts of town also, but several of these in a few blocks area can indicate the presence of clientele that might not be desirable as tenants. We are just trying to determine if the area is likely to be burdened with crime or drug dealers. It is far better to buy an apartment complex with a McDonalds and Starbucks nearby. Drive by the businesses near your home and see the type that is there. Those are the type of businesses you want your tenants to be exposed to also.

Deciding if the general area and businesses are going to pass our inspection is easy. If it looks like a war zone with undesirable people hanging around then it is not for us. If the business area looks like you could send your teenage daughter out after dark to buy a half gallon of ice cream, then it is probably fine.

If the area has not been a cause for rejection then we are off to inspect the property itself. I might take a quick drive through the complex on this first look, but usually it is better to get your buyer's agent and the selling agent to set up a tour. Have the selling agent arrange to get into a few representative apartment units. You want to see each of the types of rentals available at the property.

Inside The Complex

Does the property have a gated entrance? In general, tenants like the security of a gated entrance. They are not always needed, but their presence sets off a red flag to consider problems with crime at the complex. I have never been a big fan of gated communities, as I do not think they stop much crime. I have often driven into these by following another car and I am sure a criminal could do the same. If the expense has already been absorbed by the property and there is no obvious crime problem, then the gate would be an asset.

Look at the parking lot. I always count the number of parking places to verify the information shown on the sales brochure. I look at the quality of the asphalt and the white lines in the parking lot. If the parking lot is in need of resurfacing, it needs to be noted. The cost of redoing the parking lot is a major expense and it should be included as a consideration in any subsequent offer to buy the property. Also, look at the quality of the cars in the parking lot. This will give you an idea of the type tenants in the building. Nice cars that are clean and in good condition will indicate tenants that are also nice, clean and in good condition. How many cars are in the parking lot in the middle of the day? We want our tenants to be working. There will always be some cars there, but in the middle of the day we want to see a great many empty parking places.

Is the landscaping pleasing and well kept up? Apartment complexes usually have a yard service that comes once a week. There may be some pruning needed, but the general look has to be good. I often drive through the properties we own with the eye of a new tenant. I want the landscaping to be reasonable. It does not have to be perfect, but it cannot have obvious signs of poor care jumping out at prospective renters. We like enough open areas that contain landscaping to give the property a park like appearance. We would prefer mature trees and bushes, but are willing to wait for them to grow if the rest of the property rings our bell.

Once on the property, you can see the siding up close and determine if there is a significant dry rot issue. Fir plywood siding, commonly called T-111, is very susceptible to water damage problems. Even if it is painted regularly, there is good chance dry rot damage will occur. It is often trimmed with horizontal boards at the bottom of the wall and horizontal "belly" boards in the middle of the wall. These trim boards allow water to follow the vertical groves in the siding, run in behind the trim boards, and get trapped by the metal flashing between the plywood sheets. This trapped water will eventually rot the horizontal trim boards as well as the siding itself. This is a very big headache for owners of property with this kind of fir plywood siding. We have owned property with this siding and hated it. We would only consider buying a property with T-111 siding if it was in very good condition, or if we planned to have it all replaced after the close of escrow. Our offering price would be reduced by enough money to make any necessary repairs or replacements to the siding.

The other horrid siding is a horizontal pressed board siding with a coating on it. It is usually embossed with wood grain and comes looking like three or four smaller horizontal boards of about four inches each. In theory, if it is kept painted and waterproofed it should work fine. In practice, it is never waterproof and the pressed board construction absorbs water like a sponge. It is hard to believe a siding product could be worse than T-111, but this stuff definitely is. If you are considering purchasing a building with horizontal pressed board siding then plan to have it all replaced as part of your offer. This product belongs in the garbage dump.

You should have gotten information on the age of the building from the sales brochure. Now is the time to check the property for signs that will tell you about its age. In the chapter on Construction, we list information on windows and other construction materials that have changed over the years and on how to date a property based on which materials it contains.

You probably would not have gotten this far in your evaluation of the property if it had too many units per acre. It was common in the 1960s and before to try to get as many apartments on a piece of property as possible. Most complexes in this vintage will not have the open spaces we want. During this building time frame, flat roofs were also common. If you get to this point in your check of the property and did not previously know about its density or flat roofs, then now is the time to forget the complex. These are both deal killers. Density for the reasons stated above and flat roofs because they leak and date the property.

Windows are a major clue on the age of the building. Windows have changed often over the years and, barring the replacement to more modern windows, will give you a good idea of when the structure was built. There is a table on windows in the Construction chapter showing when certain types of windows were in use.

When checking out the interiors of the units, remember to filter out problems that are fixable. These might include new hardware due to sloppy painting, or new hinges on doors. Replacing doors is a modest expense to get them looking more modern. Older apartments often have very darkly stained wooden doors that give the apartment a dark feel. These can be replaced by new white six panel doors to brighten up the place. Some deficiencies in the unit may not be fixable at all. If the apartment is too small in square footage, there is no way to make it bigger. An apartment that is very dark tends to be more difficult to rent, and it is not easy to put in more windows.

You would like the apartments to be pleasant and comparable to other nice complexes in the area. The fewer improvements you need to make inside the better. Some improvements to the inside are very expensive. If the cabinets in the kitchen are old fashioned there is no easy fix. If you want to upgrade the kitchens, you are going to have to spend the money. Most times when you change cabinets, you are going to change the counter top, sink, faucet and anything else affected by the change, which might even include the floor covering. Replacing old appliances is also an expensive fix. As we upgrade kitchens and replace appliances, we change all appliances to white. White is bright, clean and acceptable to just about everyone. Minor upgrades for new light fixtures, cabinet pulls or towel bars are modest expenses. If it is going to require extensive upgrades to get the apartments to a competitive level then you need to make sure your offer allows for this expense.

I like to check the swimming pool fence to make sure it meets the insurance company's safety requirements. Pool fences need to be 5 feet high and the space between vertical pieces needs to be less than 4 inches. There must also be less than 4 inches clearance under the fence. This minimum is required to make it very difficult for a small child to get their head through the rails and cause injury or death. Before we were aware of this requirement we purchased a complex that had a pool fence that was only 4 feet tall. We had to change the fence to meet this safety requirement at considerable expense. Better to get it out during the negotiation period and receive some concession for the cost to bring the fences up to code.

Similar to the pool fence are the balcony and stair railings on the property. They too must meet the less that 4 inch rule between railing verticals and under the railings. This can be a major expense to change all the stair, landing and balcony railings in an apartment complex. Make it part of your value calculations. Get the seller to bring them up to code during escrow or to provide an allowance for the work.

If the prospective property is still in the running to be considered for purchase, I ask myself, "Would I want to live there?" If the answer is no, then it is probably not for you. It is not easy to promote a property to others if you do not like it yourself. If it is nice enough for you then it is probably nice enough for the good tenants you want to attract. Good renters want to live in a nice area and next door to nice people just as you do.

If it is still in consideration after all this checking, then it is time for more scrutiny with a pencil and a calculator. Have your real estate agent obtain information on rent rolls, income and expenses, and any additional information available from the seller's agent that will help you figure the values of the property.

Calculating the Value of an Apartment Complex

The value of an apartment complex is a function of its income. You only need to know the net rents, expenses and a market capitalization rate to calculate value.

There are not that many variables: rents, vacancy factor, other income, an expense estimate, and a cap rate. Any broker trying to market a complex by "cost per door" (meaning cost per unit), square foot cost or replacement cost is probably covering for an overpriced property.

Be careful using figures supplied by the seller, as income is usually inflated and expenses minimized. Figure what an apartment should rent for less any concessions given, and less a vacancy allowance (usually figured at 5 percent, but can be more.) This should give you an amount you can reasonably expect to net each month (the amount you take to the bank.) Other incomes, such as laundry, late fees, etc., should be added to rents to give an accurate total on expected income.

The manager's apartment is calculated into the income as if it was rented. It is also included in the expenses as management cost. This is the best way to handle it because per unit expense estimates include the manager's apartment.

We review expenses presented by the seller, but use the figures we have on our own properties. Allow for any new property tax or insurance increases. Be cautious of properties in counties that you are unfamiliar. Water, sewer and trash costs can be much higher than expected. It would be a mistake to use income and expense figures supplied by a real estate agent representing the seller; it is much more accurate to use figures based on our own experiences in the past with similar properties.

You should look at the seller's expense documents to catch any larger-than-normal costs because of the area in which the property is located. Different counties and different cities can have big differences in expenses sometimes. If the figures presented by the seller are accurate, you should be able to spot these and will not be surprised after escrow closes. Two unexpected expenses that we have been caught with were trash pickup and water costs. One city required every apartment owner to use the same trash removal company at higher than expected costs. We had assumed we could switch companies to our lower cost trash collector we used at other complexes.

At the same apartment complex we also did not realize that water rates were sky high. This was a different county than we were used to and we were blindsided by utility costs much higher than our normal rates. The prior owners had mitigated the water costs by contracting with a company to prorate the monthly water bills and charge each apartment for the water usage. By continuing this system, we were able to pass the water costs on to the tenants and not impact our bottom line. Tenants are more likely to conserve water when their bill reflects a prorated amount of the water used.

When estimating expenses for an apartment complex, it is necessary to consider features of the property that will increase expenses more than normal. Many apartments built before 1990 used a large central water heater in each building to supply hot water to each apartment in that building. The large water heater also had a large storage tank and a pump system to distribute the hot water. This is an efficient system overall, but the cost of heating the water is billed to the complex and not the individual units, which can be a large expense for the owner. In addition, the tenants have no reason to conserve water, as they not paying the bill. This is a significant expense for the owner and needs to be included on any expense estimates used to determine the value of the property. Apartments constructed more recently have individual hot water heaters in each apartment, with the utility cost paid by the tenant.

Apartment complexes that have a spa provided will have higher utility costs than a complex without a spa. The spa is usually kept hot 24 hours a day, year round. The energy for the heat and the electricity for the pumps are also significant costs and must be included in final expense figures for value calculations. A spa is a good selling feature to a prospective tenant, but does not translate into higher rents for an apartment. We have seen a few properties without a swimming pool. In the case of no pool, expenses will be reduced from the normal complex, which most times include a swimming pool.

If you are still considering a property that has one of the bad sidings, allow an annual figure in the expense estimate for repairs to the siding that will surely be needed. There may be some additional landscaping expense depending if there is a lot of acreage or something special about the grounds that might need to be considered in the expense estimate.

The annual expense per unit figure will come from averages you have experienced with your own properties in the past, plus additional amounts to cover the costs that are particular to the property being evaluated. If this is your first apartment complex purchase and you do not have your own past expense records to base estimates on, then you are going to have to rely on your real estate agent's help, as well as advice from friends and business acquaintances you might have.

Finally, add "Reserves" to the expenses. This is the money set aside for major repairs that do not occur on an annual basis. These are for roofing, exterior painting, parking lot resurfacing, and swimming pool plastering or new equipment. In 2013, this reserve amount ranged from $150 to $250 per unit per year, based mostly on the amount of exterior maintenance the complex was expected to need.

Interest expense is NOT included in this formula because interest, as part of debt service, is paid out of the Net Operating Income.

Discretionary capital expenses that make the property more valuable are not included in expenses when figuring the value of an apartment complex. These expenses are not necessary, but are upgrade improvements to the property. These might include building a storage shed, adding balcony covers, or remodeling the laundry room. These do not need to be done and they do not usually result in increased income from higher rents. An improvement such as a fitness room may result in being able to raise rents, but it is still a capital improvement rather than a normal day-to-day expense.

Sometimes the seller's figures will omit the cost for new appliances or replacement of carpets and put them in the capital expenditure section. They reason that these large expenses are not a day-to-day expense as they only occur every several years for a particular apartment. The test for normal expenses is whether you have a choice in making the expense or not. In the case of carpets and appliances there is no choice; if they are bad you must replace them, and therefore they are included as normal expenses. Remember, a capital expense does not have to be done. It may improve the property and may even make it more valuable, but it is not included on the expense figures in determining the value of an apartment complex.

Do a little looking at comps for other apartment complexes that have sold recently to determine a market cap rate for the property. Real estate surveys by brokers usually have an estimate of the "going" cap rate.

FORMULA:

	Market Rents	(Gross Income)
Minus	Concessions	
Minus	Vacancy Factor	
Equals	Net Rental Income	
Plus	Other Income	(Laundry, Late Fees, etc.)
Equals	Net Income	(Amount Taken to Bank)

Minus   Normal Expenses   (Do not Include Interest)

Minus   Reserves Allowance

Equals   Net Operating Income (NOI)

NOI divided by CAP RATE equals Value

EXAMPLE WITH REAL NUMBERS:

For our example, we are using the following numbers:

1. A 40 unit apartment complex with 20 each of 1-bedroom and 2-bedroom units
2. Market rents are $700 per month for 1 bedroom and $900 for a 2-bedroom unit
3. Tenants are given a $25 discount (concession) as a signing special
4. We use a standard 5 percent vacancy factor
5. Other income from laundry, late fees, etc., comes to $500 per month
6. Our estimate of regular expenses comes to $4,000 per unit/year
7. The complex has a stucco exterior so we use $200 per unit/year for reserves
8. A survey of current cap rates for similar apartment complexes is 7 percent

CALCULATIONS:

Market Rents (20 x $700) + (20 x $900)

= $32,000/month......................................$384,000 per year

Less Concession (40 x $25)

= $1,000/month.......................................$12,000 per year

Less Vacancies

($384,000 - $12,000) x 5 percent......................... -$18,600

Net Rental Income..**$353,400**

Plus Other Income $500/month $6,000

Net Income..**$359,400**

Less Expenses   (40 x $4,000) $160,000

Less Reserves   (40 x $200) $8,000

Net Operating Income **$185,400**

Value equals NOI / Cap Rate   ($185,400 / .07) = $2,648,571

If the property has "deferred maintenance" – repairs that should have been done but were not – then an estimated amount for those repairs must be subtracted from the above value to arrive at the price the property is currently worth. If the deferred maintenance has resulted in a reduced market rent then the property falls into a depressed property category. You will need to think about the deferred repairs and market rents to determine what the market rents will be when repairs are completed.

Apartments are not emotional purchases like buying a house. Yes, you want to like it, but it is strictly a business decision. Do not get sucked into paying too much by some real estate agents sales pitch. If the complex cannot support the value by earning enough income, then the asking price is too high. Apartments are an investment based on a return. The return is directly based on income and expenses.

We once looked at a nice apartment complex that was marketed for about 25 percent more than its real value. The seller tried to convince us that is was worth more because of the nice area in which the complex was located. It was true, the apartment complex was in a nicer neighborhood; but if the niceness of the area does not result in higher rents or reduced vacancies, it does not make the property worth more.

Several years later, I saw this same complex still for sale, being offered for a more realistic price. The seller had been forced to put on a roof and make major siding repairs as well as drop the price 20 percent.

Appraisals

When a property is purchased, the lender will require an appraisal to make sure the value is correct for the loan requested. These appraisals can be costly for large properties, but there is no way around the expense. It is a bit of a scam sometimes when you pay a large down payment on a nice property and are requesting a modest loan. It should be obvious to anyone with a minimum amount of sense in the real estate business that the loan to value is better than good. However, logic does not enter into the system and the professional, book-sized, expensive appraisal must be done. For example, we were getting a loan for a commercial property with a Starbucks and a Subway as tenants. We planned to put 50 percent down. This was a good investment on a class A property with class A tenants and we were going to put half the money in as cash. We were required by the lender to obtain a multi-page appraisal costing over $4000 (in 2006.) This was the first and last loan we ever applied for with that lender.

Apartment Appraisal Form

Input Information		Date:	December-13

Complex Name	Rocky Mountain Apartments
Complex Street Address	1423 Main Street
City, State, Zip	Denver, CO

Type of Units	Number of Units	Monthly Rent	
1 bedroom, 1 bath	22	780	17,160
2 bedroom, 1 bath	36	865	31,140
3 bedroom, 2 bath	1	1,200	1,200
			0
			0
			0
			0
			0

Yearly Expense Estimate per Unit	4,500

Current Cap Rate Estimate	6.50 %

Notes

Uses 5% vacancy

Does not use other income

Calculated Totals

Total Number of Units	59
Total Monthly Income	$49,500
Total Annual Income	$594,000
Total Estimated Expenses	$265,500
Net Operating Income	$298,800
GRM	7.74
Value	$4,596,923

Cost per Unit

	$77,914

Besides the need for appraisals during escrow for either a new purchase or refinancing, from time to time appraising the value of your properties is a part of good accounting. I appraise all of our properties, both commercial and residential, at the end of each fiscal year. We take a loss or gain on our books for the year based on this appraisal. We do it as part of our estate planning for our kids and grandkids, to be able to gift the allowable dollar amount each year in the form of a percent of the value of the company. We like to close out the fiscal year with up-to-date property values and capital accounts for all the partners. Accurate value appraisals are also useful in dealings concerning valuations for property taxes reductions.

We use the Excel program to calculate apartment appraisals using the same formula as shown above in the calculation of the value of a complex. The Excel spreadsheet is programed to allow for 5 percent vacancies, a credit to debt ratio of 1.2, and other standard assumptions that are all calculated automatically when the required information is entered. This required information includes the market rents and number of each type apartment, the estimated expenses for an apartment for a year, and a going cap rate.

We do not consider any other income in this annual appraisal. We ascertain an average market rent by looking at the prior year's rent reports and averaging the rents collected for each type of apartment unit. For expenses, we use our prior year's operating statements, adjusting the number by factors that are special for the particular complex. A complex with a spa heated all the time will show slightly higher annual expenses than a complex without a spa. This goes also for complexes with central hot water systems paid for by the owners. These complexes will show higher annual costs than apartments where the tenant must pay all their own utilities. I keep emails and other information on sales statistics to know what the going cap rate should be at the time of the appraisal. I will keep copies of such emails and average the cap rates listed, which I will use on our appraisal form. Copies of the cap rate information and copies of all our apartment appraisals are kept on file with our financial records for the year.

Commercial properties are handled slightly differently. Some of our commercial properties are full triple net while others are full service. When times were good, most commercial properties were triple net, meaning the tenant either paid all the expenses directly or billed by the landlord. However, when the economy tanked in about 2008 all kinds of deals surfaced for commercial property. The landlord could bill the tenant directly, partially bill them, or just forget it and pay the expenses themselves. When appraising the property we only need to come up with a net operating income (NOI.) The value of the property is easily determined by the NOI and a cap rate that is appropriate for the property. The income less expenses and reserves will equal the net operating income. It is then an easy mathematics problem to figure the value based on the current cap rate for the property.

For our apartments, we use our own Excel form. It is only necessary to enter the name of the property, the number and rents of the different types of units, an estimated annual expense amount and an estimated going cap rate for the property. The Excel program calculates all the other values based on the parameters we have programmed into it. It is easy to justify your appraisals if you keep current cap rate estimates from brokers, refer to your prior years expenses and average your current rents. It is hard for the IRS or anyone else to challenge your appraisals when you have the documentation to justify your calculations.

No Friends in Real Estate

A close friend who worked for a very large real estate management company introduced me to this. His company owned or managed over 15,000 apartment units all over the country. He dealt with new purchases and was responsible for evaluating and putting together offers and negotiating purchase contracts.

On one particular purchase, he was working with a representative from the seller's real estate broker whom he knew and considered a friend. During the course of the negotiations, the "friend" agreed to a $50,000 credit for some deferred maintenance work that needed to be done. The deal was struck and off went the document for finalization. My friend, the buyer's representative, told his boss of the agreement for the $50,000 and was pleased with how it had all gone.

However, when the final documents were ready to be signed, the credit was not in them and the seller disavowed any knowledge of any such agreement. My friend's friend had screwed him over and left him hanging.

Yes, you will have people in real estate you will consider friends, but some of the other basic rules should keep you out of trouble: read all the documents, trust everyone but cut the cards, and remember to make sure all is as it is supposed to be. Always put agreements in writing so everyone will understand the terms. Yes, a handshake is your word, but when it gets down on a piece of paper, it is better for everyone.

Real Estate agents you Cannot Trust and Why

Unfortunately, there are more real estate people in this group than in the ones you can trust group. This is partly because they need to make sales to survive, and they can fall into the trap of becoming a used car salesman touting all that is good and minimizing the shortcomings. During the mid-2000s, I saw many, many properties that were priced well beyond reality. It was a time of buying frenzies and it was easy to be caught up in the need to buy a property with a guy in a three-piece suit telling you what a great deal it was. An inexperienced buyer could easily fall into the trap. There were many properties sold during that time that had to result in people losing a great deal of money. I saw properties sold in the mid-2000s with an asking price of $100,000 a unit, only to go for sale again in the late-2000s for

$75,000 a unit. Someone had relied on a slick real estate agent and lost a ton of money.

Scott*

Some agents are like Scott: he is not a bad person, nor is he trying to lead you into a bad property to make a buck, but he does not do his homework and is a wealth of misinformation. We have chatted with Scott from time to time while looking at properties. He works for a large company and seems to acquire a great many listings. We have looked at properties he has, but he never gave us the feeling he knew what he was talking about. Maybe it was just a personality conflict, but we never got the feeling of trust we want in a person that we are going to use to invest our money. He did act as the selling agent when Randy was our buyer's agent. Randy kept him on the ball and it all worked out fine.

I would not hesitate to work with Scott, but I would feel that I needed to check everything and make sure the purchase was heading in the right direction.

Kurt *

I never met Kurt in person. He was a real estate broker from the San Francisco bay area that I had talked with on the phone several times. This started during the time we were looking for our 10-31 replacement properties, and I was willing to talk to anyone. He would bring me information on possible properties, always telling me what a great place it was or what a great deal it was. One time he told me about a property which I had already looked at and knew to be an overpriced dud. Kurt went on about how great it was. Right then and there, I made a red mark next to his name as someone I could not believe. Either he did not know what he was talking about or he was intentionally misinforming me to make a sale. Either way he would never sell me a property in the future. He failed several of my basics to live by. If an agent does not have good character traits, dump him or her and move on to one you can trust.

Dennis *

Dennis worked for Kurt, which put him in the two-strike category. I had talked with Dennis on the phone many times about possible properties. This was still during the time we had 10-31 money to invest in replacement properties. I let every agent I talked to, including Dennis, know that whichever one brought me a property first would be my buying agent. These were in the days before Randy, and I wanted agents to think of me first when a new property came onto the market.

Dennis told me about a terrific property that had just come up for sale. It was in a good area and contained 106 well-maintained units. It had all the good stuff, like a fitness center and community room. It sounded great. My wife and I went out, looked at it, and agreed with Dennis that it was a nice property. The asking price was $100,000 dollars per door (per unit). The problem occurred when we looked at the income and expense report and the rent rolls. Of the 106 apartments, 70 of them were studio apartments renting for $650 per month, which was reduced to $625 on a six-month lease. The rough rule of thumb is that, for a complex to be worth an average of $100,000 per unit, it should have an average monthly rent of close to $1,000 per unit per month. This place was not even close.

Dennis produced a letter from the leading lender in town stating they would lend on it at that price. That did not make sense. I read the letter from the lender and it offered a one-year, interest only loan. It was hardly a ringing endorsement of the property. It would have been a set up for failure. A one-year interest only loan on a property that was overpriced and had incomes insufficient to keep the venture afloat would end in disaster. Dennis has been on the bad list ever since.

Letter of Interest

If you are going to move forward with the possible purchase of a property, then the next step is a Letter of Interest. I usually make an offer based on the above value figures. I do not offer less to give room for a negotiated compromise later. I feel it is better to figure the value and present it to the seller. I usually include how I arrived at the price based on rents, vacancies, etc. If the final offered amount is based on facts, you can defend this price very easily. The seller cannot argue with logic very well. Figure the value, tell it like it is, give the reasons, and let them deal with it.

You do not want to insult a seller by offering a lowball price that is obviously not realistic. Treat the seller fairly, give an honest offer, and go from there. In 2006, we had sold our duplexes and were looking for replacement property. We looked at a very, very nice apartment complex in the Roseville Rocklin area. The problem was that the property had been a low-income, assisted property with a special loan guaranteed by the state. It still had some units with restricted rents, but this did not affect the property much. The problem was that the loan had to be assumed, and it was paid down to a low level. We loved the property, but knew we could not get a second loan. We did not have enough money to bridge the difference between the existing loan and what the property was worth.

We tried to see if the owner would carry back part of the down payment, but they wanted to cash out and refused to give us a small second on the property. In our last meeting with the owner, I told him his property was worth 12 million dollars, but I could only offer 11 million as that was all I could afford. I apologized profusely, telling him I recognized the value of the property, but there was just no other way I could buy it. He rejected our offer, of course, but appreciated our honesty with him.

Purchase Agreement

When both the seller and the buyer have agreed on the basics of the purchase, a purchase agreement is drafted. This is usually done by the buyer, but can be done by either party. While the LOI is a non-binding agreement, the purchase agreement is a contract that binds the signers to the terms of the agreement. It is very important to get all the terms of the transaction in writing to ensure that both sides understand their rights and obligations.

All commercial real estate brokers will have standard purchase agreements available for you to use. This is where the real estate agents earn their money; by making sure the purchase agreement covers all the variables and protects your interests in the purchase.

It is not unusual to add an addendum to cover anything that is not specified on the standard purchase agreement. Be sure you understand the agreement, the terms and your obligations and responsibilities. Failure to meet the terms of the agreement following the timetable stated can cost you money. This is a legally binding contract that both parties must follow.

Read Due Diligence Materials

When you are purchasing a property, there is a "due diligence" period. During this period, the buyer can back out of the deal for any reason. The seller is required to provide documents to the buyer, as specified in the purchase agreement. These documents include rent rolls, repair records, lease agreement, contracts with subcontractors and any other documents that could affect the purchase. A good purchase agreement will list all the documents required. Always include a time frame for reviewing the documents, and specify that the time does not start ticking until all documents listed are received.

Take the time to read all the documents. This is a big job, but very impor-tant. It will give you lots of information after the purchase in the manage-ment of the property, but more importantly, it can uncover problems you might not have even considered.

If you do not understand a document, ask questions. The seller is obligated to explain any unclear portion of the documents and answer your ques-tions. If you are not satisfied with the answers or do not understand what the documents are about, you can simply say that you are not buying the property. If the seller wants to sell the property, it is in their best interest to provide answers in a timely manner.

During the due diligence period the buyer can have the property inspect-ed as needed to satisfy the buyer that all is as it is supposed to be. These inspections are done at the cost of the buyer. If problems are found dur-ing the inspections, then it becomes a negotiated issue between the buyer and seller.

These inspections can, and usually include an inspection by a pest control company. Who pays for the inspection and who pays for any work done is specified in the purchase agreement. We usually buy properties "as is" other than active termite infestation. This makes it easy for the seller and still gives us protection if there is a termite problem.

Keep copies of all due diligence documents with your records for the prop-erty. Many documents are not needed again, but contracts and agreements that will pass forward with the purchase need to be understood and avail-able for reference at a future date.

In the mid-1980s, we bought a duplex in the same area as the others we owned. It was the same floor plan as the others and built in the same man-ner. For some reason, when it was built it was constructed too close to the ground, without adequate clearance under the floor joists. These duplexes were built with raised, wood floors as opposed to the mostly concrete floors used today. During the course of the escrow for the duplex, the pest report indicated that code requires 12 inches of clearance under the floor joists and this structure only had 9 inches. The estimated cost to remove the excess dirt was $4,000. This was a sizable amount of money in 1985.

Our 15-year-old son, Michael, was trying to earn money and we offered this job to him at the amount estimated by the pest company. He got a couple of his friends to help; after all, it was only 3 inches of dirt.

The building covered about 1600 square feet; multiplied by 3 inches that makes about 15 cubic yards of dirt, or enough to fill two normal sized dump trucks. I do not think any of us really calculated the volume of dirt at the beginning, but it became obvious quickly. To remove this dirt working in an area of only nine inches clearance under the joists meant that they had to crawl on their bellies using hammers, short handle digging tools, and rakes. They constructed a plywood path, for a low cart they made, to be able to pull the dirt to the tiny access hole in the back of the house. They strung lights and worked for weeks. Every time I saw their operation, I was reminded of the movie *The Great Escape*, about World War II prisoners who dig a long tunnel to freedom.

Once the dirt was piled in the backyard, it had to be wheelbarrowed to every low spot in the neighborhood or hauled out. It is amazing how big a pile of only three inches of dirt can make. They stuck it out and got the job done. They earned their money on this job. This was the same son that cleaned the dog lady's place, further adding to his motivation to get a college degree.

After the Purchase

For each of the apartments we have purchased, we printed a flyer with our phone numbers and names and personally visited every apartment.

Many tenants told us they had never seen an owner before and only had the phone number of an answering service. We gave them our emergency number, which goes directly to my wife's cellphone. It did not take long before all the tenants knew that they better have a real emergency if they called; not only would they be talking to a real person, but it was the owner of the property.

On this introduction visit, we gave each tenant an invitation to an open house around the pool to meet us again, along with our other managers and workers. We would have drinks and refreshments at the pool on the designated date, and as many of our workers and sub-contractors as we could get. This was a great start to our taking over the property. Tenants knew who we were and that we were in charge and approachable.

Chapter 5

RESIDENT MANAGERS

Information Needed at Apartment Complex Level

A good resident manager can make or break your company. They need to be firm, yet pleasant and deal with tenants fairly. When we began, we did all the jobs involved with rental properties ourselves, but as we got bigger, we could afford some management help and our lives got easier. It is good to remember the bad times along with the good, like a call for a backed up toilet on Christmas Eve. Once we got to being able to afford a resident manager, we could devote our time to ways of improving our operation

Below are the ways we handle the resident manager duties in our company. There are several other ways to do the same thing. We show how we hand day-to-day jobs to help others understand a possible way and to use our experiences to help them find their own solutions.

Office Work

The resident manager is responsible for handling phone calls to the complex, showing apartments to prospective tenants, directing workers on the property, and handling the paperwork needed to run the office. The manager handles payments from tenants, completes a deposit report and deposit slips. Safeguarding the payments received is an important part of the manager's duties.

The computer is the center of the resident manager's office, as it is in just about all other offices today. A manager needs knowledge of applications like Word and Excel. The computer will contain all the forms and day-to-day documents needed. We maintain a Manual of Operations in each office computer with our rules, regulations, and operating procedures.

In each office computer, we provide letterhead and fax forms customized for the individual apartment complex. Each computer has custom flyers, notices and a collection of photographs of the complex. Special company forms designed by us can also be found in office computers.

Office Hours

Having regular office hours is a definite advantage in renting property. There are always some potential tenants that just happen to drive by and stop in to look at an apartment. However, in smaller apartment complexes, the manager is only a part-time job. There is not enough income to afford a full-time manager with regular office hours.

Probably around a hundred units would justify a full time manager with regular office hours. This would not be 40 hours a week in the office, but posted times they would be working in the office. Weekends are really the best time to catch a prospective tenant who works during the week and is looking for an apartment, but our managers generally do not work Sundays other than to be available by cell phone if needed.

In our complexes with fewer than 100 units, we allow our managers to work flexible hours. They can be in the office as needed, but also walk the grounds and deal with tenants. If they plan to be in the office on any kind of regular schedule, they can post the days and times on the office door.

This is up to the manager's preference for running the complex. We do require the office phone number to be posted on the door along with our 24 hour emergency phone number. Our managers have cellphones that are tied to the office phone by call forwarding, so any call to the office will get to the manager.

We have a note system in which, if the manager is not available, the tenant or prospective tenant can fill out a half sheet note form and drop through the mail or rent slot. We try to make it as easy as possible for people to reach our managers without having to have someone in the office all the time or have regular office hours.

Dress Code

Managers and supervisors should be dressed reasonably nicely. Our definition of reasonable would be clean, normal, and suitable for the job. Probably the best description would be "nice casual." We have seen management companies require more business wear, but we have never required such dress. Workers should be in work clothes suitable for the job.

Parking

Every tenant's vehicle(s) must be registered with our on-site manager. This gives us a record to follow up with the tenant in hopes of avoiding a costly tow. We use a standard form from the Apartment Association to notify owners of vehicles in violation of parking guidelines. All charges for towing will be charged to the vehicle owner following the below parking guidelines:

Vehicles will be kept in a clean and operable condition. License plates and registration tags are to be current at all times. Vehicles with expired license plates or registration tags will be towed at the owner's expense pursuant to the Vehicle Code.

Guests and tenants who park in fire lanes, red zones, reserved parking or undesignated parking areas will be subject to tow at the owner's expense. Vehicles parking in handicapped spaces not displaying proper disabled person's plates or placards are also subject to tow and/or citation from law enforcement authorities.

We require tenants and guests to observe our speed limit of 5 mph when on the complex property. Parking of boats, campers and recreational vehicles is prohibited unless approved by management. Major vehicle repair is prohibited. Disabled and unattended vehicles will be towed at the owner's expense.

In some complexes, covered parking spaces are assigned to tenants by management; we attempt to provide parking spaces convenient to their apartments. These are reviewed from time to time. Covered parking space numbers are not the same as apartment numbers to make it more difficult for a burglar to determine if a tenant is gone. Some apartment complexes do not have assigned covered parking.

Pet Policy and Service/Companion Animals

We have researched information from a variety of sources to formulate our pet policy. These sources have included insurance companies, Animal Control, lawyers, and the Apartment Association. We have found that there are certain breeds of dog that are known to be harmful or to present a potential risk to people.

As owners and landlords, we are obligated to reduce and eliminate risks to all our tenants; therefore, we will not allow these particular potentially harmful animals to be kept as pets on our properties.

Breeds not allowed are Akita, Boxer, Chow, Doberman, Pit Bull, Presa, Rottweiler, and Wolf. Other than the above breeds, tenants are allowed one pet that does not exceed ten pounds. We require an additional security deposit of at least $300 for pet occupancy. Dogs are not permitted to be loose. When not in an apartment, they must be tethered or on a leash. Loose or roaming dogs will be reported to Animal Control.

All tenants with a dog or cat must have renter's insurance with a minimum of $300,000 liability coverage. This coverage must include animal bites. The policy must list the apartment complex, manager and owners as additional insured. Tenants must provide landlord with proof of insurance.

Pets are not allowed to cause discomfort, annoyance, nuisance, or in any way causes a complaint from any other resident. Action will be taken by the landlord to remedy the cause of such complaint. Owners are also required to pick up after their dogs.

Any individual animal that displays vicious or dangerous behavior towards any other tenant, management, or maintenance personnel will result in the landlord revoking permission to keep the animal.

Service dogs and, more specifically, medically prescribed companion dogs, can create problems for property owners. These animals must be allowed no matter what your pet policy is. The number one defense is "meeting" the dog. Although you must allow companion animals, you are not required to accept a specific animal that displays aggressive or loud behavior.

Renting Guidelines

Below are listed some of the key points when dealing with a new tenant and the rental application process. Taking care of these details at the beginning will keep a manager out of trouble later.

We verify that the person meets our minimum qualifications, such as being at their current job for a minimum of one year. We will allow an exception to this if the renter has a co-signer with a good job history. If the tenant looks like a good possibility we can also charge a larger deposit if they do not meet the job requirement.

The first step is to fill out the rental application completely and have the new tenant sign it. Their signing of the application gives us the permission to run a credit check on them. Make a copy of the applicant's driver's license and paycheck stub. If they look like a really good possibility get their security deposit immediately and fill out the "Offer to Rent" section with, "subject to application verification," on the bottom of the form.

We charge a new applicant a credit check fee. This is our cost to run them through one of the credit checking companies. We only do credit checks on people that we believe would make a good tenant. We verify rental and job information first before running a credit check. If the applicant does not pass the information and job screening then we do not have to spend the money for the credit check.

The prospective tenant must pay the credit check fee, full security deposit and first month's rent before moving in. Any rent proration or credit check fee reimbursement, are taken in the second month of occupancy. The security deposit and first month's rent must be paid by money order. We prefer the credit check fee be paid with a money order, but we will accept cash or check.

When showing an apartment to a prospective tenant it is usually better to not show units that are not ready and still in the turnover process. Most people have a very poor ability to visualize what the apartment will look like after you complete the work. If possible the resident manager can show their own apartment or the apartment of a tenant they know well and shows well. Be careful showing apartments that have different amenities than the one coming up for rent.

Dealing with Tenants

One of the first responsibilities of a resident manager is to deal with tenants. The resident manager is the first line contact for tenants and can solve many problems before they become more serious. Tenants have a great ability to come up with issues and problems to make a resident manager's life interesting to say the least.

In one tenant problem, we got a report of a shooting at one of our duplexes. The coast was clear so we went over to investigate. It turned out that our male tenant was going somewhere with his family. He took the first kid to the car on the driveway and tucked him into the car seat then returned to the house to get the second child. On his return to the house, he left the car door open and in the tenants absence a large dog came on the scene and got into the car.

The tenant's return with child number two was met with a large growling dog in his car and one of his kids strapped in a car seat. He hurriedly returned child number two to the house, retrieved his revolver, and proceeded to shoot the dog several times, as well as his car. Fortunately, the kid in the car seat was a small enough target to escape without injury. The car was not so lucky.

In another tenant story, we rented to a reporter for the major newspaper in town. The reporter and his family had lived up in the Mountains somewhere and he wrote a newspaper column on rural life. They were very nice, down-to-earth people. They only stayed in my duplex for a few months when they gave notice to move. I went to the property for their move out and the almost new carpets were black from what looked like oil. Outside I saw the problem. Under the two cars parked on the driveway was a heavy coating of oil on the concrete that extended down to the gutter. It was a horrible mess. After they were gone, I was cleaning the driveway with solvent when a neighbor came over and told me that my tenant had just gone under the car and removed the oil drain plug and let the oil run out on the driveway.

It was pretty unbelievably stupid. As a country boy that was the only way he knew to change the oil in his car and truck. That is how it is done in mountain country. Of course, that was before the EPA had enlightened everyone on the hazards of motor oil waste. Sometimes you just never know what goofiness a tenant is capable of doing.

It's Not Personal, Just A Business

It is easy sometimes to be caught up in someone's bad behavior and become irate yourself. Put yourself above it all by remembering, this is a business; we do not want to make it personal by becoming angry with a tenant or worker. It will happen, of course; we are all only human, and it is normal to lose it occasionally. If you realize that other people are going to be a pain at times and that personal conflict is part of the job, you will not be surprised when it happens.

Treat everyone nicely. The good people will appreciate it and the bad will just be irritated. It is just a business; treat people in a businesslike manner and it will put you above the run-of-the-mill management people.

Four Basic Rules

When renting to a tenant, we include the basic guidelines for getting along in our complex with their rental agreement, and discuss these guidelines in person. Breaking the below rules will get them asked to leave:

> Rule 1: Pay your rent.

> Rule 2: Get along with your neighbors.

> Rule 3: Do nothing illegal.

> Rule 4: Take care of your apartment and our property.

We want them to fit in with other tenants and to be a good neighbor. All four rules make the life of a manager much easier. We make it clear that we will not tolerate a tenant that breaks the rules. If they cannot live in our complex and obey our rules then they are going to have to go.

We need tenants to pay their rent on time so we will be able to take care of all the financial needs of the complex. This is a business; money comes in and money goes out to pay bills. If the rent money does not come in then there will not be enough money to go around.

We do not want tenants annoying other tenants. We want all of our tenants to get along. Just a little courtesy will go a long way. It does not take long before bad tenants will force good tenants to leave. If you allow bad renters to cause problems, before long you will only have bad ones when all the good tenants have moved elsewhere.

If a tenant breaks the law, do not turn your back on it. Stop it or call the law enforcement agency. Tolerating this kind of behavior will turn your complex into a hellhole of bad people with little regard for laws or good sense. Always act quickly and decisively in dealing with illegal issues. You want every tenant in your complex to know you not going to have this in your property. If tenants think they can get away with it, they are going to make your life miserable. Be fair, firm and consistent and the tenants will know they are going to be held responsible for their behavior.

A tenant that has a disregard for our property or others' property is going to be a constant source of trouble. Insist that they take care of the property of the complex. If a tenant damages property then they are going to have to pay for it. It does not make any difference if the damage was done accidentally or if a guest of theirs caused the damage, it is still the responsibility of the tenant. Do not take the damages out of their security deposit until they leave. Instead, bill them to pay with the next month's rent. The amount owed for repairs is deducted from their payment first and the rest is applied to rent. In this way, if they do not pay enough for both the repair and the rent, the rent is short and is susceptible to a three-day notice to pay. You want the word around the complex to be that the management is not going to allow the property to be mistreated, and that those who do so will be required to pay for repairs. Tenants who repeatedly display a lack of respect for property should be asked to move.

Owners Make Their Money When The Last Tenant Pays Rent

It would appear that with all the rents collected, laundry room income, late fees, etc., the property owner would be making a great deal of money. The income can be good, but only when everyone pays their rents and expenses do not get out of hand.

During the course of a month, there are many expenses that must be paid. These are due even if the tenants pay their rents late or not at all. Wages, taxes, insurance, repairs, etc., have to be paid each month. At the end of the month, if the income exceeds the expenses, the property owner makes his profit. In reality, the landlord's profit comes from the last people that pay their rents each month. Bills are paid from income until all the bills have been paid, and then the rent collected after that becomes profit.

I was in the office of one of the complexes once late in the month and a tenant came in and told me he could not pay his rent. I pulled out my wallet and asked him how much he needed and pretended to look at the money in my wallet. He was surprised, of course, and said he did not want me to pay his rent. I told him it made no difference whether I paid his rent for him or he did not pay it at all. Either way it was right out of my wallet. His past due rent was part of the profit for the complex.

A tenant could perhaps reason that part of their rent goes to pay the mortgage, taxes or other expenses, and part of it goes to pay salaries and profit on the business. Those expenses are paid totally from rents paid early in the month, with the left over rents paid at the end of the month going toward profit. Any unpaid rents or vacancies will come directly out of the profits for the complex. That is why owners are always concerned with vacancies. A vacant unit is a direct drain on the profit of the company.

Collecting Rents

Near the end of one month and the beginning of the next month, the manager needs to check the office daily for rents. Most tenants pay their rent by putting it through the mail slot or rent collection slot at the office. We want these picked up often so they not lying on the floor. We have the manager stamp the back of the check with our bank deposit stamp to prevent anyone else trying to cash it if somehow it gets lost. Always have a special place in the desk to put the checks or money orders received. A small box or an envelope will work to keep them in one place. Do not just leave them in a pile on the desk or mixed in with other paperwork. It is easy for a check to get lost when it becomes mixed in with other loose papers.

As soon as possible, record the rent paid on your Rent Deposit Report. Check at that time if the amount paid is the correct amount owed for the month. If the amount is not equal to the balance due, you must notify the tenant of the shortage. If a rent is overpaid we will carry a credit forward for the tenant, but it is also a good idea to let them know so they can adjust their payment for the following month.

At the beginning of the month when many payments are being received, it is a good idea to get the money to the bank often. Complete a bank deposit slip, being sure that the total on the deposit slip matches, to the penny, the amount shown at the bottom of the column on the Rent Deposit Report for the deposit being made. List checks and money orders on the deposit slip with the apartment number. There is no need to use bank numbers on the deposit slip. Always double-check your entries for errors. The deposit slip is made in duplicate, with the original going to the bank with the deposit and the copy going to our main office at the end of the month with the monthly Rent Deposit Report.

We want bank deposits to be made frequently so that tenants' checks are debited against their accounts and the check clears before too much time has passed. Many people do not pay much attention to their bank account balances; if they see that there is money in their account they might spend it, even though our rent check is still sitting in the manager's desk waiting for a deposit to be made.

Keeping a record of received payment by making a copy of each check or money order is the best was to be sure we could verify what we received from a tenant. It takes a little more time, but it is worth it when there is some dispute on what was on the check received.

Late Fees

The late fee is used to encourage tenants to get their rents in before the late fee takes place. I am amazed sometimes that tenants that are unable to pay their rent on time, but can come up with the additional late fee month after month.

Tenants who do not pay their rents on time require the manager to do extra work in accounting and notification. If everyone paid their rent on time the manager's life would be easier.

The late fee should be charged in all cases of late rent due to the tenant failing to pay. Do not waive the fee to be a "nice guy." The purpose of the fee is to encourage tenants to pay on time, and giving them a pass on the fee defeats the purpose. If there is a question as to when the rent was paid, or if we failed to properly post it, then we cannot expect the tenant to pay a late fee. If you are a good guy and let a tenant slip on paying a late fee, then everyone in the complex is going to find out about it and want special

We do not want to drag out a payment plan by extending and changing it as the tenant's finances worsen. As soon as it starts to go backwards, it is time to ask the tenant to move. We like to help good tenants, but many times we have gotten two or more months behind with no hope of recovering the lost rent. This is bad for our company and does not help the tenant in the long run. We are in the business of renting apartments, and want to keep them full. We do not want vacancies, but sometimes a slow paying tenant with behavioral issues will force us to give the tenant a notice to move.

Taking Cash From A Tenant

It is never a good idea for tenants to know that rents are paid in cash and that cash is in the office. It is tough to refuse to take cash from a tenant who wants to pay rent, but we do not want our managers carrying cash, which puts them at risk for robbery or injury.

All rental offices should post a "NO CASH ACCEPTED" sign. Paying in cash should be discouraged. However, on occasion we allow managers to accept cash payment as a service to our tenants. The tenant is always told that this is not our policy but that we will do it for them this time. The manager can use the line, "It is okay for now as I am just leaving for the bank."

Great care must be used to safeguard the money. Usually the manager takes it to a safe location. This is definitely a gray area of management, as we want the rent money, but we do not want problems for our managers.

Tenant Works For Part Or All Of Their Rent

Over the years, we have had maintenance people that were also tenants, or who became tenants after they had been doing work for us. Those who are regular workers as well as tenants will be included in our "Worker Holding" program, explained below and in the Administration chapter earlier.

treatment too. Do not get caught in this and charge late fees as they are due. It is just part of the job, nothing personal.

When a tenant's rent check is returned from the bank for insufficient funds, the tenant will incur a bank charge for the return check and a late fee as the rent will now be past due. A tenant can only be charged one late fee per month. If, for example, a tenant pays part of their rent late, they are charged a late fee, but they do not incur an additional late fee for the unpaid amount. Banks always notify their customers (tenants) before we get a bounced check notification. A good tenant will come into the office and arrange to take care of it before we even know it is a problem.

We encourage tenants to pay on time with a sign near the office reminding them of the cutoff date for late fees. We do not want the income from late fees; we would much prefer the rent to be paid on time.

Keep On Top Of Slow Paying Tenants

When a tenant fails to pay or gets behind in their rent, it is the manager's responsibility to contact the tenant as soon as you know there is a problem. The three-day notice is given, but it is also important to talk to the tenant face to face. There is a big difference between a good tenant who is having a temporary financial problem, and a poor tenant that has been constantly late in paying rent or has caused other problems.

We are willing to work with a good tenant to help get them past a short-term problem. The manager can get a commitment from the tenant for a payment plan. Stretching payment over a period of a couple months can, many times, allow the tenant to catch up on money owed and prevent an eviction on their record. Once we establish a payment plan, however, we expect the tenant to uphold their part by paying as agreed. The manager has to stay on top of this and get the rent collected if possible.

Occasionally a regular tenant will do some work and, instead of paying them, we credit it against their rent. It may be from some work or part of a repair that the tenant just took care of without our prior approval. If it is reasonable, we will give them a credit towards their rent. It is shown on our monthly rent report as a negative in the "Other Income" section, and we indicate in the remarks what the work was so it can be coded into our accounting system.

It is a little more complicated if we approve the purchase or repair ahead of time. This puts the tenant into the category of a worker on the property. Our workers' compensation policy does cover this kind of worker and our liability policy will protect us. However, it opens us up a little to problems from a worker who is not one of our regulars.

We try to avoid giving work to tenants who are having a hard time paying their rent. We do not want to have to provide work for these people. We have been more lenient with work done by relatives of the manager living on the premises. In all cases we want the work to be done prior to the rent being due. Work done in one pay period goes to pay rent in the following month.

Worker Holding Program

Our regular workers, that are tenants, can use all or a part of their pay to go towards their rent. Their timecards are forwarded to the main office for the following payday. They will be issued a paycheck with a pre-designated amount withheld for their future rent in our workers holding fund. Usually, the apartment manager knows the amount, as it is the same each payday. If there is any question as to the amount being held, it is necessary to confirm the amount with the main office.

When you are using funds from the workers holding account, show the rent amount in the upper section of your Rent Deposit report. On the lower section show the same amount as a negative entry. This will balance the rent above and not affect the amount of a deposit. Code the lower entry "Wk" for "worker." There will be no explanation needed in the remarks section for regular workers.

If a regular worker's pay is less than the rent due in the following month, then the resident manager needs to record the amount earned on the current Rent Deposit Report and forward the timecard to the main office. The amount earned will be carried as a credit for the next month's rent.

Three-Day Notices to Evictions

Three-Day Notice

Rents are due on the first of the month. They are subject to a late fee if not paid on time. We allow a few days' grace period, as shown on their rental agreement, before the late fee is applied. If the tenant has not paid their rent in full by the end of the grace period then we give the tenant a three-day notice. This notice is a standard apartment association form called "Pay or Quit." This form notifies the tenant that if the rent is not paid, or they do not move in three days we will file for an eviction with our attorney.

If the tenant pays the rent with a late fee in full within the three-day period the matter is closed. If the tenant fails to pay the amount due in full within the three-day period, we will file on them. If the tenant pays a portion of the due amount we will accept the partial payment, crediting any late fee first; we then issue another three-day notice for the balance of the rent and start the clock running again on eviction. This is important if you go forward on eviction, as it is easier to get a judgment for rent than it is for rent and a late fee.

Many times in the past, we have worked with good tenants to set up a payment plan or catch up plan for back rent. We will, however, still issue a three-day notice to protect our legal rights for an eviction if they fail to keep their part of the agreement. It is always difficult to tell which renter will actually pay and which one will end up with an eviction. You just take your best educated guess based on their past performances and cross your fingers.

If they do not pay, it is time to file for eviction. It is necessary to put the rent on one form and the late fee on another. Judges sometimes disallow the collection on the late fee, so we want that to be a separate issue.

It is usually best to be very strict on this procedure. We want the tenants in the complex to know that if they fail to pay their rent, we are going to move to evict them as quickly as the law allows. We do not want them to feel they can fail to pay rent, use the money somewhere else, and get away with it. We want them to know that they had better pay their rent first or they will have to face eviction and a judgment against them from the court.

When we are evicting a tenant for non-payment of rent, we always file for a judgment against them for rent and all fees owed to us, as well as any damages caused by them to the property. Again, we want all tenants to know that we are going to come after them if they do not pay.

30-Day And 60-Day Notice To Leave

When a tenant has not paid their rent and there is no hope of recovering the amount owed to us, we will file for eviction. If the tenant has paid their rent but has broken our other important rules then they are subject to be given a notice to move. We will always give them a written warning and explain the importance of not being a bother to other tenants or of not damaging the complex property. A copy of this written warning will be kept on file in case we have to go to court. We are not in a hurry to get rid of a paying tenant and have to go through the headache of eviction. The eviction is bad enough, but we also have the expense and work to make the apartment ready for the next tenant.

When it becomes obvious that it is not going to get any better we will give the tenant either a 30-day or 60-day notice to leave. It is not necessary to explain why we want them to leave. We have been advised by our attorney to only tell them that it is just not working for us and that we feel it would be much better if they found a different place to live. They might scream and shout, but do not give in to telling them what a horrid tenant they are and we have had it with them. We just think it is time for a change, and that is it, period.

We usually serve the notice in writing after they pay the rent for the month. That way we have a month before they are in default on rent and we might have to go into a full-fledged eviction. This is not a pleasant task, but dealing with a tenant that is not getting along with others, damaging our property, or doing something illegal is far worse.

We are required to give a 60-day notice if the tenant has been a resident for longer than a year. If they have been a resident of the complex for less than a year, we are only required to give a 30-day notice.

As talked about in the Administrative Chapter, we prefer the month-to-month tenancy so that we are able to get rid of troublesome people with no reason required. A person on a lease has many more rights and it is necessary to show that they are in violation of some provision of the lease.

It is very, very important to give bad tenants a notice to move. If you allow them to remain in the complex and continue to annoy other tenants, the outcome can only be the loss of other tenants who give notice and move just to get away from the bad tenant. If you do not give notice to bad tenants then the good tenants are going to move and you will only have bad ones. When you are getting rid of a bad tenant, it is a good idea to make sure other tenants in the complex are aware that you are taking care of the problem so they do not give notice to move themselves. Move fast when you identify someone in this category and get them going; your good tenants will appreciate it.

Evictions

When a tenant is just not going to pay their rent, or they have not left after being served with a notice to move, the next course of action is an official eviction. We follow the steps outlined from our eviction attorney. Once the three-day notice has been given and the three days has passed, we can file. This would be after we have exhausted any other options for the tenant to be able to pay.

If the eviction is due to the tenant not moving after a notice to move, we can file for eviction after the 30 days have passed. If they received a 60-day notice then they should be still paying rent on the first of the next month. Failure to pay this rent will put them into the category of being evicted for non-payment of rent. We would give them the usual three-day notice for failing to pay and file for eviction as soon as the three days had passed. On this three-day notice, we would note that the original 60-day notice to leave is not cancelled.

One of our more unusual evictions occurred with a tenant that came to be known as the 40-year-old plumber. Tom was a great tenant. He and his wife took care of the property and always paid their rent on time. He had a decent job as a plumber working for a medium-sized company. All was well until Tom turned 40 and decided that he should not be working for someone else, he should be working for himself.

He gave notice to his employer and began looking for jobs on his own. He found a few, but far too few to maintain the lifestyle they were used to. He struggled and was unable to find enough jobs working as his own boss to keep the income coming in and to pay all their bills. It was not long before his rent check came late, then later. We worked with him as we would do for a good tenant and came up with a payment plan, but he was unable to keep up the payment schedule we had agreed to.

He was in a downhill spiral with no end of financial problems in sight. When it became painfully evident that they were not going to get back on a firm financial footing we told them that they should move out. When they did not move, we reluctantly filed for eviction. In the course of the eviction, Tom answered the notice, which would require a court appearance by him and us. This would extend the process by a few weeks.

At the court hearing, when the judge asked Tom if he had anything to add on his behalf, Tom stood up and told the judge and the court that we were the best landlords in the world. This was why he answered the eviction notice: so that he could tell the court how great we were. It was nice to hear how great we were, but it cost us three weeks of lost rent by going to court.

They were served in the normal process to vacate the property, but did not do so until the last day. We accompanied the sheriff to physically get them out of the building. When we arrive at the property, we found that Tom had moved all his possessions to the front yard. There was a very large pile of his belongings in the middle of the lawn. Inside, we found Tom vacuuming the carpets. He had cleaned the place completely and was leaving it in great condition. They moved out of the rental and moved across the street into a friend's place, leaving their belongings in our front yard.

Over the course of the next week, Tom moved from neighbor to neighbor every couple of days, while his pile of possessions got smaller and smaller. After about a week, he and all his stuff were finally gone. Tom was just a nice guy that could not handle his midlife crisis.

Asking A Tenant To Move Without A Full Eviction

Sometimes a tenant can be encouraged to move before the eviction process starts or before it gets too far along. A good manager will chat with a tenant in the process of being evicted. Giving them a talk about how an eviction is going to affect their credit rating, and about the problems of having an eviction and collection on their record for 10 years, might encourage them to think about just moving sooner and avoiding the whole thing. Knowing that an eviction is going to cost us attorney fees upfront and the loss of income from the apartment not generating any rent, we sometimes might forgive some of what is owed, or offer a cash incentive to them if they move immediately. We would lose any chance of an eviction judgment from the court but we could still attempt to recover some of our losses from collection agencies.

Pulling this maneuver off is not easy and it requires finesse, but occasionally it will work and we cut our losses and more on. This is more palatable if the tenant has been a reasonably good tenant in the past that got into financial problems. If you can come to an agreement with them and they move, it is a good deal for everyone except the attorney.

Inspections

Walk Grounds Daily Or Often

The best way to know how your complex is doing is to look at it often. Walk the grounds daily, or at least several times a week. Walking around, looking and making mental or written notes will put you in a position to keep your property in top condition and discover problems while they are small.

While checking your complex, empty any trash cans and pick up waste papers, cans, etc. It is part of the job to tidy up the grounds. The trash can near the mailboxes is especially prone to being filled quickly with all the junk mail tenants quickly discard. Tenants will appreciate an apartment complex that does not have trash all over the place. Picking up around the grounds prevents trash from building up and blowing around in the wind.

I think many tenants are more careful with their trash if they see the manager keeping things neat.

In the early days of the McDonalds hamburger chain, Ray Kroc, the founder, used to walk the parking lots of stores and even the immediate neighborhood picking up trash and used ketchup packs. He insisted that, inside and out, the stores would be spotless.

Pay particular attention to the dumpster area. This is usually the worst spot on the property. From tenants missing the opening to the dumpster, people looking for cans and bottles in the dumpster, and the waste removal company, this area is usually a mess. Yes, cleaning up this mess is nasty business, but it has to be done. Gloves are essential, as well as a broom, dustpan and whatever else it takes to clean it up. If you find a bag of trash alongside the dumpster, look inside it to find a letter or other document that will show the address of the culprit. Knock on their door and ask them to do a better job of hitting the opening to the dumpster.

Make sure the pool area is tidy. Empty the trash container at the pool and pick up around the area. Any items left by a tenant can be saved for a short time, but stuff left at the pool is subject to disposal. Straighten pool furniture, tables, and umbrellas. Note any damaged furniture or other items needing replacement or repair. Check if the pool itself is clean. The pool service company usually comes twice a week. There will be times when leaves or blossoms are falling, or the wind is blowing when the pool will not be perfect, but as a general rule, it should be in good shape. The pool maintenance company is supposed to complete a log of service done, kept in the pool equipment area. It is one of the manager's duties to make sure this log is maintained in accordance with county health department regulations.

During times when there is a heavy dropping of leaves or blossoms, the manager may need to dump the skimmer baskets occasionally or do a little extra leaf removal with the pool skimmer on a pole. A trick during especially heavy leaf falling times is to fill the pool above the tile an inch or two. This will put the water level too high for leaves to be taken into the skimmer on the side of the pool. This prevents the skimmer from becoming clogged and causing damage to the pump from lack of water.

Each apartment complex should have a power blower to remove leaves from the pool deck. This is blown once a week by the landscape crew, but this will not be enough during some seasons of the year. During your walk of the property note whether there is a need to blow the pool deck.

During your walk of the property you are also looking for signs that the yard sprinklers are not doing a good job. Overly wet areas can be an indication that there is a broken sprinkler head or water supply line, or that the timer has this zone watering for too long for this time of year. Likewise, an area where the lawn or plants are turning brown is an indication that they not getting enough water. Make a note of where the problem is for repair. This can be caused by a turned off valve, an incorrectly set timer, a bad automatic valve or a broken line somewhere.

These yard sprinkler problems can be caught early by your frequent walks of the property and can be repaired before they cause more severe damage to the landscaping. Most brown lawn spots will turn green again quickly once regular watering is restored.

Make a note of any maintenance needs or safety hazards. During your inspection you will be able to see problems early and get them repaired. Tenants will appreciate that management stays on top of repairs. When needed repairs are not taken care of in a timely manner, tenants will be unhappy. By having a list of needed repairs, you will be organized when a maintenance man is available and working on your property. Use your list to order any repair parts so they will be available when the repairperson arrives. A small amount of organization here will get repairs done and keep the property looking great.

If your complex has a restroom, it will be necessary to check it daily. A messy, dirty restroom without paper products will give tenants the feeling that it is a second-class complex. Be sure that there are toilet paper and paper towels. The soap dispenser should not be empty. Picking up papers and general light cleaning are done frequently. A more thorough cleaning, including mopping the floors, is needed from time to time. Your walk of the property will include the minimum cleaning of the restroom, with a note if a more thorough cleaning is necessary for later in the day.

Make note of areas full of cigarette butts. It is your job to pick up cigarette butts dropped by tenants. A better solution is to tell the tenant to use an ashtray rather than littering the area with butts. A tenant that repeatedly throws cigarette butts on the ground is given a written warning. We can also clean up after them and give them a tenant damage bill. Repeat offenders who will not pick up after themselves should be asked to move. I cannot imagine an apartment complex manager being happy to pick up cigarette butts from an inconsiderate tenant. A manager has to take care of the problem or pick them up himself.

Problem tenants can also be identified during your walk of the property. Junk around their apartment, old furniture in public view and an accumulation of stuff on their patio or balcony is a sign of poor housekeeping. If you suspect a problem from your walk of the property, give the tenant notice to enter and inspect their apartment. The word will get around the complex that management will not tolerate poor behavior from tenants.

Look for problem cars, such as those with no registration and non-running vehicles. Vehicles in violation of the parking policy should be noted and taken care of later. Over time, a good manager will learn which cars belong to which tenants and will spot problems early.

Checking From Time To Time

Walk the grounds occasionally after dark to check cars, parking and problem tenants. A walk in the evening will turn up tenants who are noisy or playing music too loud. We want our tenants to enjoy themselves, but not at the cost of disturbing others. During the evening inspection, make a note of any burnt out light bulbs.

Occasionally, the pool deck, fencing and patio furniture should be hosed off. This does not need to be done too often, but frequently enough to keep the pool area looking pleasant. The pool company will try to keep the pool water at a proper level in the middle of the tile, but on the day you hose things down you can leave the hose in the pool to fill it. Set a timer if you do. It is very easy to forget and let the pool overflow.

During times when leaves or blossoms are falling, it will be necessary for the manager to use the pool skimmer to remove them. An excess of debris floating on the surface of the pool will eventually be sucked in the wall skimmer of the pool and clog things up.

The restrooms will need a good cleaning occasionally. They should be checked daily, but every so often you will see that they are in need of a more thorough cleaning. The laundry room is in this same category. The daily inspection will take care of the day-to-day cleanup of lint and left-behind clothing; however, like the restrooms, a more thorough cleaning will be needed occasionally.

Occasionally it will be necessary to be on "cobweb patrol." Grab a cobweb duster and make sure the area at the office and mailboxes gets a cleaning up. Check for cobwebs at the pool fence, laundry entrance and the walkways to any vacant apartments.

Semi-Annual Inspections

Twice each year we schedule a walkthrough of every apartment in every complex. Tenants are notified in advance and we use a team of the complex manager, the supervising manager and a repairperson. During these inspections, we check and change batteries as needed in all smoke and fire detectors and install a new furnace filter.

One of the purposes of this inspection is to find problems while they are a manageable size and make repairs. We are especially concerned about any water leaks that will cause more damage if left unchecked. This also ties into our efforts to keep our units free of mildew problems. We check around tubs and toilets for water damage, as well as under all sinks and lavatories. Windowsills, areas around windows, and walls of bathrooms are also on our checklist.

We look at the tenant's housekeeping. If the tenant is not taking care of our property and trash is evident in the unit, we will give the tenant a notice to clean up the place and re-inspect in a reasonable amount of time, usually two weeks. We may also give them notice that we are raising their security deposit in the anticipation they are going to have excessive repairs and cleaning when they move. If conditions in an apartment are bad enough, we will give the tenant either a 30 or a 60-day notice to move. We do not want to deal with tenants that refuse to take care of our property.

We have a repairperson accompany the inspection team to make small quick repairs right on the scene. They will have a few tools and access to parts from our shed. They cannot spend a lot of time making repairs, as we need to keep the inspection team moving. They can return the same day after inspections are done and take care of the easy fixes. The notice to enter allows the repairperson to return on the same day for repairs.

We use a form (of course) to record the findings of the semi-annual inspection. There is a line for each apartment horizontally and a series of checkboxes for each area of the inspection. This "Semi-annual Inspection Log" form is detailed in the chapter on Forms. In our county, we are required to complete an annual self-inspection form for each apartment. We use information from our semi-annual inspection form to complete the county form and attach a copy of our form to it.

Forms, Reports and Paperwork

We use a combination of Apartment Association forms and forms we have developed ourselves. Forms and reports are part of life in most businesses. We use a variety of forms and reports to document rents collected, as well as the availability of apartments for renting and the ordering of supplies. The chapter on Forms shows many of our forms and reports and information on their completion. Here we are only going to list the most common forms used by resident managers.

The computer at each complex contains the forms needed for day-to-day operation. It contains a variety of forms including letterhead, FAX cover sheet, the Turnover Work List, the Semi-annual Inspection Log and the Apartment Interest List. Our forms are the same or similar at each complex to allow managers to fill in as needed more easily. Forms can be printed or used right on the computer. If used on the computer it is necessary to "Save As" first so you do not end up using the original form for the work you are doing.

If you only wish to use the form and make a printed copy, do not save it at all. Type what you want and print it. When finished, simply click off on the upper right corner "X." It will ask you if you want to save the document. Click "No" and your work will be gone and the original form will be the same as it was when you started.

Apartment Interest List

We keep this list on the manager's desk to record information on prospective tenants. When someone looks at an apartment or wants information, we try to obtain information on them so we can follow up later. When people are looking to move they are going to look at several apartments, and most likely will not be able to remember some of the differences in complexes. If we can call them back and chat a little about our place, it will put us a little ahead of other complexes. Many times this is the only push a prospective tenant needs to become a resident of one of our apartments.

Managers Credit Card Log

Once a month, managers are required to send in their credit card expense sheet. They are notified by the office, usually after the 20th of the month for your report. This report lists each transaction made with the company credit card along with any explanation. The credit card receipts are stapled to the report and they are sent to our main office.

Move-In Form

We use a standard move-in form from our apartment association. This form indicates the condition of the property at move-in and will be compared to the condition when the tenant leaves. It is very important to accurately complete the move-in form, as it will be critical in establishing a tenant's responsibility to pay for any damage done while they occupied the apartment.

MOVE-IN SPECIALS FORM

Resident managers maintain a list of tenants that have gotten special move-in rent in their complex. This is a simple line form similar to the availability report. It contains the basic information on any specials we have given on an apartment to assist a fill in manager or supervisory person. It is kept on the desk or other easy to find place.

Notice To Enter

Unless it is an emergency, we are required to give a tenant 24-hour notice before entering their unit. This is a common courtesy respecting the tenant's privacy. The notice can be given directly to the tenant or taped to their front door. The notice should list why we are entering their apartment.

Parts And Office Supply Order Forms

Monthly – by the 20th of the month – the complex managers are required to inventory the items in their storage shed and place their order for replacement parts. Not all parts are stored in the shed; this varies from complex to complex. Check your parts and complete the order form. Office supplies are also ordered at the same time. These order forms are sent to the main office and your replacement parts and office supplies will be delivered to you within a few days.

Rental Application And Rental Agreement

We use the standard rental application form provided by the apartment association. We have added a few addendums, recommended by our apartment association, to take care of the variety of special points, notifying tenants of all the required information. Likewise, we use the standard rental agreement form from the apartment association and supplemental forms they recommend.

Rent Deposit Report

This is our main form for reporting all the monies collected and deposited in the bank each month. Individual rents by apartment are entered, as well as money collected for late fees, credit check fees, bank fees and any other money collected by the manager and deposited in the bank. The report is done by the calendar month and copies are emailed to our main office several times during the month. The report keeps track of current rents for each apartment, any past due amounts, and the current balance owed.

As checks are received, they need to be stamped on the back with our deposit-only bank stamp. This will make the check un-cashable if it is lost or stolen. Always make a copy of the tenants check or money order. This gives us a record of exactly what was paid.

Deposits are made several times during the month by listing the checks and money orders received one at a time by apartment number. Each column of the rent deposit report is a separate bank deposit. The form totals the deposit for you at the bottom and this total must match the total entered on the bank deposit slip.

Security Deposit Reconciliation

When a tenant leaves, it is necessary to give the tenant a refund on their security deposit less any charges against it for outstanding rent or damages. Our form is copied from the apartment association form with minor modifications to fit our operation. This form and any refunded amount must be given to the leaving tenant within 21 days. Refund checks are mailed from our main office, so it is necessary to get the required reconciliation form to administration in a timely manner. If the turnover is not complete within the 21 days it will be necessary to make an estimated of the repairs needed and send the security reconciliation form to our office with the word "Estimate" at the top.

Tenant Information

We maintain a current list of all tenants, the make and license number of their car, phone numbers, email, and other important information a manager might need in the normal course of work. We also keep employer information, as well as the employer phone number. In the remarks section we can list any special needs of the tenant or their next of kin.

Unit Availability Report

This Unit Availability Report lists each apartment that is currently vacant and those that will be coming vacant soon. It tells when an apartment is expected to be ready to rent as well as the rent amount, any specials offered, and security deposit amounts. This is just the minimum amount of information to quickly see what is available to a prospective tenant. This form is emailed to our other nearby apartment complexes to keep all managers up to date on what is available, so they can refer potential renters if they do not have an apartment for them.

Work Orders

We use a store-bought repair order form. It is in three parts using NCR paper. The top page is white, middle yellow and the bottom sheet is pink. The white and yellow sheets go to the repairperson and the pink stays in the book until the work is done. When the work is completed, the worker will return the yellow sheet to the manager. At this time the pink sheet is removed from the book and discarded and the yellow sheet goes into the file for the apartment. The white sheet is used by the worker for billing or a timecard.

Make sure the forms contains the date, apartment number, work to be done and if permission to enter has been arranged. It is also nice to include the tenant's name.

Make the Property Appealing to Tenants

Curb Appeal To Front Door Of Unit For Rent

The importance of a first impression for prospective tenants cannot be overemphasized. An apartment manager has only one chance to make a good first impression. The look of the complex should make people want to live there.

Start with the curb appeal as the prospective tenant arrives at the property. Lawns should be trimmed, leaves raked, and plants pruned, and the property should present an inviting overall look. With normal maintenance, lawn sprinklers are working and there are no areas of dead grass. There should be at least one planter with flowers near the entrance driveway. Curb appearance should be free from weeds, papers and trash, and any deferred maintenance issues.

The driveway area from the street entrance to the office must also present an attractive appearance. It is mandatory to keep the area clean and trash-free, with cared for landscaping. Parking at the office for "New Tenants" should have a sign posted.

Planting flowers near the office makes the complex attractive and inviting. Like the entrance to the complex, the office area must be free from weeds or any deferred maintenance problems. If the pool is visible from the path into the complex, the office or the path to the vacant unit, it should be well cared for with pool furniture straightened.

Signs at the office for hours, etc., should be printed and professional. Hand-written signs should be discouraged. There should be a phone number listed in case the manager is elsewhere. Make sure there are flyers available outside the office with information on the property and a rental application.

The office itself needs to be neat and businesslike; a minimum of papers on the desk, and a minimum of or no items stacked on the floor. Windows and tabletops should be clean. Temperature in the office should be pleasant, neither too hot nor too cold.

The path taken from the office to each vacant unit needs to have the same high level of cleanliness and care we require from the entrance area to the office. As the possible tenant walks from the office to the vacant unit, they should continue to observe a well cared for complex.

The front porch and front door area of each vacant unit again gives us a chance to reaffirm to the prospective tenant the quality of our apartments and our complex. The front door and trim of the door should not need painting. Many times front doors and trim are scraped from move-ins and move-outs. These should be checked during turnovers and the paint should be touched up as needed.

Exterior areas near the front door must be free of cobwebs and trash. Exterior siding in this area should be maintained constantly with frequent paint touch ups. Front porch lights should be free of dead bugs and should not need maintenance, and there should be a nice doormat at the front door.

Other apartment units near the vacant unit should likewise be clean and in good condition. Do not permit old chairs, ashtrays, cigarette butts, or junk near apartments. Kids' toys, bicycles, etc., should be neat and stored to keep the complex from having a cluttered look. Do not allow broken or bent window blinds in neighbors' apartment windows.

Most of these curb appeal to front door tips are really just good common sense. If you want to sell a product then you need to spruce it up. The new tenant is going to want to rent our property partly based on the good vibrations they get even before they go inside.

Doll Up Units

Vacant units show better and will rent better if they are dressed up a little. It only takes a few items to make a unit look homey and inviting to a prospective tenant. We talked about making sure the front door area is clean and free of cobwebs; plants are trimmed and there is a new or clean front doormat.

Always leave a couple of lights on so the unit will not be dark upon entry. Better to spend a little extra on electricity than to have an apartment seem dark and uninviting. A hall light works well, as does the range hood light.

Use enough lighting to brighten the place up. If the apartment is in a particularly dark part of the complex, leave more lights on.

We usually put a valance on windows in either the kitchen or dining room. Most bathrooms in apartments do not have windows, but if they do, it is also a great place for a valance. A small curtain rod with a valance is a very inexpensive way to make a room cozier. A similar valance can be put over the sliding glass shower door at the bathtub. These additions add some color to a normally dull area.

Always put bath towels in the bathrooms to add color. These towels are not left in the unit. They are part of the decorating package to be saved and used on other units in the future. A couple of small kitchen towels can also be put in the kitchen.

Use a few decorative items like artificial flower arrangements, large kitchen bowls or platters. We have used empty bell canning jars with beans, macaroni, etc., in them and a ribbon around the top to finish it off. These easy, inexpensive items make an apartment look like a home.

A garage sale is the perfect place to pick up all kinds of simple decorator pieces for almost no money. In one day you can find enough stuff at a few garage sales to last for years of decorating units in your complex. Basically, ugly stuff you would not have in your own home works great, in limited quantities, to doll up a vacant unit and make it more appealing to prospective tenants.

The unit should be clean and fresh and smell good. With carpets recently cleaned, the apartment should smell just fine. A little "smell good" stuff, like potpourri, might help. We use mild plug in air fresheners. An old real estate selling trick is to put a pot on the stove of something that smells good – just a little, so when someone comes in they get that warm, comfortable, home feeling.

Make The Units Livable

We always make our apartments ready for a new tenant to move in. There should be a full or nearly full roll of toilet paper in each bathroom. We put in a new toilet seat for every new tenant. This has been one of our policies since we started managing apartments: clean, fresh toilet seats for all new renters. We buy toilet seats in bulk and buy a nice inexpensive model.

In the kitchen, we supply a roll of paper towels, a paper towel holder, ice trays and a cutting board. The cutting boards save our counters. Sometimes we put a couple bottles of water in the fridge. We usually put brand new drip pans under the burners of the range.

We want the apartment to be ready when the tenant moves in. If they have to use the bathroom, there is toilet paper available. If they need to wash their hands there is a roll of paper towels waiting for them.

Turnovers (Make Ready)

The manager is the person that supervises turnovers, also known as "make ready." Turnovers are the work needed when one tenant moves out to get the apartment ready to show and rent. It is important to finish a unit quickly so it will be ready to show as soon as possible.

The manager will have seen the apartment when doing the final walk-through with the departing tenant and will already have some ideas on the extent of the work needed for the turnover.

GETTING STARTED WITH THE TURNOVER

Very few apartments are ready to rent after a tenant leaves. Be sure the apartment has the minimum items in our make-it-livable list. There will always be at least a modest amount of work to do, and many times there is considerable work to do. To keep this work organized, we have guidelines when doing a turnover on an apartment. Always leave the heat on low in the winter months to prevent pipes from freezing and to make the apartment warm for the workers doing the turnover. Likewise, in the hot summer months we set the thermostat for the A/C at a reasonable temperature for workers and for showing the unit.

The resident manager is the turnover supervisor. You begin by taking the following items with you to the apartment: turnover work list, set of new door locks, roll of toilet paper, a large trash can, a roll of paper towels, a plastic shoe box, a notepad, and a ball point pen. It is our policy to change locks with each change of tenants. When the maintenance person arrives, there will be a set of locks in the unit to make the change.

The turnover work list and a ballpoint pen are always the first items into the apartment and the last to leave. The pen stays in the unit for future additions to the work list. The notepad is for the manager to make notes to take with them to the office later; these notes will help in ordering special parts or lining up the right subcontractors. It is important to get any special parts ordered early so they will be available to the workers when they are in the apartment. The plastic shoebox is used to catch all the small parts, preventing them from being left on the counter or accidentally dropped down the garbage disposal.

If, during the final walk through with the tenant, you notice considerable work to do, bring a few large plastic trash bags and a couple 60-watt light bulbs, if needed, when you return to the apartment to begin the turnover work list.

Fill out the turnover work list, inspecting the unit from room to room, as well as the patio and front door area. Keeping repair jobs on the work sheet by rooms will make it easier for the repair personnel to keep organized.

The turnover work sheet has several jobs printed at the beginning that we do on all turnovers. We always change the door locks, change the toilet seat, check the smoke detectors and change the furnace filters. This section of the form also reminds the workers to provide ice trays, a roll of paper towels, toilet paper, new cutting board and a new front door mat.

The apartment complex manager keeps abreast of the progress of the turnover. The manager orders special items for the unit, calls and schedules repair people and outside contractors, and checks the progress daily. It is also important to check the quality of work to make sure it is done to our specifications and quality guidelines.

The owner or a designated mid-management level supervisor should be available to assist apartment complex managers as needed to keep the turnover on track. We have a supervisorial level of management over several managers. This supervisor is the next level up in the chain of command. However, we also have an overall maintenance manager that is responsible for larger maintenance problems for the company. The maintenance manager helps determine products we use, maintenance procedures, and inventory we stock.

Pert Chart

To assist apartment complex managers in keeping turnovers at their complex organized, we provide guidance in the form of Pert Charts and Turnover Progress Charts.

Pert charts are used in many construction trades, as well as other industries, to keep a project moving forward in the least amount of time by doing the individual tasks in the correct sequence. It is obvious that you need to putty holes in a wall before you paint it, but many other jobs that appear to be unrelated need to be done in a specific order to eliminate duplicate efforts and the need to back up and do something over again.

The chart also helps keep track of work when more than one worker is doing jobs on the same apartment. Jobs that are done will have the corresponding box checked off. The subsequent worker knows to work down the chart to the next job.

The chart is laid out top to bottom with connecting lines between boxes. The jobs in the boxes are done after all the boxes ahead of it are completed. For example, "Remove Trash" is before "Structure Repairs," which are before "Plaster Repairs."

Follow the chart from top to bottom. Do jobs in sequence. Think of the boxes as valves and the lines as water flowing. As work is completed, the valve opens and the water flows to the next valve. Any box with all the work completed before it can be worked on. Complete all activities before moving on. For example, taking the plastic shoebox, etc., is done after making the inspection and work list, but before removing trash. It can be done at the same time as, before, or after jobs in the same line, such as ordering special parts and scheduling subs. These four jobs are not dependent on one another. Likewise, lower on the form when painting is completed, there are three boxes that can be done in any order; however, all three of these need to be completed before moving to carpet. As work is completed, you can cross out the box and move to the next job. Most of the boxes in the chart are self-explanatory.

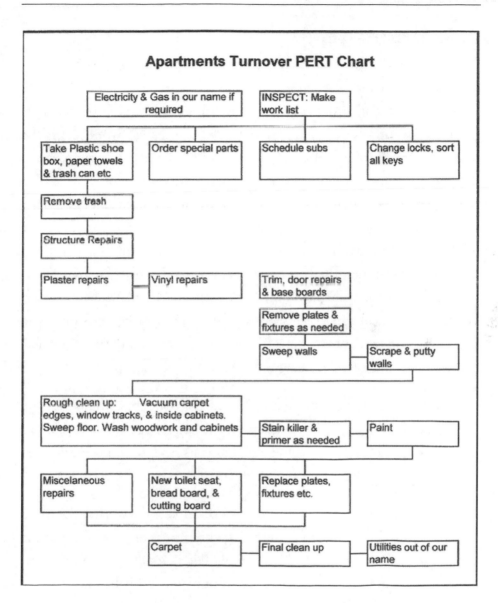

Apartments Turnover PERT Chart

An experienced building and property maintenance person will probably be able to follow the correct sequence of jobs, but they have the pert chart to keep them on track if need be. The single-page pert chart is for work in a single apartment. When a complex has multiple units being turned over at the same time, the manager uses a Turnover Progress Chart to keep track of it all.

Turnover Progress Chart

The turnover progress chart is like a horizontal pert chart. It is not as detailed as the pert chart for an individual unit, but does list major jobs of the turnover sequentially from left to right. It is designed to guide the manager through the turnover process and allow them to assign work to get the turnovers done in the shortest possible amount of time. The pert chart is designed to show the work order for a single apartment or project. The turnover progress chart will list all the apartments being worked on in the complex on a single form so the manager can keep the maintenance people working on the most important job at that time. Our mid-management supervisor above the managers will use a Master Turnover Progress Chart for all the apartments being worked on in all the complexes being supervised. This level of supervisor can use the chart to make decisions as to where the work needs to be done considering all the complexes and where workers need to be redirected.

Our form lists important information for each apartment being worked on in the complex. The first few columns on the left contain some basic information on the unit. The remaining columns list the jobs to be performed in sequence left to right to complete the turnover.

Generally, the maintenance workers should complete the work sequentially from left to right, completing one job before proceeding to the next job to the right. The jobs are logically listed. For example, structure repairs are before drywall, and trim work and rough cleanup is before painting. Sounds logical, but in the rush to get a unit ready to rent it is easy to skip a step and have to back track, losing time.

The turnover progress chart keeps the jobs in the right order and makes the turnover move forward quickly and efficiently.

COMPLEX TURNOVER PROGRESS CHART

Unit	1 or 2 BR	Up or Down	Trash out	Structure repairs, drywall, vinyl, tile, trim, doors & base	Rough clean for paint, cobwebs, vacuum edges, base, window sills, cabinets. Wash trim	Wall Prep Pull nails, spackle, caulk	Paint	Misc repair, fixtures, plates and blinds	New Carpet	Final clean. Toilet, tub, mirrors, windows, storage, patio, etc. Paint touch up if needed (incl.ext paint). New toilet seat, ice trays, cut board & door mat. All stuff out.	Clean Carpet

Turnover Priorities Chart

Managers should use the below priority guidelines in scheduling work when we have multiple vacant units. Consideration should also be given to how much work is needed to complete a turnover.

Priority	
1	An apartment where you have a tenant that has money in hand and wants to move in NOW
2	A tenant wants to take possession in a couple days
3	Tenant needs to move in next week
4	The complex has no vacant 1 bedroom units ready to rent
5	The complex has no vacant 2 bedroom units ready to rent
6	There is only one rent ready vacant unit available in the complex of either 1 bedroom or 2 bedrooms
7	One bedroom units are usually done before 2 bedrooms
8	Units that are of opposite elevation from rent ready units in complex. If you have a 1 bedroom downstairs unit ready, then an upstairs 1 bedroom unit would have a higher priority over another downstairs unit.

Odd Tenants and Disasters

Over the course of our years renting property, we have encountered a number of situations that were out of the ordinary to say the least. Following are a few short stories of some of those incidents. Some were amusing, some were costly and most we would not want to repeat. I have included them here to show some of the type problems a property owner and resident manager are sure to come across in this business. These are just a sample, keeping in mind that tenants have an infinite capacity to come up with strange and bizarre situations for a to deal with.

Motivation For College

Eleanor, also known as 'the dog lady,' had been a great tenant for years. She had been a perfect tenant as an older female living alone. She paid her rent and did not bother anyone. The problem arose when she took in two large stray dogs into her duplex unit. She already had a cat and a smaller dog. We did not know about the big dogs until the neighbors begin complaining about the odor. Our investigation showed that the two large dogs had puppies that now were also grown into large dogs. They were kept in the garage, which housed the five dogs. The garage contained Eleanor's stored odds and ends, and months of dog poop and urine. It was a nasty situation. Inside the house was not much better with a cat and another dog living there.

We confronted her about the problem and her explanation was that the dogs were not hers; they were strays that belonged to someone else. We went round and round with her about the dogs, and always got the same result: they just were not hers. She refused to get rid of them and we gave her a 30-day notice to move. She did not move, but she did continue to pay rent during the 30-day period as well as the eviction period that followed. She ran out all the time during the eviction process and had not moved anything when the sheriff served the lockout notice. We met the sheriff on the day she was supposed to be gone and she had not moved any of the animals or her belongings.

When we got to the unit on the day she was thrown out, the sheriff had gotten the dogs into her car and she took a few things with her. We took possession and inspected the unit. The place was full of trash a couple feet high with paths through it to walk. Pet feces and urine were everywhere and the filth had soaked into the carpet and walls. After Eleanor had retrieved what she wanted, we got a large dumpster and hired our middle son, Michael, to empty the house into it. Once the trash was out, he pulled up all the carpet, then all the particleboard under the carpet. He did a good job doing nasty work. We could never be sure what influence this job and others we gave him had, but we always thought it inspired him to be our first child to get a college degree. I do not think he wanted to make a living doing the type of jobs we had provided for him.

Sewage Under The House

We were called to a duplex we owned because the tenant complained of a bad odor. When we arrived, there was a sewer gas-type odor in the unit. We looked around for a drain that might be dry. If a trap under a sink loses the water in it to evaporation, then the sewer gases can back up through the dry drain. Nothing seemed to be causing the problem. We decided to check under the floor. This duplex was built in the 1950s and was a raised wood floor with a crawl area.

As soon as we opened the access door to the under-floor area, we found the smell. The entire area under both sides of the duplex was full of liquid. We wished it were water; it was raw sewage. We spotted the problem, a clean out cap that had blown off. These caps do not just blow off by themselves; they are blown off due to a backed up sewer pipe.

The real problem was somewhere in the sewer line that had caused a complete backup, blowing the clean out cap, and filling up the underside of the building. Not only did we have a big sewage problem, but none of the toilets, bathtubs, or sinks in the building could be used.

Lesser landlords might have gotten out of the real estate business right then and there, but not us. We got hotel rooms for the two sets of tenants to stop the problem from getting worse. Then we got a septic tank specialist company to come and pump out the underside of the house. Next, we got a plumbing company to run a TV camera through the roof vent pipe, down the sewer line until they found the blocked area. They could determine where the end of their line reached and marked the spot in the backyard under the concrete patio.

A little jack hammering of concrete and some digging down about 5 feet got our workers to the cracked pipe and the roots that had caused the problem. The pipe was fixed and the whole thing was back together within a couple days with a new patio poured the next week. This, like many jobs that seem overwhelming, fall into that category of projects that fit the old Chinese proverb, "Once started, half done." It always looks better after you get going.

Chapter 6

FORMS

The forms listed in this chapter are the common forms used in our company. We developed most of them ourselves with reference to standard apartment forms found elsewhere. All organizations will use forms, their own or from companies specializing in providing the necessary forms to run a residential real estate company successfully.

Apartment Interest List

This form is kept in the office to record the names and phone numbers of visitors to the complex that might be interested in becoming a tenant. It is a single line log that also contains what type of apartment they were looking for, move in date, and any other remarks pertinent to them.

Cleaning List

Our company uses a cleaning list guide to assist workers in cleaning a unit and keeping track of work done. The sheet is divided by rooms or area cleaned and includes a check column for the date and initials of the worker. Many of the notes in the cleaning list are just good common sense, but are included to provide a complete list of the work needed and good cleaning techniques.

The form is not only a guideline for us in our cleaning, but it is used to let tenants know what we expect of them when they leave. It is given to a new tenant when they move in so they can see what we are looking for when they leave. In this way, they get a heads up if they want to get a substantial part of their Security/Cleaning deposit back.

It is a good idea to give a copy of this form to the tenant when they give notice to move to encourage them to clean the apartment. When they leave, we expect the apartment to be as clean as it was when they moved in. If the tenant has a copy of the form, it will give them a guide and motivation to clean the apartment before it is an issue when they move out.

Credit Card Log

We have a Business MasterCard account that allows us to issue credit cards to managers and others workers to make purchases for the company. Each card so issued has a different credit card number, but they are all included on the same monthly statement. The statement lists expenditures by card number for ease of accounting.

The Credit Card Log form is completed by holders of each credit card for their expenditures in the monthly statement period. After the cutoff date of the month, managers or workers will receive an itemized list of the charges shown for their credit card. This itemized list is checked against the Credit Card Log to make sure all expenditures are listed. When complete and checked, the form with the credit card receipts are forwarded to our office.

The form is pre-printed with the last four digits of the individual's credit card, along with the name of the cardholder. Our form includes the vendor, date of purchase, amount, what the item was and the complex for which it was purchased. We have a place for remarks to explain any complicated purchases.

Move in Specials Form

This form is used to list specials we have given on apartments. The resident manager maintains this form for the benefit of another manager or supervisor that might be filling in at the complex.

The form is a simple line form similar to the availability report and contains all pertinent information about the special that had been given.

This form includes:

> Apartment number
> Date tenant moved in
> Special rent amount
> Length of time special price will be in effect
> Date rent goes to the regular amount
> Regular rent amount after special price is finished

Notice to Enter

Most communities require giving tenants a notice before entering their apartment. A 24-hour notice is common but it can be longer in some places (this does not include entry in case of an emergency). We use a simple "Notice to Enter" form from our local Apartment Association that lets the tenant know the approximate date and time we plan to enter and the purpose of our entering.

On our form we site the State Civil Code pertinent to the requirement for the notice. The form is given to the tenant in person or taped to the door of the apartment.

Other Income Form

This is an office-only form we use to list income that is not associated with or listed on the Rent Deposit Report. Things such as income from the laundry room contract, utility reimbursement company or refunds we might receive are listed on this form.

The form is an Excel spreadsheet with all our complexes across the top and possible income sources in the left hand column. One form is used for a single deposit and the form totals the deposit. A bank deposit slip is completed, and the form, deposit slip and all related documents are stapled together. Computer entries are made from the form and then filed.

Parts and Office Supplies Order Forms

We use a parts order form for our complexes to order common parts and office supplies on a monthly basis. The order forms are customized for each apartment complex and contain only the items they stock in their sheds or office. Once a month the manager uses this inventory order form to list how many of each item they want. Within a couple days, the order is filled from our central parts storage area and delivered to the apartment complex.

This saves the manager from having to shop at several different stores to keep their sheds and offices full of needed parts and office supplies. This system makes it easy to keep inventories up.

Rental Application and Rental Agreement

We use a standard "Application to Rent" form available from our local Apartment Association. This type form is also available in stationary stores, as well as on the internet. It asks all the important questions and is compatible with standards in the industry. This rental agreement includes many sub-forms designed to protect property owners and renters.

Rent Deposit Report

Every apartment complex needs a method of recording rents and other incomes. We use an Excel spreadsheet to keep track of the monthly transactions for rents, late fees, credit checks, etc. The totals for each column of the form must match the amount on the bank deposit slip. Decimal points and commas will be put into your currency entries as needed.

This form is used on the computer to record tenant rent payments. It can also record late fees, security deposits, and other incomes received at the complex. Each column of the form represents one deposit. There are seven columns for deposits. The eighth column is marked Bounced Checks and is used to deduct bounced checks. On our form this column prints in blue to differentiate it from the rest of the entries.

The manager only makes entries into the columns marked 1 through 7 and the Bounced Checks column; all of the totals, Past Due and Balance columns of the form are calculated for the manager. The current rents column may be changed if needed. When you change a rent amount in the current column it will be automatically carried forward to future months unless it is changed again.

As a tenant pays rent it is entered in the next bank deposit column in the row with that apartment number. Rent payments are shown on the top part of the form. The lower section is used for "Other Income." The column numbers in the bottom part of the form are the same as in the upper section. For other income, list the apartment number and the code for the type income, in the extreme left column. The amount will go in the column corresponding to the next bank deposit. For example, a tenant pays $850, $800 is the rent and $50 is a late fee. Enter the $800 in the upper portion of the form opposite the tenant's apartment number. In the lower section of the form, in the same column, enter $50. Use LF and the apartment number to indicate a late fee.

Always make a copy of the tenants check or money order. This gives us a record of exactly what was paid. Either keep the check, money order copies in file at the complex office or forward them with you Rent Deposit Report for the month to our main office.

At the bottom of any of the first seven columns, the entire bank deposit is totaled automatically. This must equal the bank deposit slip exactly.

This form is emailed to our main office. It should be sent early in the month after the late fee date has past. Each time a deposit is made the form is also forwarded to our office by email. When the month has ended a hard copy of the form along with all the deposit slips and any other associated documents are sent to our main office.

Security Deposit Reconciliation

Our Security Deposit Reconciliation form is an Excel form in the computer, customized for each apartment complex. This form should be complete on the computer as the program will add and subtract entries as needed to complete the form. After completed be sure to "save as" in a file for the tenant, keeping the original form ready for the next time needed.

The form has sections to list the original amount paid by the tenant, as well as money owed by the tenant. Any rent owed to us is listed along with repairs and cleaning that is the responsibility of the tenant. There is a section to list utility fees incurred by the tenant and not paid. If the tenant has a credit for rent or anything else it is shown as a "minus" number and will be added to their security deposit held by us.

It is important to make your entries into the form as accurate as possible. We are required to supply the leaving tenant with detailed information on deductions to their security deposit and a refund if any within 21 days after leaving.

Semi-Annual Inspection Log

This form is used during our semi-annual inspections of each apartment. It is a line log form with a single line for each apartment. It has check boxes for the smoke detector, furnace filters, mildew check, water leak problems and general housekeeping by the tenant. There is a comments box to add any additional notes on the unit.

Three-Day Notice

We use a standard "Three-Day Notice" form supplied by our local Apartment Rental Association. Like the Rental Application, these forms are also available from stationary stores and the internet. We like the standard form as it has all the correct information required in case we subsequently file for an eviction. The form is sometimes called, "Pay or Quit."

Turnover Progress Chart

This is a line-type form with a line for each apartment in the process of being "Turned Over" or made ready. It reads from left to right with the different jobs listed across the top in the sequence normally completed. The form makes it easy to keep track of several apartments being worked on and what stage they are in and what needs to be done next. The manager simply checks the boxes from left to right as the work is completed.

There are companies that supply wall charts that do the same function with apartments listed in the first column and the jobs checked off as done. These are very easy ways to keep track of a fairly complicated turnover sequence, keeping the progress moving forward and not doing jobs at the wrong time.

Below is our sequence for work on our Turnover Progress Chart:

1. Remove all trash from unit
2. Structural repairs

3. Drywall

4. Vinyl

5. Tile

6. Doors, trim and base (in that order)

7. Rough cleanup for painting
    a. Remove cobwebs, vacuum edges of floor, sills and cabinets
    b. Wash trim

8. Wall prep
    a. Pull nails
    b. Spackle
    c. Caulk

9. Paint

10. Miscellaneous Repairs
    a. New toilet seat
    b. Replace fixtures
    c. Replace plates
    d. Replace or install blinds

11. If installing new carpet, it is done here on the form

12. Final Cleanup
    a. Clean toilet, tub, mirrors, windows, storage, patios, etc.

13. If cleaning carpets, it is the last thing on the form

Turnover Work List

The turnover work list is used each time a tenant leaves and the apartment must be "turned over" for the next tenant. Before beginning the inspection of the unit and completing the form, look to see if there are any outstanding work orders for the apartment that can be done with the turnover.

After completed, the form is left on the kitchen counter of the apartment for workers to see and use. Special tools and parts lists are made using this work list. This form is the first item you take with you when preparing to work on a recently vacated apartment and it is one of the last items removed from the apartment when all work has been completed.

The turnover work list should include the work to be done entered in a clear manner so maintenance personnel will understand what is needed. We include any special tools or special parts that we do not stock in our storage sheds on this form. The manager or the maintenance person can make a shopping list from our form to purchase all the special parts needed for the turnover.

We have a column to indicate if the repair is caused from tenant damage. This will alert the office to include this cost on the tenant's final security deposit reconciliation. Completed Turnover Work List forms are forwarded to our office to be used in calculating the amount of refund due the tenant on their security deposit.

The manager inspects the apartment from room to room, noting repairs needed on the Turnover Work List form, following the below guidelines:

1. Check for any outstanding work orders.
2. Inspect every room, closet, and exterior.
3. Turn on every light.
4. Run water in every plumbing appliance.
5. Run heat or air conditioning.
6. Windows:
    Look for missing or damaged screens.
    Note broken or cracked glass.
    Note damaged mini blinds, verticals or curtains.
    Look for moisture or water damage on sills.
7. Kitchens
    Check all appliances.
    Run disposal.
    Run dishwasher.
    Check under sink for leaks.

       Check for hot water.

8. Bathroom

       Flush toilet.

       Look under basin for water leaks.

9. Flooring

       Check all floor covering

       Decide if carpet will need to be replaced or only cleaned

       (If vinyl is in need of repair, check with the maintenance manager if ceramic tile might be used as an upgrade to the apartment)

Unit Availability Report

The Unit Availability Report is maintained to give quick reference to apartments now available and those that will be available in the near future. It is designed to be transmitted by e-mail to our other apartment complexes, as well as our main office. In this manner, all our complexes are aware of vacancies in others and can refer possible renters to the apartment complex best suited to them. The form lists all the apartments by a line entry, and includes such information as what stage of turnover the unit is in and the approximate date the unit should be ready to rent.

We list how many bedrooms the apartment has and whether it is an upstairs or downstairs unit. Monthly rent, any rent specials and the amount of the security deposit is on the form. We list the assigned parking place to the vacant unit so workers will be able to use the space during the turnover process. When the new tenant moves in the line for that unit is deleted from the form.

Each time information changes it is necessary to forward the updated form to all other apartment complexes and our main office. This is done using this file as an attachment to an e-mail.

Work Orders

We use a store bought, inexpensive repair order form. It is in three parts using NCR paper. The top page is white, the middle is yellow and the bottom sheet is pink. The white and yellow sheets go to the repair person and the pink stays in the book until the work is done.

Complete the top of the form with the date, apartment number, and any other information needed by the repairperson. In the main body of the form, write the repairs to be done and the name of the tenant. Indicate if it is okay to enter the apartment or if giving a 24-hour notice is needed.

The person doing the repairs will write on the yellow copy what was done and any other information pertinent to the job. He returns the yellow copy to the office, at which time the pink copy is removed from the book and discarded. The yellow copy is filed in the folder for the apartment for future reference if needed. The white copy is either retained by the repairperson to accompany his time card or in the case of an outside vendor, sent to our main office to match up with the invoice for payment. If some work is only partially completed it is usually easier to make a new repair order when the yellow sheet is returned.

Work Order List

A list is maintained of future repairs, changes or improvements for each unit. Oftentimes these jobs or repairs are made when the apartment becomes vacant and are completed with the normal turnovers. However, it is a good idea to check the list when day-to-day repairs are needed in case some of them can be done at that time. These are all repairs or changes that do not need to be done immediately but can wait until it is more convenient.

Chapter 7

MAINTENANCE

There are many ways to handle maintenance. Listed here are my ideas based on what I have learned over the years. What I talk about here is "a" way to do things, not "the" way to do them. I have always liked jobs done right, not "good enough for a rental." Yes, we want to be economical in our expenditures, but sometimes it is false economy to put in a cheap item only to have to replace it sooner than needed.

I always think about improvements to the property against how much the improvement will benefit the company. Will it result in higher rents or reduced vacancies? Or will the work make the property more valuable and result in a higher sale price if we should decide to sell it?

The day-to-day maintenance on the property should bring it back to as good as or better than it was before the repair was needed. For example, a kitchen faucet is leaking and needs to be replaced; instead of replacing it with another old-fashioned two handle faucet, put in a new single handle faucet. It takes the same labor to install the upgrade faucet as a low-end one. Small improvements over the years add up to big increases in value.

Always maintain your properties with the thought they will be for sale some day and you are going to want them to show well for prospective buyers.

We had owned duplexes for over 10 years before we could afford an almost full time repairperson. He was taking care of most of the maintenance work, as well as landscape work, including cutting all the front lawns. As we got larger, more and more help from maintenance people was needed.

Kits

I like kits. Kits are tote boxes or containers with tools and parts for a specific job, like a turnover kit, detail kit, and cabinet knob kit. I have always liked the kit idea because you can grab the tote and have all the items you need to do a certain job.

Turnover Kits

We used to maintain large plastic storage boxes with a great many parts common to the apartment complex. These kits did not have any tools, but did provide most small to medium parts a repairperson might need. The problem with this kit is that it consists of two large plastic storage boxes and was not convenient to the workers. Most preferred to make a list of what they needed and get the items from the storage sheds we maintain for each property. Some maintenance workers still use the turnover kits, but we do not maintain them any longer.

Detail Kit

The detail kit has taken the place of the turnover kit, providing more specialized parts and tools that maintenance people might need. It has a small hammer, Phillips and slot screwdrivers, a pair of pliers, a small crescent wrench, a utility knife and paint can opener.

The detail kit also contains touch-up appliance paint in colors common to the particular apartment complex. White, almond and bisque will work for many touch-up situations.

A few parts are included, such as doorknob and hinge screws, and a few cabinet hinge screws. We also include a can of Goof Off, Elmer's glue and putty in a color to match the cabinets. The detail kit is in a large tote-type plastic box to make it easy to take to the apartment being worked on.

Cabinet Pull Kit

This kit has all the items needed to install cabinet pulls in an apartment. It is always good to standardize pulls in a complex so you can stock one kind in the storage shed. Many complexes are built without cabinet pulls to save money, but after a time, cabinets are damaged by fingernails. It is smart to put in pulls to save cabinets from further damage.

Establish a standard placement of pulls. We place ours 3 inches up or down and 2 inches horizontally. Other dimensions will work, but you want to be consistent. As kitchens are upgraded with new cabinet doors, the old doors can be used in other units to replace damaged cabinet doors. If cabinet pull placement is standardized it becomes a great deal easier to swap one door for the other without having to fill a hole from a cabinet pull that was in a different location on the door. It is just about impossible to fill a hole in a cabinet door so that it does not show. When pulls are placed in the same spot on all the cabinet doors in the complex, swapping one door for another is an easy task.

The cabinet pull kit contains:

> A supply of new cabinet pulls
> Supply of 8-32, Phillips, round head bolts in 1, 1 ¼, 1 ½, & 1 ¾ inch sizes.
> 3/16 inch drill bitt
> Phillips screwdriver
> Pair of scissors to cut plastic bags with pulls
> Template with correct placement of pulls

Most cabinet doors use an 8 x 32 bolt one inch long; however, many times the drawers will take a longer bolt. There are mostly 1 inch bolts in the kit with a few of the longer sizes for special circumstances. We set our templates at 3 inches from the top or bottom and 2 inches from the sides of a cabinet door. Drawer pulls are set in the center of the drawer.

When it comes time to add pulls in an apartment, the maintenance person can grab the cabinet pull kit and have everything they need, plus an electric drill to get the job done.

Breadboard Hole Plug Kit

In our apartment complexes, we have eliminated breadboards and now furnish a cutting board to each tenant. Wooden breadboards become dirty and unsightly very quickly. We put a fake cover over the old breadboard opening in the cabinets.

The kit contains several pre-made bread board, hole plugs. Each plug is two inch tall by the width of the old breadboard and made from the same material and finish as the existing cabinet doors and drawers. We also have a selection of #8, Phillips, pan head screws in lengths from 1 inch to 1 ½ inches. We supply a stubby Phillips head screwdriver to work in the tight area behind the old breadboard opening, and a few small wood pieces for backing. The kit gets the job done without having to spend time making or looking for all the components needed.

Parts and Inventories

When we began our company and only owned a couple duplexes, we did not have a big need to keep a supply of repair parts for our properties. As we grew, it became easier to maintain a few commonly used parts in our toolbox or in our vehicle.

When we were large enough to hire a part-time handyman for some repairs it became evident that maintaining a modest supply of common parts would save us money and time. If we sent the repairman to a rental, he would have to evaluate the problem and then run off to a store for the part. If he found some additional part needed later, it was off again to the store. The travel time was eating into our meager profits.

Storage Sheds For Parts

Our first move to an organized parts inventory was to rent a small space in a nearby public storage company. We pretty much just bought a few regular items and put them in the storage without much organization. It was not long before we got a bigger storage unit and even started storing toilets and appliances, such as a range or dishwasher. The organization was somewhat better, but the time going to and from the storage unit was still too much.

Our next step in our evolution in parts inventories was the construction of our own storage shed near the properties. We built a 120 square foot shed. Small sheds of 120 square feet or less do not need a building permit. We added shelves and semi-organized our paint, parts and tools. Being close to the jobs made this shed fantastic and allowed us to maintain a nice selection of common parts. We did try to make it strong enough to discourage theft. We used 5/8 plywood sides with a plywood interior also. Vents to the shed had interior bars. We figured that there was no way you could break into it without making noise.

The storage shed has become a fixture of our rental properties. Each apartment complex has a storage shed for parts. All the sheds are laid out in a similar manner. A repairperson can go from one complex to another and expect to fine similar parts. The sheds are large enough to hold all the normal parts used plus paints, ladders and other day-to-day repair items.

Storage sheds are keyed alike for complexes that use the same repair people, and the sheds are keyed to a master key for the property managers.

Managers were originally responsible for ordering parts from suppliers to maintain the inventories in their own sheds. We began a system for managers to make a monthly order of the most common items in their sheds from a central supply and have it delivered to them. We maintain a large supply of common parts at a storage area that is part of a commercial property we own. Managers send their monthly supply requests, which are filled and delivered to them. We place monthly orders to suppliers to refill our supplies. We try to maintain a two-month quantity of parts at each complex and a three-month supply at the central supply. Maintaining a large inventory in our central parts storage allows us to purchase parts by the case or in bulk to get the best price.

Our storage sheds and central parts supply now have parts in bin boxes with labels showing item, supplier, supplier's stock number and other pertinent information for inventory and ordering. It looks like a hardware store. Being organized, with replacement parts on-hand and easy to find, makes repair work much easier. It's kind of like playing store when I was a kid; I love it.

Standard Inventories

As we began stocking more and more parts we developed a Standard Inventory sheet showing all the items we stock, which complex uses the part, and all other ordering information such as supplier, stock numbers and minimum order amounts for the best price.

This standard inventory is done in a Word table format. This allows us to sort the table by supplier, complex or any other information we keep. We maintain one main inventory for all complexes, but can sort and delete unwanted information to produce an inventory sheet specific to a particular complex.

With the purchase of each apartment complex, we walked each type of unit and made a list of all parts we wanted to stock. These parts are added to the standard inventory sheet. We make a list of other specifications for the unit that we do not carry as inventory items, such as window covers, screen sizes, cabinet door sizes, etc. These items and many similar items are not stocked in our sheds, but listed on a specification sheet, for that complex, contained in our Manual of Operations.

In addition to our Standard Inventory, we have several special inventory lists and sheets, such as a light fixture schedule, light bulb schedule, window cover schedule, and rekeying sets parts. For example, the light fixture schedule contains all the different light fixtures we normally stock, plus special non-stocked fixtures, along with where they are used and in which complex. In some complexes the hall light fixture is the same as a bathroom fixture in another complex. The light bulb schedule lists all the bulbs we use and where, and in what complex they are used. We only stock a few types of the most common bulbs. The light bulb schedule lists them all by type and wattage to make it easier to replace them with the correct bulb.

Monthly Parts Delivery System

When we began, we had the individual managers at an apartment complex try to keep up their stocks of the parts stored in their sheds. This was always a hit and miss situation, with some managers much better at ordering supplies than others. The managers with some experience in building had an easier time with parts. Supervisory personnel, including myself, ended up checking on sheds frequently and made lists of parts to keep them supplied. After years of trying to be efficient in ordering parts for each complex, we came up with a system where the most used parts were bought in bulk by our company and warehoused in a storage area we owned. In this way, managers only needed to check a portion of their inventory of parts once a month and send in their orders to our main office. We like to keep a two or even a three-month supply of these most-used items in each complex and another three-month supply in our main warehouse.

We began this supply system by listing which parts were used the most. These parts were identified in each shed by painting their storage bin blue so it would be easy for the managers to check during their once a month order. We made a separate inventory list and order form for each complex containing only these items. Other less used items in their sheds only need to be reordered every six months to a year.

In our main parts warehouse we stock all the most used items, which are inventoried by a storage bin number. Our main office inventory of these items shows which vendor supplies the item. We keep about a three-month supply for all complexes of these items and buy them in bulk. We usually make a fill-in order once a month after supplies are delivered, but we have enough parts on hand for at least two months at any one time.

This system does require one of our workers to fill and deliver orders each month. The payback is in the savings from buying our parts at good prices and in bulk quantities. The worker's time is more than balanced by our supervisor personnel not having to monitor apartment complexes parts inventories. Keeping our storage sheds full of parts makes repairs much easier and eliminates the need for a repairman having to head for the closest Home Depot or Lowes to pick up a part.

Repair and Maintenance Procedures

We maintain a number of maintenance procedures to standardize the work done on our properties. This makes it easier when multiple maintenance personnel are working on a complex; they will all know the basic jobs and the way we want them done. Most of this information comes from years of working on rental properties and my experience in building contracting. Doing a job right makes the property more valuable and tenants happier. We are never satisfied with "good enough for a rental." We want it good enough for owners who like their properties maintained to a high standard of quality.

Little Hints on Maintenance

Like many jobs and professions, you learn little trick of the trade. These are ways to get jobs done better or easier by doing little short cuts or knowing the way to make the apartment look better without spending a lot of money and time.

Door Bumpers

When you are installing door bumpers, put them on the door instead of the wall. When on the wall, they are vulnerable to being hit with a vacuum cleaner and being broken. On the door they are swung out of the way when the tenant is doing cleaning.

Bypass Doors

Sliding bypass doors need to have the outside door nearest the entrance to the room. When a person enters the room and looks at the doors, the door in the front will be closest to them and cover the space between the doors. If it is the other way around you will be able to see the crack between the doors. This is just a little trick to make the room look a little better.

Bi-Fold Doors

On a bi-fold door, the pull handle goes in the center of the door farthest from the hinge. This is done so that when the door is open the pull is facing the opening of the door. It is easy to pull the door in this direction. If the pull is on the door closest to the hinge, when the door is open, the pull will be on the outside and it is just about impossible to push from the outside to close a bi-fold door.

Removing Trim Boards

When removing casings, baseboards, or trim, cut the paint where the trim boards meet the wall with a utility knife before trying to remove. If you do not cut before removal, you will pull off paint from the wall and need to make plaster repairs. Many of these trim pieces have been there for many years and will have had several coats of paint. Cut the paint and save the headache.

Door Knobs

When replacing a doorknob, change the bolt also. It does not take much time for door bolts to get paint on them. Door bolts also wear out; especially bolts on keyed entry locks. There are only two screws to remove and replace the bolt with a new one, and you will not only save time later, but will have a better looking job right now. This same logic goes for the strike plates. Strike plates do not wear out, but they do get worn-looking and many times have paint on them. All these parts come with the doorknob being replaced and it is easy to do it right and replace with new parts.

When you finished installing the doorknob, you should save any extra parts like screw and strike plates. They can be put into the plastic shoebox if you are changing a front door knob, or put into storage in our sheds. We stock both strike plates and miscellaneous door screws if needed to replace used parts from a doorknob box.

Door Hinges

Door hinges are another matter. Hinges are very often painted by poor painters and ignored by repair personnel. We buy hinges in bulk and store them in our sheds. Our cost on hinges is about a dollar apiece. The couple bucks spent on new hinges makes the door, and the unit, look much nicer and newer. When you are changing hinges do one at a time. You can put a wedge under the door to hold it in place and remove the hinge by removing the screws. Do not take out the hinge pin; it is much easier to unscrew the old hinge and replace with a new one while the door is still in place. If the door happens to have three hinges you do not even need to use a wedge; two hinges will keep it in place while you replace the third.

Concealed Towel Bar Set Screws

The tiny set screw that attaches the towel bar or toilet paper holder ends to the backing plate should be on the bottom. Small point, but I have seen them on top more than once.

Fiberglass Bathtub Refinishing

Plastic bathtubs are susceptible to discoloration and holes from tenant damage. If a tenant drops a heavy shampoo bottle or other item, it can knock a hole in a fiberglass tub. There are companies that can patch the hole and totally refinish the tub with an epoxy spray coating. This repair comes out very professional and look as good as new. This is the same process as the refinishing of plastic laminated kitchen counter tops.

Range, Fridge And Dishwasher Parts

When you are replacing major appliances, save some of the old parts. Apartment properties will usually have the same brand and model refrigerators, ranges and dishwashers. If you have a container in the shed, you can cannibalize some smaller parts and save them for an appliance that is missing the part down the road. These parts include range knobs and the handle for the oven. The elements are usually not worth saving unless they have been replaced recently and appear in good condition.

If you have room in the shed, it is nice to save refrigerator door shelf guards and crispers. These are common missing items when a tenant leaves. The cover for the butter shelf is also a common broken or missing part.

Save dishwasher wheels and silverware trays, or even the entire pull out dish rack. By saving these smaller parts on dishwashers, ranges and fridges, you will make the replacement of a part in the future an easy task instead of a trip to the appliance store.

Painting Hints

When rolling paint, use a disposable roller and disposable paint pan liner. We stock both in our sheds and buy them in bulk. It is not an easy job cleaning a roller. It is much less expensive to throw away the used roller and liner than to burn up labor hours trying to clean them. We also stock one-inch and two-inch disposable brushes for a quick touch-up without having to clean the brush. These are especially good when using oil based paints, stains, polyurethane, or varnish.

Keep a list of the paint colors used in each apartment. Note the brand, type and color so you can come up with a touch-up paint for the next time and not have to paint the entire unit every time. It only takes a few minutes to record the paint information, but causes wasted time, effort and money when you do not know what paint to use.

Clean the top of the paint can or five-gallon container before putting the lid back on. If you do not clean the top, the lid will not fit correctly and the paint will be ruined before it can be fully used. With the top of the can filled with dry, old paint, the next time the can is used it will be impossible to get the lid to seal and air will screw up the paint. A minute or two of labor to clean the top of the can will save 10 times the money in paint cost later on.

Buy paint from a paint store. They are professionals and have the expertise to advise you and keep you from making a mistake. They can match colors and stand behind their products. There are several good stores to select from when you need professional paint guidance. Check them out and pick the one that you like the best. I avoid getting paint from the big home improvement stores. My experience is that they cannot match an existing color as well as the professionals, and in some cases cannot match the color even when they have their own color formula.

Semi-Gloss Or Eggshell

For years we painted walls in flat paint, and kitchens, baths and trim in semi-gloss. Our next change was to paint everything in semi-gloss, at the request of our managers, because they like the easy cleaning that semi provides. After a few years of semi, all of our places looked like hospital waiting rooms. Our next move was to paint everything in eggshell, which we are still doing today. Eggshell is a good compromise as it is easy to clean and has a low sheen to it that is attractive. It also does not require priming over spackle repairs as semi does. We use a slightly off-white color.

Range Drip Pans

We replace range drip pans on almost every turnover. These drip pans are often discolored and dirty. We buy a variety of drip pans in bulk and are able to change out a range for less than 10 dollars. New drip pans, like new hinges, make an apartment look clean and new. We stock a universal drip pan that fits most ranges except General Electric. We also stock GE drip pans for the older and newer models. These are stocked in our sheds and are easy to bring to the unit with the other repair parts needed. Take care to use the correct drip pan.

Cabinet Doors

Most cabinet doors used in apartments are of the lowest quality available at the time the apartments were constructed. Most of our complexes used cabinet doors that were just particleboard covered in a contact paper. These doors can chip or get ragged when the contact paper comes loose from the edges or large pieces are ripped off. There are companies that make replacement doors, but we have not found any that can duplicate the original poor construction.

Our solution is to take an apartment unit with bad doors and replace all the doors in the unit. We can buy a similar, better quality cabinet door in a color that matches the rest of the cabinet. Save the old doors and drawer fronts, even badly damaged doors can be cut down to a smaller-sized door or drawer front. As units later need replacement cabinet doors, you can use the good ones you have in stock or make them from a larger size. When making a cabinet door smaller, it is necessary to paint the newly cut edge in a color that matches the old cabinet door edges. Have your paint company make a quart of matching edge paint for each color door you might be working on. When you have used up so much of your supply of used doors that you cannot replace a needed one, then it is time to replace all the doors in a unit again and replenish your supply of usable replacement cabinet doors.

When replacing a cabinet door, leave the top hinge on the door and the bottom hinge on the cabinet. In other words, unscrew the bottom hinge from the door first leaving it still attached to the frame; then unscrew the top hinge from the frame and leave it still attached to the door. Take the old door and place it on the floor or work bench with the new door next to it. Move the top hinge from the old door to the new door making sure it is screwed in the same distance from the top of the door. Now return the new door to the cabinets and screw the top hinge into the frame using the existing holes. The door will now swing in place to the old hinge still attached to the frame and will be easy to attach in the right place. This requires very little measuring and comes out perfect every time.

Air Conditioner Troubleshooting

In the apartment unit, check that the circuit breaker is on and the furnace filter is clean. Check if the fan comes on when the "Heat/Cool" switch is off and the "Fan" switch is on. If the fan does not come on, then there is no power to the fan or thermostat. Check the circuit breaker or fuse to the fan receptacle. The normal position for the switches is for heat or cool to be selected and the fan switch to be on "Auto," automatic.

Are pipes going into the unit cold? When working correctly, the pipe going into the unit from the compressor outside should be very cold.

Outside you should check if the compressor is running. If it is running but not getting cold then you are going to need the A/C repairman. If the compressor is not running, check the fuses or circuit breaker near the outside unit. Many outside A/C compressor units use fuses instead of circuit breakers. If fuses are used, you will need a continuity checker to determine if the fuse has burned out.

Weeds or obstructions around a compressor can restrict the cooling of unit and keep it from cooling properly. The compressor needs air to dissipate the heat. Also, look for a broken thermostat wire at the compressor unit. Kids or gardeners can trip over the wires and pull them out; we have also had dogs chew the wires, causing a malfunction.

Look for something stuck into the top of the compressor unit causing the fan not to turn. We have experienced kids putting sticks into the top of the compressor unit. If the cooling fan is not turning, the outside unit will overheat and shut off.

Work Orders

The resident manager uses a work order form to list jobs that need to be done. This form is not used for turnovers, but rather for repairs in occupied units, in the common areas of the complex, or on the grounds. The work order is a three-part form, which will include the date, apartment number, tenant name and the work to be done. It may also give information about permission to enter the unit.

The worker gets the white and yellow copies of the form. When the work is completed, the yellow copy is returned to the office with any repair information on it, including a note that it is completed. The white copy is submitted with the worker's time card for pay.

Semi-Annual Inspections with Simultaneous Repairs

During our semi-annual inspections of each apartment, we have a repair-person accompany the resident manager and the supervising manager to each unit. The inspections are mostly made by the managers, while the repairperson can check the smoke detector, replacing batteries as needed, and replace the furnace filter. We take a supply of nine-volt batteries and filters with the inspection team.

The repairperson can also make small repairs right on the spot, and should take a tool belt with the normal small tools. On these inspections, it is easy to tighten up a towel bar or faucet or complete other small jobs. Make a list of repairs that will take a little more time or need some special part we stock in our sheds. If time permits, you can come back to this unit on the same day and make these quick additional repairs. We have given notice to enter for the day, and returning to make a repair on the same day makes it easy.

Employees versus Outside Contractors

We have found that our work is not normally a full-time job for a maintenance person. We carry them as outside contractors and pay them by the hour. This is a tough area; an owner does not want the expense and responsibilities of having employees, but they want the workers to be readily available as the quantity of work demands. We use outside contractors as much as possible.

Locks, Keying and Master Keys

Somewhere in the late 1980s when we only owned a few duplexes, our son was managing an apartment complex and figured he could make a few bucks rekeying locks instead of having to call a locksmith each time a tenant moved out. He bought a rekey set and taught himself how to change the pins in a lock to match a new key. He learned how to rekey the lock so a master key would work in it also. In that way a manager had a single key that would open all the locks. Each of our complexes has a keying kit, extra locks, bolts, screws and strike plates.

We have standardized locks for all complexes by type and finish. In this manner, locks from one complex can be used on any of the other complexes. We use polished brass doorknobs, as they are the least expensive.

My son taught me the process, and we too became our own locksmiths with a master key system of our own. Since that time, we have maintained our own supply of back-up locks and spare parts. As we got bigger, we got more sophisticated. We started a system using plastic shoeboxes, which contained a full set of doorknobs, including dead bolts and keyed-alike entry locks. The box also contains extra screws, strike plates, and a cylinder tool for working on locks. Each apartment complex maintains three or more plastic shoeboxes, each containing a complete exchange of dead bolts and keyed entry locksets.

Changing Locks At Turnover

When a tenant moves and locks need to be changed, a complete box is taken to the unit along with all the old keys. Locks are removed and new locks installed. All the old, serviceable locks and keys are put into the plastic shoebox for future use. If there are any missing or damaged parts, they should be replaced as soon as possible to complete the locks in the box and be ready for the next time. There should be a minimum of four keys in the box. The best two keys are the keys we keep and the other two will be given to a future tenant. The shoeboxes should be rotated, using locks on turnovers that have not been used in the longest time. Be sure all keys end up in the correct place after changing locks. All old keys will go into the plastic box with the old locks and be put back into storage. The new keys will need to be put on the correct key rings in the office.

Master Keys And Special Keys

All office doors, storage shed, and, in some cases, other doors on our properties are keyed on a master key. These keys are in the possession of managers and some maintenance people. Assistant managers have keys that work on the office and other required doors at their complex only. Master keys are not the same for all properties. Each complex has a secondary key know as a tenant's key. This key fits the swimming pool gate and laundry room. Complexes using Kwikset locks will also be keyed to our master. Each complex also has a maintenance key. This key will allow maintenance personnel to gain entry to sheds and other doors, but not to the office.

Keys To Vacant Units

Each apartment complex needs a system of providing keys to maintenance personnel or sub-contractors. We have used a container in the manager's office with all the keys to the vacant units. The manager keeps control of the keys and who has them. The downside is that the manager has to be in the office, or someone on site has to have an office key, for the unit keys to be accessed.

A better system is to buy a supply of doorknob key lock box, similar to the ones used by real estate companies on houses for sale. We use these on all our complexes with a common code number. Any maintenance person or outside vendor can work at any apartment complex and gain access to the vacant units.

Key Shop

We currently maintain our own "key shop" in one of the storage areas at one of the complexes. We have a large supply of dead bolts and keyed entry locks as well as all the parts used with them. The shop has a key cutting machine. Locksets in plastic boxes are brought to the key shop and exchanged for ready-to-go sets. Locksets can be serviced and keys cut as needed. Ready-to-go sets contain four keys, so we can give the tenant two and we keep two. We can also cut keys for mailboxes as needed.

Turnovers

Turnover, or "make ready," is the process of cleaning up and making any repairs needed to an apartment when one tenant leaves. The resident manager of the complex will start with bringing needed items to the unit and begin a Turnover Work List. This work list is kept on the kitchen counter along with a ballpoint pen. Sometimes the manager completes the work list, and other times the repairperson might do some of it or even all of it. This list has columns to note any tenant damage. There are columns to list any special parts that must be purchased or any special tools needed to complete the job.

The manager will also provide a trash can, a roll of toilet paper, a roll of paper towels and a plastic shoebox to hold any small parts during the turnover process. There should be a set of replacement front door locks and maybe some large plastic trash bags if the manager thinks there will be a large quantity of trash.

Using the work list, the repairman should make themselves a list of parts and tools needed for the work. A list of the parts needed from the entire work list will enable the maintenance worker to pick up as many as possible of the needed items at one time from our sheds or from a vendor.

The first thing done is to change the locks. Most tenants are responsible, but some cannot be trusted. We want the locks changed early to protect tools that might be in the apartment. See the section above for more on changing locks. The second job is to remove all the trash from the unit. It is always easier to work in an apartment when the debris is gone. This will include any old appliances that are going to be discarded.

The Turnover Progress Chart shows the sequence of work to do during a turnover. It reads left to right, and jobs are done in the order shown. We may also have a Pert Chart for the particular turnover if there is a great deal of work to do. Use the charts to help keep you on the right track of getting jobs done in the correct sequence. The Turnover Progress Chart and the Pert Chart are explained in much more detail in the Management chapter. Be sure you do not let painting begin until all the prep work and other jobs higher on the progress chart are completed. The supervising manager will have a Master Progress Chart. On this master chart, all turnovers in all complexes are listed. The supervising Manager uses this Master Progress Chart to be able to determine priorities between complexes.

On all turnovers, we check and make sure the smoke detector has a good battery. We also replace the furnace filter. During the final stages of the turnover, we replace the toilet seat with a new one, and provide a cutting board, ice trays, and a new front door mat.

The resident manager is the person in charge of the turnover and making decisions regarding priorities. They may be assisted by the supervising manager and the maintenance manager. In our Construction chapter, we have guidelines for specific jobs that you may encounter during a turnover.

Care and Maintenance for New Refinished Countertops

It is important to refrain from using the new countertops for a minimum of 24 hours after installation. If temperatures are lower than normal room temperature then the waiting period is longer.

During the first 30 days after the installation of the new countertop, clean only with mild, liquid dish soap. After 30 days, you can use a nonabrasive liquid or foam cleaner such as Dow Scrubbing Bubbles. Never use an abrasive sponge or cleaning implement.

Never use bleach, harsh chemicals, caustic materials, or abrasive cleaners of any kind. Destruction of the finish may occur through improper use of acid bearing compounds. All chemicals must be kept away from the finish, including cosmetics, hair dyes and perfumes.

The newly refinished countertop will not be fully cured until 30 days have passed. Clean the finish regularly during this curing period with mild soap and a sponge to remove any dust or foreign substances that might have settled. Do not pick at any bumps or particles on the surface. Picking at minor bumps or particles can damage the new surface. After the 30-day curing period, any particles will come off with normal cleaning.

Never cut or chop on the countertop at any time. Always use a cutting board. If a tenant needs a new cutting board, we will supply one at no cost to them.

Chapter 8

CAPITAL IMPROVEMENTS

Definition of Capital Improvements

A Capital Improvement makes a property better, nicer, more salable and hopefully more valuable. Replacing carpets or appliances is not a Capital Improvement. These replacements bring the property back to where it was before the items needed to be replaced.

Adding a patio, sliding glass door, microwave, or better landscaping are examples of Capital Improvements. Capital Improvements fall into two categories. The first is work done to the building that will ultimately make it worth more, but will have little or no chance of increasing rents. These are improvements such as an upscale roof, new siding, or other improvements that might appeal to a future buyer but have little chance to increase the income of a property.

The second type of Capital Improvement is geared to produce a return in the form of reduced vacancies or raised rents. The increase in income should substantially pay for the improvement. The ideal improvement will generate more income than the improvement costs. Improvements that appeal to a prospective tenant will help keep vacancies low. Some improvements, which can be expensive, are desirable enough to generate an increase in rent that a new tenant is willing to pay. These may include adding washers and dryers to a unit or adding a fitness center.

The test to see if the expenditure is a Capital Improvement or a routine, regular expense is whether or not you have to do it. If it is discretionary, then it is probably a Capital expense. If a refrigerator in a unit goes out and must be replaced, it is not discretionary; you have to replace it. Therefore, it is a normal, routine expense. If you replace the refrigerator with a stainless steel model with an ice maker, then you move into the Capital Improvement area. You made the property better and nicer with the upgraded fridge. The difference in cost between the two models is definitely a Capital Improvement; however, most would categorize the entire purchase as such.

Some expenses can fall into different categories depending on how you deal with the repair. For example, if a fence needs repairs work of a minor nature, it would be a routine repair expense. If the fence were so bad that you need to replace a significant amount of it, then it would fall into the Reserves category as a major expense that does not occur on a regular basis. If you replaced the wooden fence with a block fence then it moves to the Capital Improvement area.

You are probably wondering why we should make such distinctions when categorizing whether an expense falls into everyday expenses or into a Capital Improvement category. Regular expenses are included in the total expenses of a property when figuring the Net Operating Income, (NOI). Capital expenses and money spent on Reserves are not included when calculating NOI. The value of a property is a direct function of its Net Operating Income (Net Operating Income, divided by the current Cap Rate, equals the value of the property).

This is very important when selling the property to justify your selling price. It is also important when the property comes due for a refinance. The amount of the loan will be directly affected by the NOI of the property. If expenses are not correctly categorized then your operating statements and real estate schedules will not reflect the correct amounts to show the health of your company.

Regular, routine expenses are also included on your annual report to the lender on the property. Discretionary expenses, reserves and capital improvements are not included on these annual bank reports.

Easy Improvements

The below improvements should be done by every apartment rental owner. They are inexpensive and make your property more appealing or will result in a greater chance for profit.

Park Benches

A few park benches placed around the property give the property a nice feeling. People rarely sit on these benches, but the tenants like them. They give your open areas a park-like look. Generally, a nice park bench is available at home improvement stores for a reasonable price. In the spring they are also available in many discount stores as well as the big national drug stores. This is an easy, inexpensive way to make your property nicer.

American Flag

All of our properties have an American flag flying out front. Some use wall mounted flagpoles, but a real flagpole concreted into the ground is even better. The flag is placed near the office and between the entrance driveway to the complex and the office if possible. It is in a place that any vehicle that drives into our complex will see the flag. Yes, we are patriotic, and yes, we love this country. We hope our prospective tenants feel the same way.

Banners And Signs

There are a number of very inexpensive improvements to your property that promote it to passing motorists. Make sure there is a large sign that has the name of the apartments visible to the public. It should be large and easy to read, and in a place that will be seen by all who come by. The sign should also include your phone number in a font size large enough to be read easily from a long way away. You want someone passing by to see the sign and be able to read the phone number without their glasses. This is inexpensive advertising for your complex.

Large banners also promote your property. These are inexpensive and available from a sign shop or online. You do not want too many words on your banner. You want it to be easily read by someone driving by without having to put on glasses. A banner only needs to grab attention, with words like "Now Renting," "Move in Special," or some other short, eye-catching phrase.

Decorator Paint Colors

We have experimented with some decorator paint jobs in units. This is an inexpensive upgrade. Instead of painting the entire unit white or off-white, we painted the living room a darker, earthier color, making the room warmer. We tried to use a neutral color so as not to conflict with a prospective tenant's furniture colors. A color in a lighter tone, such as a brown-gray mixture, gives the room the look of a more expensive apartment.

One of the complexes we purchased had apartments already painted in designer colors. This is trickier, as someone looking for an apartment may not like the colors. Surprisingly, new tenants who must be getting tired of the normal white in every room have liked them.

The cost of decorator paint is the same as white. It may cost a little more in labor, but all in all the cost is minimal for the improvement gained. If you can rent an apartment quicker with a decorator color on the walls, it is a good investment.

Computer Phone

An inexpensive change in your phone system can result in a substantial savings in phone expenses. We have replaced our office phones with a computer phone system. A computer phone system is paid by the year at just a fraction of normal phone charges. It works through the internet and includes call forwarding and messages. It has all the features of a normal office phone, but is much less expensive. Using a computer phone helps keep your bottom line on your expense sheet down a bit and your profits up a bit.

To Maintain the Value of Your Property

There are some important improvements you can make that will prevent your rental property from becoming damaged, less valuable, or dated. Many are easy to do and are not that expensive. It is often more costly not to do them and then have to pay more in the future for repairs. It is important to maintain the value of your property in the event you sell it at some time in the future.

Cabinet Pulls

Replacing cabinet pulls maintains value and is cost effective. Buy the nicest, inexpensive pull you can find. The cost of adding pulls to kitchens and bathrooms is outweighed by the improvement to the apartment, which keeps your property at the highest value possible.

Cabinet pulls are more important than just making the kitchen look better. The pulls prevent the cabinets from becoming scratched by fingernails. Years ago, big developers and contractors left off cabinet pulls and sold the public on the "clean look." It was really done to save them money. Cabinet pulls, plus the labor to put them in, cost the builder extra money. By leaving them off and being clever enough to convince the consumer that the building was more attractive without them, was more money in the bank for the builder. This was especially important to large builders building hundreds of houses. A savings of $100 on one home will result in a savings of $10,000 on a hundred homes.

Apartment kitchen and bathroom cabinets are usually of minimum quality. Many times they are made with particleboard or cardboard and a thin contact paper material over it to resemble wood. The thin outer cover is susceptible to damage from fingernails. It does not happen overnight, but after a while the cabinets will have scratches under the doors. This damage is not easy to repair. It is not like wood that you can sand and stain to match the original finish. It some cases you must rebuild the entire frame of the cabinet front.

Providing pulls on cabinets will not result in fewer vacancies or raised rents, but it will save money in the long run from fewer cabinet replacements. Leaving cabinet pulls off is false economy. You can save a few bucks now, but you will pay more in the future for repairs.

Try to standardize pulls for all the rental units you own. Standardized type and placement makes it easier to swap doors between units and allows you to buy pulls in bulk at the best price possible.

Yard Sprinkler Systems

Sprinkler systems to irrigate you property are important to prevent your landscaping from becoming dry and ugly. You want the property to be nicely landscaped with a great many green bushes, trees and flowers. The investment in sprinkler systems is money well spent. When we had duplexes and relied on the tenant watering the yard, it was a disaster. The yards never looked their best and from time to time we had to replace bushes and lawns.

We added sprinklers systems to water the front yards. These systems had a timer to automatically water without the tenant having to do anything. We utilized large "Rain bird"-type heads wherever the yards were big enough for them. Sprinklers are costly to purchase and a lot of work to install, but is well worth it to keep your property looking its best and allow trees and bushes to grow and add beauty.

Glass Shower Doors

Most rental properties, including apartments, are constructed with tub-shower combinations with a shower curtain. These usually lead to water on the floor that can lead to wall dry rot or floor damage. This is especially bad on a second floor unit where water can run through the ceiling to the floor below. Glass shower doors are not put in rental units when constructed because they are expensive and add to the labor cost of the building.

We have always replaced shower curtains with glass shower doors. These doors do not just help prevent water damage, but are more attractive in the bathroom. We often decorate them with a colorful valance over the top.

Providing Barbecues

Tenants using a barbecue or a hibachi on their patio or balcony deck can be a fire hazard. The fire department does not like to see open flames anywhere near the building. Even small propane units are discouraged. Your insurance carrier might also require a policy of no barbecues on patios or balconies. We like to provide a barbecue area for the tenants to make it easy for them and discourage more dangerous cooking near their apartment.

We have provided a few commercial charcoal type barbecues for the tenants' use in a convenient part of the complex. Sometimes it is in the swimming pool area; other times we have put them in a convenient part of the property, usually in a grass area. It is always good to put them near a picnic table or park bench. This small improvement is appreciated by tenants and makes the property more livable as well as safer.

Other Capital Improvements

Some improvements help reduce vacancies as well as make the property more valuable or result in being able to increase rent amounts. These improvements make the property more appealing and will add value to the complex when it is sold. The reduced vacancy should increase income and thus value, but there is also a benefit of making the property more attractive to a prospective buyer if the property is put up for sale sometime in the future.

A more attractive property can also help keep rents at a higher level. We try to make improvements that are cost effective. Meaning that the improvement cost is not that great when compared to the possibility of additional income that might be generated from it.

Yards And Landscaping

Improvements to yards and landscaping will be a benefit for years to come. Trees should be planted as soon as you identify the need. Trees take a long time to grow and considerable savings can be realized by planting smaller, less expensive trees as soon as possible. Plants and trees will need to be picked by geographical location. Check with a local nursery for recommendations for your area.

Trees

You should always plant trees with the thought of how big they are going to get when full grown. Make sure there is enough room for them and that roots are not going to impact walks or sprinkler systems. Keep them at a distance from the buildings also. We have had roots under slab floors lifting or cracking the floor inside the unit. It is also important to plant new trees away from main sewer or water lines. Tree roots can cause major headaches when they clog or damage water or sewer lines.

Types of trees to consider will vary as to the location, space and purpose of the tree. I have listed a few suggestions of trees we have used. These plants will not be suitable for all parts of the country. Talk to your local nursery to get information on what works best in your area.

Aptos Blue is a type of redwood that grows fast and thick. You can usually expect them to grow 4 to 6 feet a year and they can easily reach 50 feet tall or more with dense foliage. They will become 20-plus feet wide with very big trunks. They are great to block out an undesirable view and their fast growth and inexpensive cost make them very popular.

Crepe Myrtle (or Crape Myrtle) is a small flower-bearing tree very popular in our area. They only grow about 20 feet tall. They can have a large amount of flowers, usually white or red. These flowers bloom much of the spring and summer and are great to add color to your property. They do drop their flowers over a long period of time, so do not plant them near the swimming pool.

Wax leaf privet is a bush that can grow into a small tree. They are a fast growing bush with dense dark green leaves. They are commonly used as a bush, but if allowed to grow tall and pruned properly, will become a small tree.

Fruitless pear trees are desirable because they are a very symmetrical, beautiful tree of medium height. They have dark green leaves, but no pears, of course. In our area, we use the Bradford Pear tree. They do not drop pears, but they do have blossoms in the spring. The tree will be totally covered in white flowers and very beautiful until they drop and need to be cleaned up. Bradford Pear trees are not good around the pool for the blossom issue.

Fruitless plumbs are of medium height with very dark red leaves. They are great here and there to break up the all green landscaping. They will grow to about 20 feet tall. They have no fruit, but do have pink blossoms in the spring.

Bushes

Bushes, like trees, need to be planted early so they have time to grow. They are less costly than trees and grow more quickly, so it is not as critical to get them planted immediately. Get the major trees and bushes in for your landscaping improvement early them move to the other yard needs.

Bushes that thrive in full sun are the Wax Leaf Privet, Indian Hawthorn, Boxwood, Mock Orange, Escallonia and Oleander. All are hardy and attractive. The Oleander, Escallonia and Indian Hawthorn have flowers to add color to the area. Carpet roses are a low growing, sun-loving bush that provide flowers for much of the year.

Hydrangeas, Gardenias and Aralias all do well in full shade or at least filtered sun. The Gardenia and Hydrangea have flowers. Aralias are a large-leaf, tropical-looking bush. The Hydrangea has very large lower clusters that bloom all summer. It needs shade and plenty of water. Azaleas are another flowering bush that does well in filtered sun with loose soil.

Flowers

I like flowers at the entrance to the complex and near the offices. I want prospective tenants to be greeted with flowers upon entrance to the property and when checking in at the office. Annual bedding flowers are planted each spring, but some flower-bearing bushes help keep the property colorful year after year. Roam through the nursery and talk to the nursery workers to get more ideas.

Bedding flowers are not like trees. With trees, you are stuck with your decision for probably the rest of your life. With annual flowers, you only have to live with them for a season and then they are gone. Picking flowers is easy. Whichever is the biggest, most colorful and the cheapest is the best. Pansies are available early in the season. Marigolds, Vincas or Periwinkles do well in full sun. Begonias and impatiens need filtered sun or shade.

Petunias are great sunshine flowers. They grow fast, have many blossoms and will fill large planter areas. They are a vine-like plant, so you need room for them to grow and expand.

Bedding flowers are available from about February on in our area. Many times, it is better to shop at professional nurseries. Nursery plants are usually healthier and larger, but more expensive also. The big home improvement or mass merchant store's flowers are usually on the smaller size, and are not as nice as professional nursery flowers, but they are economical and easy to pick up with normal shopping. You just need to check out the flowers when you are in these big home improvement stores shopping for other items in the spring when it is flower time.

I have found when looking for flowers, it is best to go on a Thursday or Friday. The big stores get fill-in shipments delivered during the week, and you want to do your flower shopping before the weekend rush.

Another source of flowers is your yard maintenance company. They have access to wholesale landscape and nursery items, and can often come up with much higher quality and larger plants at a very competitive price. You may have to go with your yard service guy to buy them, but our experience is that you can get much nicer plants at great wholesale prices.

The bottom line on bedding flowers is how much color you can get for the buck. Unless you invest in flowering bushes that bloom every year, you want to get as much color as possible for a minimum investment.

Planters And Other Yard Improvements

A bigger investment is putting in new planters or planter areas. In our days owning duplexes we would put in brick planters in the front yards. This would dress up the property. Filling the planters with petunias, for example, would greatly improve the look of the property. When we got into apartment complexes, brick planters generally were not used. Instead, there were designated planter areas. These can still be improved with landscape fabric, to minimize weeds, and bark or landscape rock. It does not take much effort to make a property look much better when you put in some decorator rock, a few bushes, and some colorful bedding flowers.

We spent a lot of time at this in our duplex days to dress up the front yards of the properties, making them look inviting to prospective tenants. We also wanted to make it a place our existing tenants wanted to stay.

Our duplex properties had a problem with trash cans. Each unit had a garbage can, a recycle can and a yard waste can. This was six cans per duplex, which ended up all over the place. We came up with a trash can area for each duplex. We poured concrete between the duplexes and added a three-foot high fence to hide the cans. This made room for all six cans back-to-back where they were out of sight of the street. The concrete pad tied into the walk or driveway so a tenant could easily walk to the cans to dump garbage and wheel the cans to the street for pick-up day. This simple fix took a big eye sore and turned it into an asset to the property. We finished it off with a couple bushes in front of the little fence and it looked terrific. Simple, inexpensive fixes always pay off.

Faucets

We always upgrade our kitchen faucets to a single-handle type. Many apartments are built with less expensive, old-fashioned two-handle faucets. We like to bring our kitchens up to date with the more modern single-handle control faucet.

We have also changed our bathroom faucets to a single control lever type. Like the kitchen faucets, this is a nice upgrade from the cheap looking two-handle old style. In complexes with large water heaters for several apartments, we have gone back to a decorative two-handle type; we have found that the large water heaters can have very hot water, and our managers feel it is safer for kids using two handles for hot and cold instead of the single handle. We stock both single-handle and two-handle decorator faucets for our units.

Light Fixture Upgrades

New light fixtures are an inexpensive upgrade to dress up an apartment. Like most items in the construction of apartments, light fixtures are often chosen because of their low price tag. With careful shopping, you can come up with very nice bath and hall fixtures at a very economical price. We stock a single-bulb ceiling fixture for halls and closets and a double-bulb fixture for bathroom ceilings. The average cost in 2013 was less than $10 per fixture.

We like to replace the wall light over the bathroom sink with a multi-bulb fixture using the larger decorator bulbs known as G-25 type. We want this fixture to have from 200 to 250 watts so that the bathroom will be well illuminated when visited by a prospective tenant. Four tubes, fluorescent ceiling fixtures work well in the kitchen. Make it nice and bright. An apartment that is well lighted will show better to people shopping for a new place to live.

Local electric companies sometimes have programs to replace older light fixtures with newer, more energy efficient ones. There is little or no cost, and in some cases, the labor to change the fixtures is provided. It is best to make sure you like the fixture they are providing and that it is going to be well received by renters.

Cost Effective Improvements

A cost effective improvement is one in which the cost of the improvement is easily recovered from reduced vacancies or increased rents. There are a number of improvements that are relatively easy to do and result in a positive acceptance from prospective tenants.

Ceiling Fans

We install ceiling fans with lights in all of the dining areas of our apartments. These modestly priced fans dress up the room. Apartments have very few ceiling light fixtures other than the hall, bathroom and dining. Generally, the dining room is the only place a ceiling fan will work. We believe tenants like the idea of having a ceiling fan, and it is a good feature when people are looking for a new place to live.

Microwaves

A more expensive improvement that is usually cost effective is the addition of a microwave hood over the range in the kitchen. We usually try to buy several at a time and store them until we need one. The cost can be brought down by buying in volume. The installation of the hood microwave does require labor expenditure also, but the total cost will be recouped in making the apartment easier to rent or allowing for an increase in rents. We try to complete several upgrade improvements together in an apartment to provide an upgraded unit that can demand a greater rent over the standard apartment.

Ceramic Tile

When vinyl floors need to be replaced, we try to replace them with ceramic tile. Ceramic tile costs considerably more than vinyl up front, but it will last longer. Most tenants will prefer the tile floors and, like other improvements above, this can help to keep vacancies down. Ceramic floors on their own will not allow rents to be raised enough to offset the price, but the reduced vacancies, small rent increases and the savings on future vinyl replacements makes the ceramic tile floors cost effective.

Mirrored Closet Doors

Replacing the normally plain, white closet bypass doors with mirrored closet doors gives a bedroom a very nice upgrade. These mirrored doors will make the room appear larger. This is a modest cost improvement that is well received by prospective renters.

Storage Sheds

Storage sheds do not in themselves reduce vacancies or increase rents; they make it easier for managers and workers to be more efficient. By maintaining a supply of commonly used parts on the premises, workers are able to make repairs and turnovers more quickly. The cost of the shed will eventually be recovered from the saving on labor costs of the repair personnel. Without the shed, when a worker needs a part it is necessary to drive to the closest hardware or home improvement store to get the item. In our beginning days it was not uncommon for the repair man to drive to buy a part and return, only to realize another part was needed after getting a little farther into the repair. The cost of the shed is recovered by reducing our labor cost and preventing several shopping trips a day. There is more on storage sheds in the Maintenance section.

Security Cameras

Security cameras can help with security, but a good system is a bit pricey. Small, inexpensive systems can be purchased at the big discount stores. They come with a few cameras and a multi-channel recorder. They are not bad, but the quality of the picture, most times, is poor. Still, the presence of the cameras can help prevent problems. A system with high quality pictures can set you back more than you going to recover in increased profits.

We have also invested in a single high quality camera and recorder to use on a specific problem. Once we set it up in an office window to watch the pool area trying to catch who was throwing our pool furniture in the pool. If you are going to use security cameras, buy one that allows you to recognize people in the picture. It has to be a good quality recording to be worth the cost of the investment. This investment almost falls into the next category of improvements, those that are not cost effective

All of the above cost effective improvements fall into the Capital Improvement category because they all make the property better and more valuable. They meet the basic test of being discretionary. They are a great example of how to reinvest in your property to make it not only more valuable, but to make it generate a greater income.

Improvements that are not Cost Effective, But Desirable

This section talks about improvements to your properties that will not be covered by raising rents or reducing vacancies. These Capital Improvements, however, may make the property more desirable to a buyer if it is put up for sale. They are all improvements to your property that make it nicer and perhaps more valuable.

Patios And Patio Covers

We added patios to many of our duplexes. This was done in conjunction with patio covers and sometimes sliding glass doors. Patio covers and sliding glass doors are expensive and do not generate enough additional rents to make it a good investment. We would start with a concrete patio, often with a walk to the front yard tied into the driveway. They were fairly inexpensive. We kept cost down by using one of our handyman workers for the labor.

We did add patio roof covers and in some cases sliding glass, patio doors. This improvement made a very nice addition to the property. It would not necessarily result in higher rents, but it would make the property more desirable to a prospective tenant or a future buyer. Sliding glass patio doors make a property much nicer, but it is a big cost. We only took on such an improvement if the unit was going to be vacant for a while and we had extra profits we wanted to put back into the properties. Sliding patio doors will not be cost effective considering the cost verses the additional rents that might be generated.

When we sold our duplexes, these kinds of improvements made the properties show well and caught the eye of buyers looking for a nice property. They gave our property an edge over other similar properties that had not been maintained as well nor had the upscale improvements completed.

Security Gates

Security gates are a large expense that will help reduce vacancies and in some cases promote higher rents, but the cost of the gates is so high it is not possible to recover their cost. A better idea is to buy properties in areas that do not require security gates. This expense can only be justified for a complex that is experiencing a great deal of security problems. The gates do not prevent someone jumping the fence or getting through the gate behind a legitimate driver. Tenants do like them and it is nice in your advertising to include that it is a "gated" community. You need to give this one a lot of thought.

Picnic Area

Adding a picnic area near the pool or in some central location on the property is a small expenditure that will be appreciated by your tenants. You only need a picnic table and maybe a barbecue that can be used by tenants. If the property covers a large area then more than one picnic area will probably be needed.

If you have room, putting a picnic table and barbecue in the pool area makes a nice addition. The parents can be hanging out in the picnic area cooking while the kids enjoy the pool. In the complexes where we have included a pool area picnic location, it was well received by tenants.

Pool Furniture

Always supply some patio furniture around the pool. The number of chaise lounges depends on the size of the complex. You can usually get by on one chaise lounge for every eight to 10 units in the complex, plus a few chairs and a few small tables. A patio table with an umbrella and four chairs is also desirable. If you have a picnic table in the pool area, you may not need an additional patio table. The tenant mix can affect the furniture needed. If the pool is getting a great deal of use then you are probably going to need to increase the amount of furniture.

Look for furniture and chaise lounges late in the season. The big home improvement stores are going to want to sell all their summer stock before fall and the Christmas season. As you do your normal shopping at the big stores keep an eye on the patio furniture. Sometime in the late summer it will go on sale, and you will be able to get some replacement pool furniture at great prices.

If you own several apartment complexes of varying levels of quality, you can buy new pool furniture for the best complex you own and hand down the older furniture to the less expensive complexes. Each complex gets furniture better than they had and you only have to buy new furniture for the top property.

Parking Lot Lighting

The tenants always appreciate better parking lot lighting. Make sure the lights are in good working order and all the motion sensors work properly. If there are dark areas in the parking area, improve the lighting with greater wattage or more lights. This is the kind of expense that keeps tenants happy and keeps them in your complex. It is also necessary to schedule your maintenance person to check parking lot lights from time to time. They need to turn on the timer or cover the light sensor to get the parking lights to illuminate. Check them out and replace burned out bulbs as necessary. Your tenants will love it.

Decorator Paint Interiors

We talked about decorator paint colors in a unit as a low cost improvement. The next step in upgrading units by decorator touches is to put in crown moldings or picture moldings. Crown moldings are a decorator trim placed where the walls meet the ceiling. They are put in at an angle and are, most times, painted a trim color different from the walls or ceilings. This type of trim is expensive and requires a skilled handyman to be able to cut the angles needed for the miters to fit properly at the corners. The cost of the molding and the extra labor for its installation makes it a poor investment for apartment owners wanting to spruce up their properties and make them more rentable.

A better choice is picture moldings or chair-rub moldings. Common in homes from the 1800s, picture moldings were run around the room at the ceiling or a short distance from the ceiling. They were used so that pictures could be hung from them on a wire and you would not have to drive nails into the plastered walls. They have not been used for picture hanging for over a hundred years, but are still used for decorator purposes.

Picture or chair-rub moldings are available from the big home improvement stores. They are attractive trim pieces sometimes used near the ceiling as in the past, but more likely used about 3 feet off the floor as a top for wainscoting. Wainscoting is when you decorate the room with a horizontal trim board closer to the floor than the ceiling. The paint colors are different on the upper and lower sections. Many times it is used with wallpaper or wood paneling as one part of the two-part decorating.

We use horizontal picture type molding about eight inches from the ceiling. We use a regular colonial door casing instead of the picture molding because it is the same size and costs half as much. The colonial trim looks great and is easy to buy at the home improvement stores as it is sold in bulk, in long lengths at a good price.

After the molding is in place we paint the ceiling and the molding our usual off-white. Below the molding, we paint the room in a decorator color. This trim and decorator color is used in the living room and entry area of the apartment only. We want it to be the first thing the prospective tenant sees when they enter the unit.

This combination of trim and painting is easy to do and gives your rental units instant appeal over the normal all white walls. This improvement might help increase rents when coupled with other improvement, but it should definitely make apartments easier to rent, reducing vacancies and increasing profits.

Self-Cleaning Ranges

We have put self-cleaning ranges in the upgraded units of our best complex. There are some improvements that are done because that is what is expected in a more expensive renting apartment. Self-cleaning ranges fall into this category. To compete with other higher end units you need to have the amenities tenants expect.

Self-cleaning ranges in lower-end apartments are not cost effective and are not a good investment of your improvement money. Tenants renting smaller, less expensive apartments are not going to expect to have a self-cleaning oven.

That said, one should consider the amount of money a property owner spends on cleaning a range after a tenant moves. It is the single most time consuming part of cleaning an apartment. We replace more ranges than any other appliance. Many times it is just less expensive to buy a new range than to clean, repair and replace parts on the old one. Unless you rent to tenants who only eat cold food, you are going to be cleaning and replacing ranges your entire career in the rental business.

Double Door Refrigerators

Double door refrigerators, or those with ice makers, are in the same classification as the self-cleaning ranges above. In upgraded, higher-priced apartments they are probably justified, but not in lower-end units. Refrigerators are not replaced as often as ranges, so there are fewer opportunities to make this kind of improvement. I would recommend it only be done in top-level apartments where there is a chance to recover your investment.

Ice makers

Ice maker refrigerators require a water line. Depending on the plumbing in the kitchen, this can be a problem requiring more labor costs than it is worth. In one upscale apartment we owned, we did put in ice maker fridges when we did some remodeling. We saved some of the water line costs by running one water line for two apartments. We would run the line from the unit that was most convenient and then, behind the refrigerator, put in a tee to split the line, putting an ice maker valve in each apartment.

Balcony Roof Covers

Many upstairs balcony patios do not have a roof covering them. This is done, of course, to save money during construction. Depending on which direction the apartment faces, the sun can be brutal in the afternoon, making the patio unusable. This is an expensive improvement and there is no way you going to increase profits to make it a good investment. We have added a number of these upper-deck balcony roof covers, but only when there was some other repair needed. If there is a problem with the railing, flooring, or dry rot in the rafter tails, then the additional cost of the roof covering can be justified.

There have been times when we wanted to have winter work for our regular maintenance personnel and there were not enough turnovers to keep them busy. We might put in balcony covers or some other marginally cost effective improvement to keep them working. These may not have resulted in an increased profit at the time, but they certainly make the property more appealing to a prospective tenant or future buyer.

As an alternative to roof covers, we have installed patio umbrellas or roll-down bamboo shades on units that face the afternoon sun. This is a modest cost and more uniform than if tenants provide their own sun covers.

Office Or Pool Restroom

Having a restroom near the office and/or the swimming pool is a very nice feature. There are building codes requiring a restroom at the pool depending on the size of the complex and the distances to the apartments. If a child in the swimming pool has to pee and there is not a convenient restroom, they are not going to pay much attention to codes and are going to pee in the pool.

The addition of a restroom at the swimming pool is a very costly improvement. It will not result in enough reduction in vacancies or increases in rent to even come close to covering the cost of the investment. It will, however, be included in the sales pitch to renters and add to the amenities of the complex if the property is put up for sale.

We have put in a pool restroom in one of our complexes, but the plumbing was already in place, making the job much less of a project. We also incorporated a pool restroom, shower and drinking fountain in conjunction with the expansion of the complex office. This kind of large investment in the property is part of our overall philosophy of making our properties better. It is a use of profits, putting them back into the complex in the form of improvements designed to make the property more desirable to new tenants and future buyers.

Be sure to have the restroom for tenants only, keyed to the tenant key for the property. This makes it a private restroom and not a public restroom, which would have to be ADA compliant. We want the restroom to be handicap-equipped and compatible with ADA requirements, but if it is a public restroom it opens you up to lawsuits from ADA attorneys.

Office Addition

The addition of a separate office for the complex falls into the same classification of improvement as the pool restroom. You are not going to recoup your investment in profits, but you are making your property nicer and more efficient for your manager. A reasonably sized, inviting and businesslike office makes a good impression on a person looking for an apartment. A small office without enough room for furniture or storage gives the impression that the complex is a second-rate community. Like the pool restroom, this is a good place to put profits that will probably pay off some time in the future, by making the property fall into a higher class of investment.

The office is one of the first things a prospective tenant sees at the complex. Make sure it makes your complex look professional. Nice furniture, window covers and accessories in the office will make it look warm and inviting. You do not want your office to be a turnoff to a new prospect even before they see an apartment.

Golf Carts

On larger properties we supply a golf cart for the manager and the workers. The cost of the golf cart will not cause apartments to rent quicker or rent for more money. The cart does make it easier for the manager and the workers, painters, and handymen to work more efficiently. Man-hours can be reduced by providing the golf cart to move repair parts, paint and tools to the job site quicker. It is not a big saving on one job, but in a year it can add up to considerable time saved. The cart is also terrific in moving remodel or turnover debris from the apartment to the dumpster.

Carports

Carports are a very nice feature at an apartment complex. Many areas of the United States are bathed in sunshine all summer. The average summer temperature in our area is in the mid-90s and many days reach over 100 degrees. A car parked in the sun gets hot enough to bake bread.

It is kind of a push whether the cost of the carports can justify enough extra rent to pay for them. As always, it is hard to measure whether they can reduce vacancies, but I would believe reduced vacancies should be expected. It only takes about a one or two percent increase in rents to cover the cost of this improvement. See below for the formula to figure what a return in increased rents needs to be to break even on an improvement.

I am a strong believer in carports. I always like plenty of parking and at least one covered parking place for each apartment. It is one of my must-have items. If we are considering the purchase of a complex without carports, then I am going to figure in the cost to add them into the price.

Covered Entrance To Office Or Mailboxes

Many times during the construction of apartments, as a cost-saving move, a covered entrance area or covered porch is not included at the entrance to the office. This is also a problem where the group mailboxes are located. This is a poor way to save construction costs by making it necessary for managers and tenants to stand in the rain to get their mail or enter the office.

In apartments we bought that had this problem, we extended the office roof to protect the front door from weather or moved the mailboxes to a location under a roof. With a little thought and planning, and by incorporating planters at this location, you can significantly improve the look of the office area and make it and the mailbox area much more pleasant for use by current tenants and more attractive for prospective tenants.

Be sure to check with the Post Office department before moving mailboxes. We usually just check with the mail carrier and find out what will make their job easier. Many mailboxes open from the back, so allowing ample room behind the mailboxes will be necessary and appreciated.

You are going to want plenty of light at these locations. People will be picking up their mail in the evening hours and a well-lit area is important to give them a feeling of security.

Summary of These Improvements

There is some value in these "not cost effective" improvements. They keep tenants happy and not wanting to move. There may be some value in renting units more easily. This part is hard to measure. The overall look of a property and the amenities that make apartment living more pleasant will certainly help units to rent more quickly.

If even one apartment rents just a few weeks earlier, or one tenant does not move because of one of these improvements, it will result in an increase of hundreds of dollars of additional profit for the company. In the case of preventing the move of a tenant, there are also savings in fewer turnovers preformed in the year. This is all hard to measure, but when in doubt, it is always acceptable to make well thought out improvements that will make your property better looking and more functional.

In our duplex days, we put all our profits back into the properties in the form of improvements. Many are listed above. We believed that it was like putting money in the bank. We felt that improving appearances and making properties easier to care for would make the properties worth more sometime in the future. We were not sure if it would happen in our lifetimes, but we were sure we were making the right investments of company profits.

We turned our class C duplex properties into B properties with our efforts. We originally never thought about selling our duplexes, but when real estate values skyrocketed in the mid-2000s, fortunately, we got some great advice that it was time to sell. Because of the years of fixing up our places, the great way they looked, and the hysteria of that time in real estate, they sold quickly and at a good price. All the improvements that appeared at the time to cost more than they were worth suddenly became a terrific investment. Duplexes are different from apartments. Duplex values are not as locked into Cap rates as apartment complexes are, and the value many times is just how much a buyer is willing to pay to own them. An apartment complex that looks great is also going to be easier to sell even though it may not "pencil" out based on income, expenses and Cap rate.

Some Improvements You Just Have to do Sometimes

Sometimes improvements are not really discretionary but fall into the Capital Improvement category because it just makes sense to do them. If you are going to have to spend money for a repair and you have the opportunity to make the property better by an additional investment, it may be a good use of funds. For example, putting in ceramic tile to replace a vinyl kitchen floor, as discussed previously, can save money later on. It would be less expensive just to replace the vinyl, but the extra expense to upgrade the floor to ceramic tile makes sense.

Cabinet Door Replacement

Cabinets, like most other parts of apartments, are built with the least expensive materials available at the time of construction. During construction there is no desire to make the property more damage proof, only to make the property produce a bigger profit for the builder. Many cabinet doors and drawer fronts are made from cheap wood, particleboard or even cardboard, covered with a contact paper made to look like wood grain.

When brand new they do not look too bad, but they will not hold up to the abuse of apartment life.

When it becomes necessary to repair cabinet doors, it is just about impossible to match the original colors or look. At this point we will replace all the cabinet doors and drawer fronts for an entire unit. We then save all the serviceable doors for use on other units as cabinet doors become damaged in the future.

We could replace the cabinet doors and drawer fronts with a similar cheap type door, but this is a situation where putting higher quality doors in the unit will pay off with longer life and less need to repair doors In the future.

Replacement cabinet doors are available from many sources. Find a company specializing in a wide range of types of doors and finishes. This is a big investment. The cost to replace all the doors in an apartment unit is just about the same as the rent for one apartment for one month. Keep in mind, you are going to have to spend money one way or another to repair or replace cabinet doors. Doing it right will make the apartment much more appealing, and will give you a supply of doors to put into storage for replacements of damaged doors in other units.

Countertop Refinishing

Formica countertops take a beating in apartments. Tenants are not always careful, and even when we supply them with cutting boards they may chop right on the Formica countertop. These countertops are also susceptible to water damage from liquid getting into the miter forty-five degree corners. Once water gets in the crack and the particleboard expands, there is no easy fix to get it looking new.

There are companies that will grind down swollen parts of the counter, fill in low spots with epoxy filler, and then finish the entire counter in an epoxy top coating with a color of your choice. This fix is inexpensive when compared to changing out the entire counter and replacing with the same Formica, ceramic tile, or more expensive granite type tops.

It is possible to make the old Formica look fair with silicone, but you really do not want this kind of repair to your property. This is a case of biting the bullet and springing for the cost of at least the refinishing option. If the unit is in an upgraded apartment complex then you might consider the additional cost of either ceramic tile, granite or some of the newer manufactured products. This would definitely put the repair into the Capital Improvement category, which might be justified in some cases.

Appliance Upgrades

Generally, appliances are replaced as needed with the same quality as the old unit. However, if you are dealing with upgraded apartments, which can demand higher rents, then it may be a good idea to upgrade the appliances when replacements are needed. The upgrade cost is only the difference between the standard appliance and the upgraded one, and it may be that little additional money is necessary to obtain a nice upgrade to the apartment.

Exterior Wood Siding

Wood fir exterior siding, commonly called T-111 siding, has been used on apartments for many years. When I first got into building, all exterior siding was either redwood or cedar. Both are resistant to dry rot and excellent for exteriors. Somewhere along the line, large developers and contractors building many houses got the codes changed to allow Douglas fir exterior plywood siding. This siding is very susceptible to dry rot damage and is always a problem for apartment owners who have it on their buildings.

The other major siding problem in the horizontal pressed board siding. It is made to look like lap boards and comes in either single horizontal boards or three or four horizontal narrower boards together. The material is a cardboard, pressed board covered in a thin layer of a wood grain top. This material is probably more of a problem than the plywood as it is a big water absorber.

Both materials are bad news for apartment owners. Water can get behind either material at corners or where horizontal trim boards cover splices. The only fix is to repair bad sections on a constant basis and keep the property well caulked and well painted. Both are costly for the company. There is no cost effective way to replace these materials. Pulling all of the siding off and replacing with a dry rot resistant material is an astronomical cost. We even looked into patching the T-111 plywood siding then covering it in stucco. Again, the price was beyond bearable.

If you have bought a property with either of these type siding materials, you are just going to have to live with it and pay the money to keep it reasonable. We probably will not consider purchasing a new property if it has either of these type siding materials unless we allow enough money at the time of purchase to replace it all. Not many sellers are willing to cover this cost, but at this point in our lives, we are not going to deal with siding you just cannot afford to repair properly.

How to Figure if it's Worth it

If you are really trying to make an improvement pay for itself, then you need to calculate how much the project is going to cost in parts, labor, lost rent, etc. Then you need to survey other apartments in your area to see how much this improvement is going to increase rents. When you are comfortable with these two figures, you can use the formula that the return in increased rent has to be at least two percent of the cost of the improvement per month.

For example, if an improvement costs $5000, then you need to be getting at least $100 more per month in rent to justify the cost. This is a bare minimum to have a reasonable return on the improvement. If you got $75 more per month in rent it would figure out to about a 7 percent cap rate return. A better-than-average cap rate is needed because most of these improvements will require additional replacement costs during their lives.

As an example, suppose you put an upgrade of a washer-dryer into an apartment. If the cost is $5000, then you really need to get your money back in about five years. In that period of time, either the washer or dryer, or both, may need to be replaced or have major repairs. If you were able to get the $100 per month in additional rent, you would recoup the $5000 investment in 50 months. After that, it would be a profitable improvement.

Another way to look at it is to consider if you could increase rents by only $50 per month it would take longer to recoup your initial investment, but it would pay for itself eventually. In addition, as the value of a property is a function of income; therefore an increase of $50 per month in income would increase the value of the property by about $5000. If there is space in an apartment and electrical and plumbing can handle them, adding a washer and dryer to a unit is usually a good investment.

There are certainly a number of variables in these figures and some guesstimating, but this kind of improvement should be cost effective or it is probably not worth doing.

Chapter 9

CONSTRUCTION

Age of a Building from Construction Used

There are constant changes in building construction. These changes are either from new materials, new ways of building or new trends in design. Most changes make the building better, less expensive and more energy efficient. It is possible to estimate the age of a building by the building components it contains. Of course, there could be remodels or changes made after the original construction, but most of the basics can give you an idea of the time period in which it was built.

Windows

Windows are a good gauge of a structure's age. Windows have changed often and are easy to spot from the outside. From the early 1900s until the early 50s, windows were "double hung," meaning they were a wood frame that went up and down and had a lock in the middle. Most times there was just one piece of glass in each section.

In the 1950s, we saw the introduction of steel casement windows. These were used until the late 1950s. These windows were characterized by a crank that opened the window from one side. The windows usually had several panes. These steel windows suffered from the possibility of rust and the need to keep them painted. They were quickly replaced by aluminum sliding windows in a plain aluminum color, known as a mill finish. Aluminum windows quickly took over almost all window sales because of their low cost, lack of rusting, and not needing to be painted.

Aluminum windows would dominate the market for almost the next 50 years. Even though these windows were used for a long time, the colors of the windows can give you an idea of when the building was built. The plain aluminum mill finish was used in the 1960s. By the 70s, the aluminum was now a very dark color known as "bronze." In the 80s, the aluminum was primarily white. White vinyl windows became common in the 1990s and are used today most of the time. However, you still find new construction using the white aluminum windows occasionally.

These are the main changes in windows that would have been used in apartment construction. It is always possible that a contractor got a deal on some older style windows or that the windows were changed along the way. This is just a rough guideline to be used along with other clues to verify the age of a structure.

Interior Doors

Again, change was slow for the first half of the 20th century, with panel painted doors used most of the time. Doors at the beginning of the 1900s were painted multi-panel doors of solid wood. This was a very high quality door by today's standards. By the 1930s, the doors had cheapened and were constructed with horizontal panels. Around this time, some were made with a frame and a single panel. These were still made of all wood and painted.

Table of Construction Variations by Years

	1920	1930	1940	1950	1960	1970	1980	1990	2000	2010
WINDOWS	Wood, double hung, painted			Casement	Aluminum, mill, sliding		Aluminum, bronze, sliding	Aluminum, white, sliding or double hung		Vinyl, white, sliding
INTERIOR DOORS	Wood, multi-panel, painted		Wood, single panel, painted		Wood, flat, stained		Flat, masonite painted		Six panel, painted	
BASE BOARDS	Tall with Deco top, painted		4 inch, flat, painted		2.25 inch, Oak		4 inch, Colonial, stained or painted			
		Medium tall, painted		2.25 inch, stained or paint			3.25 inch, painted or no base at all			
CABINETS	Wood, shaker type, paint	Wood, flat, painted		Steel	Wood, light stain		Wood, dark stain	Wood, medium stain	Wood, painted white	

WINDOWS

Double hung Window goes up and down	Casement Window Cranks in and out		Sliding Window goes back and forth	

DOORS

Multi panel	Multi panel	Single panel	Flat	Six panel
to 1920s	1920s to 1940s	1930s to 1950s	1950s to present	1980s to present

By the 1960s, painted Masonite flat doors were common. In this vintage we also saw a textured Masonite that came in a fake medium-stained wood grain color. By the 70s, like the cabinets, doors were a very dark stain color. White, flat, smooth doors continued to be popular from this time to the present because they are easy to work with, paint nicely and are inexpensive.

In the 1990s, we saw a pressed Masonite, textured door that looked like the old panel doors of a hundred years ago. The most common is the six-panel door, but they can come in several styles. These are very popular, as they are not expensive, but look like an expensive wood panel door. These doors are readily available today at all the home improvement stores.

Baseboards

From the early 1900s to 1950, baseboards were tall and painted. They began very tall. We own a building that was built in 1903 and the baseboards are about 9 inches tall. By 1950 they were 4 to 6 inches. In the 60s, pre-finished baseboards in a clear lacquer finish over oak become the standard. These baseboards were 2¼ inches tall. This pre-finished base was used for a long time, along with a cheaper version of the 2¼-inch base that was painted. Most rental units built in the 60s to 80s will have the painted 2¼ - inch base.

Somewhere in the 80s and into the 90s the base grew to 3¼ inches. Stained baseboards would be found in custom homes, while painted ones were more common in apartments. These were all flat baseboards with a slight curve at the top. From the 90s on, a colonial style base would be used. Baseboards by this time were made mostly of re-processed trash of some sort and known as MDF. It is kind of a combination of cardboard, glue and paper: not much quality but low cost. Apartments built in the last 10 years could very well have the colonial style base.

Often, as a money saving technique, builders would leave the baseboards off entirely allowing the drywall to extend to the floor. False economy of course, as the bottom of the wall can get beat up from vacuum cleaners; and inexpensive apartment carpet is not thick enough to hide the gap showing under the wall. This could occur in any time period, but is more likely to be found since about 1980.

Cabinets

From the early 1900s to the 1950s, most cabinets were of painted wood construction. The older ones were a frame-type door (called shaker style now) and later became more of a solid flat panel door. In the 50s, some steel cabinets were used along with the painted wood. By the late 50s and into the 60s cabinets were built of hardwood with a stain finish. The wood was usually birch, ash or oak and the finish was usually natural. The finish in the 60s was very light in color with just a slight yellow tint from the clear lacquer.

By the 1970s the staining had become dark, often very dark: some were almost black. Oak was the most used wood but birch was also used. Ash was used far less than oak or birch. In apartments, of course, they were still using particleboard covered with a contact paper material, but the color followed the stain colors in single-family homes. An apartment complex built in the 70s would probably have a dark contact paper on their particleboard cabinet doors.

The 1980s saw stain colors lighten to a medium walnut color. Most custom homes had oak cabinets with this medium color stain. Apartments would probably be using a medium oak colored contact paper in this decade. Here and there were exceptions such as white wash finish, but the vast majority was medium oak or walnut stain color.

The medium stain colors for cabinets would continue until the present. Modern custom homes can have just about anything an architect or owner can think of. White cabinet doors similar to the 1950s are back and common. They became popular again after 2000 and are often found in new apartment construction. Apartment grade cabinets in solid white are economical and favored by builders.

Flat Roofs

Apartments build in the 1960s and 1970s commonly had flat roofs. This was done to save money on the construction of the buildings. Flat roofs are the least expensive roof, but they often leak and will need to be repaired and/or replaced much more often that a slope roof. If a property has a flat roof, we will not buy it, period.

Kitchen Countertops

Ceramic tile was used on countertops until the 1960s. Formica tops became the standard soon after and are still the standard on most apartments today. After 2000, you might find some granite or other upgraded materials on a counter top, but those are going to be used only in the top class A complexes.

Other Construction Variations by Age

Although not necessarily used to date a building, many features of construction have changed through the years. Below are listed some of the more important ones.

Lead Paint

Before 1979, lead was a common ingredient in paint. Lead is a poison and the inhalation or consumption of paint chips or paint dust could be harmful to one's health. In 1979, it became against the law to manufacture paint containing lead. As environmental concerns have grown more and more stringent, regulations have come down on repainting, sanding and otherwise working on buildings built prior to 1979 that might disturb the paint.

Air Conditioning

Air conditioning has not been around that long. Buildings built prior to 1960 would be the exception if they had any air conditioning. Even in the 1960s, many apartments did not have central air conditioning, or they had wall units. Wall A/C units that have been retrofitted into older apartments are common today. By the mid-60s air conditioning began to be found more often and by the 70s central air conditioning was common.

Floors

Floors were all raised wood until the 60s. Hardwood floor over the wood subfloor was mandatory on FHA homes halfway through the 1900s. Slab floors began in the 60s, and by the 70s they were commonplace for apartments. Custom high-end homes might still use a raised wood floor, but that is the exception.

Energy

Few homes even had insulation before 1960. There was no air conditioning, and heating fuel was inexpensive. The advent of A/C went hand in hand with buildings installing full insulation. With the oil problems of the 1970's, energy efficiency became a major issue for building construction. By the 80s, dual pane windows were used and they soon became mandatory by building departments. New building codes dictated the energy efficiency of new construction, making buildings more air tight and better insulated. Air conditioning units were required to be more and more efficient as the years progressed, creating headaches for landlords dealing with replacement A/C units.

Bathtubs

Originally, bathtubs were made of cast iron. The good ones are still cast iron today. In the middle of the 1900s, steel tubs came on the market and were commonly used in apartments. They looked like the cast iron but were much less expensive. The big problem with them was that they chipped when something was dropped on them. We have all seen tubs, kitchen sinks, and lavatories from this era with large black chips in them. This is a case of false economy: the tub costs less, but fixing a chip in one is no easy task. Steel bathtubs are still available today for the unsophisticated buyer.

Fiberglass or plastic tubs have been around since about 1970. A great feature of the plastic tub is that many times they come complete with the walls. This one-piece construction makes for an easy installation and a fully water proof back. Fiberglass and plastic tubs are common in apartments and are used almost exclusively.

Helpful Hints on Common Repairs

Hanging A Door

The first step in installing a pre-hung door is to check the opening. Measure first to verify that the height and width is correct for the door size. If the opening size is correct then it is best to check plumb and level with a long level for the sides and a short level for the header. You are determining how square the opening is and what shimming might be necessary. Most important is the side where the hinges will be. This needs to be vertical. With your long level, determine if the top hinge or the bottom hinge will need shims. The stud might be perfect, but most times a shim will be needed on one hinge location to bring it into vertical alignment with the other. Measure the amount needed and cut the shim ahead of time, nailing it in the general vicinity of the hinge. When the door and frame are put into the opening, one part of the jamb will rest against the wood and the other will touch the shim, making the hinge-side of the frame perfectly vertical.

Put the door and frame into the hole against the wood on the hinge side. Place a few shims between the jamb and walls to hold it in place. Do not nail it at this time. You need to check the square of the opening and the levelness of the floor. It may be necessary to raise the jamb on the hinge-side to make sure the small crack between the door and the jamb is even around the door. Once you are assured that the crack is acceptable, you can nail the jamb to the structural wood with an 8d finish nail at the top and bottom hinge. This is enough to secure the door. The rest of the installation is done with shims at strategic locations and nailed to keep the crack between the door and jamb even.

To finish the installation, nail between the shims with an 8d finish nail. Set and use a bar to adjust the jamb until the crack is perfect. Once the casings are installed, the jamb will be locked into position.

If you are working on an existing door that rubs at the top or side, nail an 8d finish nail through the jamb top or side into the header or trimmer studs. Use a short piece of 2x4 on the jamb where you did the nailing and hit it firmly with a framing hammer. This will usually move the jamb enough to eliminate the rubbing. Finish by countersinking any nails, then touch up with spackle and paint.

Baseboards Installation

Baseboards are the last thing to do before painting. They are done after ceramic tile floors or vinyl flooring. Many older apartments use a 2¼-inch flat baseboard with a slight curve at the top. Later, 3¼-inch flat baseboards were used. When upgrading baseboards or installing them where there were none to begin with, we use a 3¼ inch colonial base. These will match most baseboards used in recent years. They are mostly flat with a routed top back into the wall.

I like to measure all the bases, allowing for an 1/8 inch short in the miters. When cutting these 45-degree corners, the boards have a way of getting bigger than you might expect. By cutting a little short, they usually are very close to perfect and easily finished with just a little caulk. I cut the entire base in our shop on a chop saw with a long table to support the base. They are numbered on the back to match the rooms. It is easy to give them a coat of paint in the shop on the bottom half of the base. The next day they are ready to install and should go in quickly. Once placed, you need to spackle any nail holes, caulk the corners and caulk the top of the baseboard if they do not meet the wall completely. A coat of paint on the top half seals the base to the wall.

Three-Way Switches

Three-way and four-way switches are used when you want a light or series of lights controlled at more than one switch location. They are commonly used in rentals at each end of a hall so you can turn the light on or off from either end. It is called a three-way switch because it has three connections on the back. Each switch only has two positions, on and off. The four-way switches, if used in between, have four connections on the back. Four way switches are used when you want to be able to control the light with more than two switch locations. In rental properties, four-way switches are seldom seen.

The basic wiring for the three-way is to begin with the switch at one end with the hot line coming in to it. On the back of the switch is one connection labeled "Common." This hot leg or line connection is attached to the screw marked Common. Between the two three-way switches are two wires; they are usually a red and a black, but the colors are not important. The two wires between the switches are attached to the two connections on the switch that are not marked Common.

From the second switch, the wire that goes to the light is connected to the Common connection. If a four-way switch is used, it will be between the two three-ways. The two wires from the first three-way switch will be connected to the four-way switch. From the four-way switch, the two wires will continue from it to the final three-way switch. There can only be two three-way switches controlling one light, but there can be an unlimited number of four-way switches in between.

The most common problem with a three-way combination is a bad switch or a loose wire. There is not much chance that the wires are on the wrong connection unless the lights never worked in the past.

Ceramic Tile

Depending on how many vacant units we have at the time, we may replace old vinyl floors with ceramic tile. Our regular workers have become proficient in the installation of floor tile, and we supply the saws and equipment needed to do a professional job. Tile floors look nicer and will outlast vinyl. Most apartments will be constructed of the least expensive and thinnest vinyl possible and it will not hold up to tenant abuse. We like to upgrade our units with ceramic floor tile in the entry hall, kitchens, bathrooms and laundry areas.

In some units we have done the entire kitchen, entry, dining, hall and bathroom. This reduces the amount of carpet in a unit and makes it easy to replace just a room or two of carpet instead of the entire apartment. The carpet in bedrooms will usually last two to three times longer than the high traffic areas of the entry, living room and hall. This savings in carpet replacement will offset some of the cost of the ceramic tile floors.

Laying out the tile in a brick-like pattern, or diagonally, will hide non-square walls. We buy tile by the pallet and try to keep the same color and pattern for as many units as possible. We save replacement tiles in storage for any repairs that might be needed.

Ceramic tile floors are not for everyone, but renters love it and our workers have made it easy to make this upgrade to our properties.

Wall Repairs to Painting

Wall Repairs

The sequence for wall repairs begins with any structural work. This is not normally required, but if it is then it is done first. After structural work is completed, then any major drywall repairs are done. Plasterwork needs several steps with drying time in between, so it needs to be started early in the turnover process, preferably, as soon as the structural work is completed.

When the drywall work is finished, any non-carpet floor work is done. This would include both vinyl and ceramic tile floors. Ceramic tile and vinyl are done at this time because baseboards will need to be installed after the floor covers and before painting. Repairs or replacement of doors, shelving and trim can often times be done at the same time as tile, but the entire tile, vinyl, and trim work needs to be done before baseboards are completed. Once baseboards are installed, we move to the actual paint prep work.

Paint Prep

I like to start by sweeping all the walls and ceilings to remove dust, dirt and cobwebs before spackling any holes in the walls. A more thorough rough cleaning will follow the paint prep work. After the walls are swept, I use a scraping tool and putty knife combination to knock off any high spots and fill any low spots with spackle. Only use enough spackle to fill the hole. There should be a bare minimum after you wipe off any excess with your finger. You do not want to spackle so much that it fills in the wall texture, which will leave a flat spot after painting. You should not need any sanding if you use just a small amount of spackle. You will also occasionally need a hammer and screwdriver to remove nails and screws before scraping and filling.

Work your way around all the rooms. When done, retrace your route around the unit with a caulk gun, filling cracks as needed. I like to have a roll of paper towels and a paper trash bag or trash container to wipe up excess caulk and dispose of the paper towel. You do not want to get caulk on the carpet.

Spackle and caulk take about an hour to dry. By the time you get through the unit the first area you worked on should be almost dry. The walls are ready to paint, but we move to our rough clean up next. We want to get all the dirt, dust and trash out of the unit before painting. This will include any debris from earlier construction that has not been cleaned up.

Rough Cleanup

Rough cleanup is primarily done to get the dirt out of an apartment prior to painting. We do not want paint rollers or brushes picking up dirt and spreading it on the walls. If the unit is going to be spray painted, we do not want dust blown around during painting and ending up on the walls.

Rough cleanup includes shop vacuuming the insides of cabinets, drawers and window tracks. Carpets should also be vacuumed along the walls at the baseboards. This will pick up any small plaster pieces, spackle or sanding dust. You do not vacuum the entire carpet area at this time, just the parts where painting is going to take place. Carpet will be vacuumed and cleaned as part of the final cleaning.

While the cleaning person is in the unit doing the rough cleanup, a few other cleaning jobs can be done. The cleaning of the range and refrigerator can be done at this time, as well as the insides of the cabinets. These cleaning jobs can be part of the final cleaning also, but they tend to be bigger cleaning jobs and since the cleaning person is in the unit already doing the rough cleanup, it is a good time to get them out of the way. The painting will most likely not be scheduled until the following workday giving the cleaning person a day's work instead of a couple hours.

Drop Cloths

The general rule is that painters never ruin carpet, but carpet installers always screw up paint. Drop cloths are part of the reason. A good, careful painter only needs a can of paint, a brush and a small box to catch drips and spills. When using a roller you need more protection, because the roller is going to dribble and toss little splatters of paint around. I like to use drop cloths, newspapers, cardboard, etc., around the edges of the wall to catch drips. Be sure your paint pan is on a drop cloth or cardboard that is connected to the perimeter of carpet protection. Do not carry your roller over unprotected carpet. From the drip pan to the wall, there should be something on the floor under the path to where you are going to work.

The protection around the walls is only a couple feet wide or less. It just needs to protect the carpet near the wall. The rule is that paint goes on the drop cloth and your feet stay on the carpet. Do not walk on the drop cloth, cardboard, etc. If you get paint on the bottom of your shoes then all the protection is going to be wasted. If you need to use a ladder, it has to be set on the carpet only or on the drop cloth only. Never go back and forth. If you get paint on the bottom legs of the ladder and then set it on the carpet after, you have wasted your efforts to protect the carpet. If you are not the careful type or the entire unit is going to be spray painted, then it will be necessary to cover all the floor areas as part of the masking of the apartment for painting.

Priming

Most dirty or faded areas, new caulk, small plaster areas, or spackle do not need priming before flat painting. If the wall has an oily stain like ketchup, lipstick or another hard-to-cover substance, you will need to use a special stain killer primer first. Special fast-drying primers in spray cans are available for covering difficult stains. Most of these contain shellac, which is an oil-based that will cover almost everything. Check with your paint store professionals and they will know what you need.

If you are painting flat paint on new walls or walls with large plaster repairs, then it will be necessary to prime the wall first or give the wall two coats. The plaster areas are going to soak in the paint and cause uneven and un-satisfactory results.

Walls that will be painted in semi-gloss paint that contain new caulk, plaster or spackle work will need to be primed before final painting. If it is on an existing wall then it is only necessary to prime the newly repaired areas. If you fail to prime these areas, all the repairs will show up as less shiny than the rest of the wall. The general rule is you need to prime repairs on shiny walls but not on flat walls. If using eggshell, satin or low sheen paint, you will still need to prime any new plasterwork, but spackle spots should be fine.

Regular wall primers will dry in about 30 minutes and can be recoated in an hour. The spray cans of stain blocker dry very fast and recoating can be done in about 30 minutes.

Painting

Painting is a big deal for me. I want the paint where it is supposed to be and not be where it is not supposed to be. Sounds logical and simple, but in practice it rarely happens without someone looking over the shoulder of the painter. The painter should not drip paint on the carpet or get paint on door handles, hinges or strike plates. I have checked a job on more than one occasion where the painter was rolling the walls of the kitchen and hit the bottom of the dark brown cabinets with the roller, getting white paint all over the bottom of the cabinet. Sure, you could only see it if you had your head low enough, but it was very poor workmanship. I have a simple rule: get the paint on the walls, doors and trim, and nowhere else, period

Often we will hire a professional painter to spray a unit, or we can use our regular workers to roll and brush the apartment. We decide which way to go based on whether it is a full paint job, best for spray work, or a touch up or partial paint job which is easier with a roller and brush. We also consider how much workload we have and how many units will need painting. If our regular workers have plenty of work then we may decide to go with an outside painting company. The below guidelines are generally for painting with a roller and brush, but some apply to spray work as well.

When painting walls, always roll first and brush after. The roller will get very close to corners, and it only takes a little brushing to finish. If you brush first you will spend more time and paint a larger area than necessary. Painting with a brush is much slower than painting with a roller. Do not try to use a paint pad to apply paint to areas next to trim or base boards. The pad will get paint from the edge of the pad onto the area you do not want to paint. The paint pads may work for the tops of casings and trim, but I find it is hard to beat the old-fashioned brush for cutting into corners, trim and baseboards.

When using a roller, apply the paint horizontally first about three feet wide, and then roll through the horizontal line of paint vertically to distribute the paint. This makes for a more even covering of paint than just painting in only one direction. Each time the roller passes through the horizontal area it picks up more paint and distributes it to the wall. Use only a light pressure to spread the paint. When the roller no longer easily covers the wall in paint then it is time for the next horizontal line of paint.

Keep enough paint on the roller. Let the paint transfer to the wall gently. Never try to push harder to get paint on the wall. The paint should flow off the roller with only light pressure. If you push hard on the roller it may seem that you are getting more coverage, but as you release pressure the roller will take paint off the wall, leaving an uneven coverage. Paint flows to where there is the least paint. If the roller or brush is full of paint being used on an unpainted wall the paint flows easily to the wall. However, if you use a dry or nearly dry brush or roller on a freshly painted wall, the brush or roller will pick up paint from the wall, leaving a non-uniform coating. Many times, this will result in a noticeable streaked look when the paint is dry. Keep plenty of paint on the roller and add more paint often. If using a brush you should also use plenty of paint. Try to keep the paint limited to the bottom half of the bristles. After you dip the brush in the paint, wipe off one side of the bristles on the side of the can. There should not be so much paint on the brush that it drips.

It is usually better to paint all the flat areas first and the shiny paint after. While painting the flat, you should paint the edges of door casings, windowsills and other door and trim items that will be painted in semi-gloss or trim paint later. The flat wall paint can get on the trim with no problem. When painting the trim after with a brush or 3-inch roller, you only need to paint the front of the trim and leave the sides or edges in the flat paint.

Clean Up

Remove drop cloths, cardboard, and anything else you brought into the apartment to do the painting. Masking tape should be removed as soon as the paint is only a little dry. If you let paint dry on masking tape, the tape will not come off easily and will sometimes pull paint off with it. Never allow the old-style, cream-colored masking tape to remain on a surface longer than a day. It will stick tight and be very difficult to remove. The new blue masking tape will not stick to walls like the old stuff and is less of a problem.

We allow cleaning of brushes in the kitchen sink, but always clean the sink immediately after. Do not let paint or residue from the brushes dry in a sink. If you use the sink, clean the sink. When closing a paint can or five-gallon container, always clean the edge first so the lid will seal properly. It only takes a short time to do it right and clean the top of the can. A buildup of paint on the top of a container will make it impossible for the lid to seal the can, and the paint left in the can will dry out. Trying to touch up paint with a partially full can of lumpy paint is no fun. Like most jobs in this business and other businesses, do it right the first time.

Caulk, Silicone or Spackle

These are all fill materials used in different parts of construction. Spackle is used to fill small holes in wood and trim boards. It will dry firm in about 30 to 45 minutes and is easily sanded smooth. It is commonly used to fill nail holes when installing baseboards, casings and trim. Spackle is far better than caulk for these applications, as it can be sanded level with the wood, primed and painted to become invisible. Spackle is the primary material used to fill nail holes and small defects in dry wall before painting.

Painter's caulk is used to fill large cracks and joints prior to painting. It is paintable and is dry enough to paint in about an hour. It is a very commonly used product in many painting situations. It is applied with a caulking gun. Caulk is sometimes used in place of spackle, but it cannot be as smooth as spackle and therefore shows up as an imperfection. Do not use caulk to fill holes in trim or baseboards. Painter's caulk can be cleaned off the fingers with soap and water.

It is now possible to buy caulk in colors to match Kelly Moore standard paint colors. This allows you to fill cracks and caulk where necessary without needing to prime and paint after. I have not seen these custom caulk colors at other paint stores yet, but they will probably be available from all the leading paint companies in the near future.

Silicone is used when it is important for the seal to be waterproof. Silicone dries to a rubber-like finish and is waterproof. Silicone cannot be painted and therefore is not recommended for use where painting is going to be necessary. Its primary use is around tubs, sealing the tub to the shower walls or to the floor. It is also used to seal the toilet to the floor and the counter top edge to the wall. White silicone is usually used, but in some cases, the clear might be appropriate.

Silicone is also used as an adhesive. It is very sticky and excellent for bonding surfaces together. We use clear silicone to glue cove vinyl base to the wall. White silicone is usually used for around a tub and clear silicone is used around the shower glass door. Silicone comes in caulk gun size tubes for large jobs and a small squeeze tube for smaller jobs. The smaller tubes are especially good around sinks and faucets when working in tight spaces.

Decorator Paint and Trim Boards at Ceilings

Crown moldings have been used for ages to trim off the top of the wall at the ceiling. They have a very attractive look, but are difficult to cut and install, which puts them out of budget for most apartment decorating.

We have used a different version of near-ceiling trim. Instead of the complicated compound miter cuts needed for crown moldings, we use a colonial casing horizontally around the wall about 8 inches from the ceiling. Because these are flat, the measuring and cuts are much easier. The colonial casing material is less expensive than the crown molding trim. We paint the trim board and the ceilings our standard off-white color, and below the horizontal trim, we paint in a decorator color.

We begin with the normal ceilings and wall already painted off-white. A mark is made on the wall at approximately the middle of the horizontal trim board. The decorator paint on the lower part of the wall is then painted to this mark. The colonial trim boards are cut to size, primed, and painted before installation. They are installed using a short spacer board about six inches long. The spacer is used to keep the horizontal trim parallel to the ceiling.

After the trim is in place, it is spackled and sanded. It will need to be primed over the spackle areas and finished with our standard off-white paint. It is only necessary to paint the areas on the trim board that were primed. We use an eggshell paint for walls and trim, so getting paint on the wall above the trim is not a problem.

Commercial Demising Walls to T-Bar Ceilings

A demising wall in commercial property is a non-bearing wall constructed up to the T-bar ceiling to divide space to fit a tenants needs. New walls are often required to meet the needs of a new tenant in a commercial property. T-bar ceilings hang on wires from the top and are not structurally suited for attaching walls. Walls are constructed under the T-bar ceiling and are fairly substantial, but of a temporary nature so they can change for a future occupant.

The first step is to protect the carpet or flooring with a sheet of plastic. Everything is built on the plastic until ready for the finish cove base, at which time the plastic is trimmed at the wall line. The 2x4 wall is built up to the T-bar, but constructed 1/8 inch short. You do not want the framing for the wall to touch the T-bar as it can raise it a little. Always run at least one empty ¾ inch raceway (empty conduit) for future phone or computer lines in any new wall.

When dry wall is applied to the new wall, the sheets are installed vertically, taking care to just touch the T-bar. Installing vertically reduces the amount of plaster at the top near the ceiling. After the plasterwork is completed, take a straight edge along the T-bar to trim anything that is too high and will intrude into the ceiling tile area. In corners we do not tape and plaster, but rather use painters caulk to fill the crack between the new wall and the existing walls. This will minimize the plaster texture overlapping onto old walls.

Any plaster that gets on the T-bar itself is easily wiped off, but the ceiling tiles must be protected from texture overspray. You cannot tape to the ceiling tiles to mask them. Use thin cardboard to mask, or remove tiles when spraying texture. It takes a little extra effort to keep the ceilings looking nice during construction, plastering and painting.

Construction Knowledge Quiz

I developed a short quiz on construction for potential handymen looking to work for us. It is basic, but does give an idea of the depth of knowledge the applicant has. The quiz is certainly not complete, but it is enough to rule out a weak candidate. The answers are in *Italics*.

1. How far apart are the studs in normal wall construction?
    16 inches
2. What size circuit breaker is normal for an electric dryer?
    30 amps
3. What size wire is normally used on kitchen receptacles?
    #12
4. Can a dishwasher and disposal be wired on the same circuit?
    Usually yes
5. In normal household wiring, what are the following wire colors used for?

    Black.................................*Hot*
    White................................*Neutral*
    Green ....*Ground*
    Bare.................................*Ground*
    Red ....*Hot (All colors except green are hot)*
6. What is the normal size of a hot water heater? *40 gallon*
7. How much water does a toilet use on each flush? *1.6 gallon or less*
8. How long is the normal bathtub? *60 inches (5 feet)*
9. How high are kitchen counters from the floor? *36 inches*
10. What is a three-way switch used for?
    To control one or more lights from two or more locations
11. What size wire is used for an electric range? *#6*
12. What size circuit breaker is used for an electric range? *50 amps*
13. What size circuit is used for a washing machine? *20 amps*
14. How many quarts of paint in a gallon? *Four*
15. What size pipe is used for toilet sewer lines? *3 or 4 inch*

Chapter 10

HISTORY OF US

I included this chronological information here to detail how we moved through our duplex buying and renting days and then into apartments. This is about how it worked for us and how we happened to be in the right place at the right time. You will find useful bits of information here and there surrounded by the events that made our real estate adventure a success.

1962 Fire Department

I left college to take a job with the Fire Department. My dad worked for the city and knew there was a fire department test coming up. His suggestion to apply was just about the best advice I ever got in my life. I passed the test and was hired just after my 22 birthday. I would luck out many times in my life, and becoming a firefighter was definitely one of my luckiest moves. It turned out to be a fantastic, rewarding job that would become my career for the next 30 years. It turned out that many firefighters had construction jobs on their days off. Our work schedule was such that a job building would work great with our shift work.

By the age of 24, we had bought a vacant lot and hired a general contractor to build a home that I had designed. I did the basic design of the house and had a building draftsman draw the blueprints. I would use these blueprints to learn to draw my own plans for future projects. I had art training and the benefit of some drafting classes and soon became proficient at producing building plans. At the height of my building days, I could produce a complete set of plans in eight hours.

As the contractor we hired for our first home completed each phase of the work, I would watch what was done and learn construction. I had a notebook, and each day I would record what I saw. Not only did I learn how different phases of the house were constructed, but also my notebook gave me the sequence that jobs needed to be completed. This education would provide the necessary skills to complete a construction project. I still was not proficient in the different trades, but at least I was to the point that I knew how it all went together.

1967 Our First Duplex

Not long after our home was completed in 1965, I began planning to build our first duplex. I had decided that duplexes were our best investment. They only needed one lot for two rentals, and in our town, most corner lots were zoned for duplexes.

I never had enough money in my early years to buy property and begin building, so I formed a small partnership with my younger brother and a couple who were one of our closest friends at the time.

With the building lot paid for, we now had to come up with a loan. I was 26 years old, had never actually built a house and never been a carpenter; getting a loan would prove to be a challenge. I got around this financial obstacle by hiring a guy in the Fire Department to help build the duplex. He had built a few houses before and, more importantly, he had gone to school with the loan officer at a local savings and loan. He had a "track record" with the savings and loan. Maintaining a good "track record" would be of utmost importance the rest of my life.

We would use this savings and loan company for loans from this point on. This saving and loan was taken over by a larger savings and loan. Then Washington Mutual took over from them. Finally Chase Bank would take over after the meltdown of 2008. The loan officers would generally just move to the bigger company and our "track record" moved on up the line too.

At 27 years old I was a captain in the fire department, had a nice house in a nice area, and a duplex rental. A couple of years later, I was a full-fledged homebuilder. I did not have a contractor's license or enough experience to qualify for one, but I had a couple projects under my belt, felt very confident, and more importantly, the loan company was confident in me.

1971

Building on budget was important to builders like me who did not have a great deal of cash lying around to bail us out if we figured costs incorrectly. In these early years, I had not considered buying rental property and fixing it up. I would not repeat this mistake in later years. I had always figured my way to success was to use my building talents to construct nice duplexes in nice neighborhoods. The problem was that nice duplexes cost more to build, and duplex lots were at a premium price. Most of the time during these years I did not have the money for the duplex lot, or if I bought the lot, I did not have the money or time to build.

1972

My early building days came to a screeching in halt in 1972 when I was moved to the Fire Department administration, full time. This was a day job, Monday to Friday, eight hours a day. I no longer had all the days off to work on construction projects. This "few months" assignment would eventually keep me on days for the next five years. I was promoted from

Captain to Battalion Chief in 1974, and I would be working days, in the training division until 1977.

1978 General Contractor License

Back on shift work and doing remodel work, I did not know what I was doing many times and my education in building was known as the red tag method from all the "Notices of Correction" I got from the building department. Nonetheless, my skills improved, and I was now ready to apply for a contractor's license. I was a good student and studied hard, passing the test easily. Now I was a bona fide, card-carrying, honest to goodness contractor.

Next was a move into constructing full buildings. I had built duplexes years ago, so it was not all that big of a deal. But now it was a contract sale, where I had to do the job to the customer's satisfaction. It was a big transition from contracting a remodel for a friend to building a custom home or duplex for a client.

1980 Custom Homes

Like most times when I was actively working in construction, the economy had become horrid. Unemployment, inflation and interest rates were running wild. This was the late 1970s to early 1980s, and it was not uncommon for interest rates to be way into double-digit territory. People who wanted to move into a new home were unable to sell their old home because interest rates made many would-be buyers unable to qualify. Sales were stagnant and prices were kept low from high interest causing unmarketable payments. All builders were struggling. Fortunately, I had my regular job at the fire department, so this was just an inconvenience and not a step to financial ruin.

I did manage to sell a couple contract sale homes. At the height of my contracting days, I had three homes going at the same time, still working my job in the fire department, plus the model home open on weekends. I was doing fine and all this activity forced me to sub out more of the work, as I became adept at organizing each project. Keeping construction projects running smoothly and bills paid was good training for later years to come when we had many rental units to manage.

1984 Divorce

In 1984, I embarked on a new life with Anita, a female firefighter I had met in the fire department. We never thought much about it in our early relationship, but we were both fascinated by real estate and the possibility of owning rental properties. My new wife had two duplexes in a poorer part of town. The kind I would not have considered in my younger days.

In the mid-1980s, I introduced Anita to construction and building. We worked together on several projects. These included building a large custom duplex as well as electrical jobs, pouring foundations, and commercial remodels.

By 1987, contracting for full houses or remodels slowed from almost a full time job to one of helping friends now and then. My days as a contractor of custom homes were over. I had beaten my head against the wall trying to build custom homes when the economy would not cooperate. I was burned out and looking for other less hectic building adventures. The less hectic part fell by the sidelines within a few years when we would own several duplexes.

1986 Duplexes

When I met my second wife, she owned her home and two duplexes. She was in her early 30s at the time and had done better than I had in real estate. She also had a real estate license for a period prior to our meeting. She had invested in low-end rental property in these duplexes. They were in a marginal neighborhood with marginal tenants, but brought in a very satisfactory income compared to their relative low cost to purchase. More importantly, they paid for themselves. I had never thought much about owning class "C" or lower properties before, but soon discovered that the income-to-cost ratio was a much better deal than the class A or B properties I had been used to.

Even though the duplexes were in a poorer neighborhood they had one terrific feature we really had not thought about when we started; they were part of a small community of 32 duplexes all together in a three-block triangle. They were landlocked. On one side was a major freeway, the other was an older subdivision, and on the third side of the triangle was a park and a residential area on larger lots. We were surrounded by areas that were fine.

Shortly after Anita and I got together, we purchased two additional duplexes down the street from the first two she had bought. They were in reasonably good condition, had tenants, and had a positive cash flow right off the bat. Like most of the property in this group of duplexes, the front yards were in poor condition, with a couple of bushes, no tree, and not much lawn. Yards were an easy fix because they were very small and the cost of a few plants, a tree and some lawn seed was within our meager budget of the time.

These duplexes were inexpensive to buy, but the rents were good enough to make it a very good investment. We worked hard, planned a great deal and seem to be lucky. Again, it was a matter of being in the right place at the right time. Getting a foothold in this closed three-block community with good rents and an enormous opportunity to upgrade our properties was just blind good luck.

Even with the low cost to purchase these duplexes, accumulating enough money to add to our portfolio was no easy task.. We came up with some creative financing before it was popular. We would put 10 percent down on the property, get the owner to carry back another 10 percent on an interest only loan payable in full in five years, and get the normal 80 percent financing from our local bank. With this clever plan, we would spruce up the property, get the rents up to where they belonged, make inexpensive improvements, and then be able to refinance the duplex. We would net enough out of the refinancing to pay off the second being held by the seller, and most times had enough left over to pad our savings account in anticipation of the next purchase.

We wanted loans with the smallest down payment possible, lowest interest rates, and the longest amortization payback period. The smaller our monthly mortgage payment, the more cash we could save in anticipation of the next purchase. We lived off our fire department salaries and keep our personal money apart from our investing money, always making sure we spent less than our income.

We had bought several properties from owners that were unable to handle the holes in the walls and doors kicked in by tenants. This was just a normal day in the residential rental business, but it drove inexperienced owners nuts. Tenants doing damage to properties and causing other owners grief were responsible for us expanding our portfolio of duplexes at terrific prices. In some cases, I think the prior owners would have just given them to us and run away. If you let tenant damage bother you, you are not suited for residential real estate. Your business needs to take in enough money to cover these repairs as a normal business expense. Nothing special, just tenants at their worst.

Many times when a property comes up for sale there will be deferred maintenance that has been left for the new owners. I did not like any deferred work left on our duplexes. We might not be able to get to everything, but it was on a list and would eventually be taken care of. There is an immediate benefit in keeping your properties in good condition with maintenance work done. Existing tenants will love it and new tenants will be more impressed with the place.

1991 to 1999, the First Buying Frenzy

By 1991 we had only accumulated six duplexes, which included the original two owned by my now-wife. In 1991, rents and values went flat and would remain that way for almost 10 years. Our rents actually went down in this period. In 1990 we were getting $600 per month in rent on a three bedroom duplex unit. In 1991 we had to drop that amount to $595 per month, and we would still be getting $595 10 years later in 2000. Rents were down in this period, but so were values. In 1991 we paid $112,000 for a duplex with three bedrooms on each side. That would be the most we paid for a duplex in this area until the end of the decade.

Between 1991 and 1999 we bought 22 duplexes. We retired from the fire department in 1991 and withdrew Anita's retirement contributions. That, added to my final check, which included unused vacation time and sick leave time, was all put into our modest investment fund. As we accumulated more and more duplexes, it became easier to buy more. Our main tool of buying at a low cost, fixing them up and then refinancing them to recover our costs and down payment, allowed us to always have an investment fund of cash when the next duplex came up for sale. Our duplexes were always the best in the neighborhood and we forced other owners to keep up their properties to compete. We dominated the neighborhood, and many other owners who decided to sell just called us instead of getting a real estate agent and having to pay a commission. We always offered a fair price and never took advantage of some other owner's problems. Values were down and the other owners knew it. They wanted out of the property and we wanted in. It was a good deal for everyone.

We became really good at buying property, making cost effective improvements, refinancing them, and moving on. The lenders we worked with loved us. We were rock solid customers of the bank: perfect credit, everything paid early, and all profits were put back into the property. Our relationship with lenders has continued to this day. They know they can trust us. We do what we say and always follow through. In all the time we have been in the residential real estate business, we have never taken cash out for ourselves. We have always used any profits to purchase additional properties or make capital improvements, increasing the value of the properties we already owned.

2000 to 2005, Real Estate Values Get Hooked to a Shooting Star

In 1999 we saw home prices moving up, but we were still caught by surprise in 2000 when rents and values began to increase substantially. Our manager had told us of a duplex for sale a few blocks away. When we looked at it, the cost was 50 percent more than we thought our duplexes were worth. The rents being asked were almost $100 more than we were getting. At first we thought they were just overpriced, but some investigation confirmed that rents had moved up and we were quite a bit behind. We had been blind-sided by this increase in rents and values. We decided we needed to raise rents, but did not want to increase too much and lose tenants. We gave everyone an across the board $25 increase per month. This appeared substantial compared to the last decade of no rent growth. For this rent increase we gave the tenants a 30-day notice. By the time the 30-day notice went into effect, other rents had jumped again and we were further behind that before.

In less than six months, we had gone from offering market rents to being $100 a month below our competition. We needed to catch up fast, as we were falling behind further every month. We did not want to lose tenants, but we had to make the move. We gave notice for a substantial amount and included a copy of the newspaper ads showing what rents were being asked. We apologized to our tenants, but promised to be lower than the average market rents from other landlords. We had a couple tenants give notice to move because of the rent increase, but cancelled their notice after they found out they could not rent as nice a place for less money from anyone else.

As values are tied to rents, we found duplexes were now worth a similar jump in prices and value. Our portfolio of 30 duplexes had jumped in value by well over a million dollars. Therefore, we did what we had always done; refinanced them. We were not sure what we were going to do, but money in the bank could not hurt.

The refinancing of all our duplexes gave us a sizeable investment fund. We began to look for other investments, primarily an apartment complex. This meant learning about apartments from scratch by looking at every possible apartment complex that came on the market.

2003, Apartments

After looking for several months at commercial properties and apartment complexes, we decided we would stay in the residential rental business in which we felt comfortable. We had enough money in the bank from all the refinancing to purchase a fairly large apartment complex, but we were too timid. We wanted to place our "eggs" in a couple of baskets and not be tied to one large apartment complex. This would prove to be a mistake made by our inexperience. Once we got into apartments, we soon learned that the more units in one place the easier it is to manage. However, in the beginning, we would split our funds and look for two modest size complexes.

In the spring of 2003, we found two nice complexes. Both were 38 units and both were built in the mid-1980s. They both had the characteristics we liked with plenty of parking, open space and mature landscaping.

They were pretty much the run of the mill, middle class, average apartments. They had more square footage than most apartments as well as a few good selling features. We liked them both because they showed well and a prospective tenant driving into the properties would be greeted by a pleasant setting.

We got the loan from the same lending bank as we had used for our duplexes, but we moved into the commercial loan division and began our dealings with the "higher ups" in the bank. Our reputation followed us to these loan officers and we had no problem putting it all together. Even though we had entered into a purchase agreement on the two complexes about a month apart, they closed a week apart. This meant we had to be organized in an unfamiliar area and had to come up with two managers and some new systems for rent reporting and bank deposits.

Because we did not really know what we were doing, we put together a letter about the sale and phone numbers to call in case of an emergency. We delivered these letters personally door to door to each tenant. The tenants loved it; most had never seen an owner before, and providing an emergency phone number instead of an answering service was well received. The phone number went to my wife's cellphone. It did not take long for the word to get around that if you called the emergency number you were going to get my wife, and if the call came in the middle of the night, it had better be an emergency. We got a few calls at the beginning, but they died off almost completely after a very few days. This emergency phone number was supposed to be a temporary stopgap effort to handle problems until we could get organized, but we received so few calls, and it was effective in handling problems, we continued it and still use the same phone number today 10 years later.

These purchases more than doubled our 'to-do' list, and there were upgrades we wanted to do at the new properties. Our son Greg came on to manage one of the apartment complexes, and 10 years later is our overall maintenance manager. For the next couple of years, we had the two apartment complexes and our 30 duplexes, which we ran like a third apartment complex.

2005, Duplex Values Went Out of Sight

The real estate market was in never-never land. Values were increasing daily and homes going on the market would get multiple offers within days. We were not really in the frenzy yet and had had our attention devoted to the properties we already owned. I had kept up on apartment prices and figured they were all over priced like the rest of real estate. We had not even bothered to refinance our duplexes again. In the summer of 2005, at a local supermarket, I ran into Randy pushing a grocery cart.

His advice to sell our duplexes and buy apartments came as news to us and eventually changed our lives. We had not paid enough attention to duplex values and Randy was right. Duplexes were selling for about $200,000 per unit and apartments were selling for less than $100,000 per unit. Rents were not all that different per unit for either the duplexes or apartments. It took us a month to make the move and place our duplexes up for sale.

The sale was more than easy. Our sale price was going to be based on current comps, less an agreed-to discount. Fortunately, on the day we set the final price, our son-in-law alerted us to a sale in our duplex area. This sale was for more than we expected and pushed the comps up about $20,000 per duplex.

We sold 28 of our duplexes in October of 2005 and moved the funds from escrow to a 1031 holding company. We would now enter another buying frenzy required by the IRS to punish people like us, lucky enough to be moving from one property to another.

2006, Buying Frenzy Number Two, or how we spent our 1031 Exchange Money

We entered into contract to sell our duplexes in the late summer of 2005. Our duplexes sale closed escrow in October 2005. We were in good shape with a couple of properties ready to go and a nice list of possible other ones. This was a time similar to a kid in a candy store with $10 that he had to spend. Every day was spent looking at property or talking about property. I was on the phone daily with several agents. We were still in good shape, playing one against the other with the sellers knowing we had other options.

By January, we had three replacement properties in escrow to purchase. We wanted to be in escrow with the rest by mid-January. This would give us three months to close escrow, which we felt should be adequate. As the January deadline closed in, we organized what we had into a priority list with how much we were willing to pay for each. We went down the list one at a time offering our price in a Letter of Interest. We called each seller's agent as well and verbally explained our position and that we did not have the time or the inclination for a long drawn out "negotiation" period. It was pretty much a take it or leave it proposition. I wanted it all done before the end of the month. Some sellers took our offer; others did not. We worked our way down our list until we spent our entire replacement fund. The bigger numbers and bigger mortgages were new to us and we were not all that comfortable leveraging the properties as we had done in our early days. We took modest loans giving us a credit-to-debt ratio of about 1.5 for our entire portfolio. Most banks at the time were happy with a CDR of 1.2. This caution in debt would pay off a very short time later when real estate values would crash.

2006 to 2008, Cayman Properties, LFI International

Over the years we had thought about the possibility of buying a property in a warm climate to spend some time when the winter months are cold and wet. We had spent time every year in Baja, Mexico, vacationing on the beach and diving. We loved these times of our life, but getting older made the 1500 mile drive look less fun and more dangerous. In 2004 we had made a list of places we might buy a condo or vacation house that was warm in winter and, more importantly, was safe. We decided that we would only invest in areas that were controlled by either the United States or Britain. This made our possible list very short consisting of only the Florida Keys, the Bahamas, the Virgin Islands and the Cayman Islands.

We began visiting and investigating the possibilities. The Bahamas was dumped from the list because the water there is not warm enough for us in winter. The Florida Keys were wonderful and we loved them, but it was mostly a fishing area and did not have the top-notch diving we were looking for. We visited the British Virgins and loved these islands, and would return several more times in the years to follow, but it was just too difficult traveling there. We had to take four flights, passing through Miami and Puerto Rico and spending two days traveling in each direction. This left the Cayman Islands, which we visited in January of 2005.

Grand Cayman turned out to be a wonderful and civilized country filled with nice people and five star restaurants. We had not really known much about these islands until we got there and found a place very much like home with strict building codes and property rights. It is like home, but they drive on the left, and observe the Queen of England's birthday. They give you a feeling you are in a special place. They are very close still to Great Britain as a Crown Colony under the protection of England.

We traveled to the Cayman Islands again in March 2006 and began looking for a possible winter retreat. We bought our dream condo on the beach in Grand Cayman in the summer of 2006. We bought the condo as part of our company and put it in the vacation rental program with our own website and on-island manager. I would eventually become a board member and then Chairman of the Board of Directors for the condominium association.

A year and a half later, in 2008, we would buy a four-unit apartment complex near downtown George Town, Grand Cayman. This would firmly establish our Cayman properties. With five units on the island, we began visiting our property there several times a year. We did work on the properties and had our son and son-in-law join us there to work. We are even working when we sit on our beach sipping rum drinks and chatting about real estate.

2008 to 2010, Surviving the Downturn in Real Estate

From 2008 to 2010 it was all downhill for real estate. Home prices were in total free fall and foreclosures were everywhere. During the boom years people refinanced their homes and spent the money on remodels or down payments on big cars, boats or RVs. When the crash came and people lost jobs as well as their homes, all these toys were also repossessed. Homes are the single biggest investment in most people's lives and the severity of the recession meant that it would be many years before most people would recover, if they ever did.

Duplexes were as bad as or worse than homes. They had been so over priced in late 2005 that when the values dropped so severely, interest in purchasing a duplex totally diminished. A duplex that was worth $400,000 in the spring of 2006 would see its value drop to under $200,000 by 2010. Many investors, including the people that bought our duplexes, had to lose a great deal of money with no hope of recovery anytime soon.

Rents were down and vacancies were up in our apartments, but only by about 10 percent. Apartment values also diminished, but in the 10 percent range based on the lower rents. The problems in real estate did drive cap rates up and apartment values down. The availability of any good properties coming on the market was limited to those who just had to sell.

In mid-2008 we did hear of a nice property that had just been taken back by the bank. It was a 48-unit condominium conversion project that only sold two units and had gone bankrupt. It was a great property that was built in 2004 and converted to condominiums between 2005 and 2007. They had missed the boom in the market. Not only did the property have two units owned by individuals but also it had seven units that had been gutted in anticipation of being converted to condos when the owner's company collapsed. We sent a Letter of Interest to the bank with a modest offer. The bank politely rejected our offer without any counter offer. We would keep track of this property for the next two years.

The property did come to our attention now and then. In November of 2008 we got the bright idea that if we had a tentative purchase agreement on the only two units that had been sold we might have an inside track on getting financing on the entire complex. This project was not going to be easy to finance. It had forty-six units owned by the bank, two owned by others and seven unfinished. We wrote letters to the 2 condo owners offering them their full purchase price back with no closing costs and no commissions, if they would give us an option to buy their units contingent upon us buying all the rest.

At first they thought it was a scam, but we agreed to a joint meeting with anyone they wanted present to help them. We gave them our plan and a written letter offering the deal. They had each paid over $200,000 for their condo. If they could be sold now might, if lucky, net $120,000. This was a good deal for us all. They were saved from paying high payments on a property that was underwater, and we had the means to purchase the entire 48-units.

We immediately tried another Letter of Interest to the bank offering considerably less than we had just six months earlier. The bank did respond this time and asked about the amount I offered. I was happy to supply them my calculations and logic on the property. Values were still dropping and cap rates had climbed. About this time the bank had failed and was taken over by the FDIC. The bank would be bought and taken over by another bank from the Midwest. It was hard to believe that this transaction could become more complicated, but now we were dealing with a bank new to the area. Fortunately, some of the officials of the old bank were still around.

In the middle of 2009, we again tried a Letter of Interest to the new bank. We had been able to keep extending our purchase agreements with the two condo owners to maintain our feeble advantage. Again we dropped our offer amount based on the further drop in values. Again the bank rejected our offer. No more was heard on the property until January of 2010.

2010

In January of 2010, we got a call from Randy while we were sitting at the airport in Houston. He told us that the 46 units were going to be listed soon and the price was just about what we had offered in our two previous LOIs. He emailed the information he had, and in the next 30 minutes sitting at the airport, we put together another Letter of Interest for the asking price.

It took three weeks to reach an agreement with the bank after many, many emails. We jumped through so many hoops we thought we might try out for Ringling Bros. We did manage to get the property into contract. Our excellent credit and our deal with the two owners to sell only to us were the deciding factors in making it happen. The two owners had stuck with us for over a year; our honesty and forthrightness had paid off.

It was hell going through the countless rewrites of the purchase agreement, but in the end, it went just as we had hoped. The property closed in April of 2010. Under the guidance of our son Greg, the seven gutted units were rent-ready to better-than-condo specifications by the end of June. It was a very nice addition to our portfolio.

2012 to 2015

As we enter our golden years, a nice cash flow and money in the bank gives us more pleasure than fixing up property and leveraging some investment to the maximum. We are playing it close to the vest so to speak. Unfortunately the economy and world uncertainty has reduced any feelings of confidence for us to continue in the buying mode, but that could always change. Buyers who paid too much in the 2005 to 2007 boom years and now need to refinance or sell are in trouble. I see many properties come through for sale that I know sold for as much as 25 percent more just a few years ago. The buyers at those inflated prices have suffered large losses. Some will never recover.

Our portfolio of properties looks great and our loan to value ratio is strong. It is no longer necessary for us to expand our holdings, but it is not out of our blood yet. We still look at properties often and are in a position to buy something. This is a lot like playing Monopoly, remembering that net worth is just a number at the bottom of a sheet of paper.

Index